Organizational Learning in China

From the perspective of behavioural science, this book systematically investigates organizational learning in Chinese organizations based on multilevel theory over the past 20 years. The findings contribute to the theory and practice of organizational learning and give insights into the construction of learning organizations.

Revisiting existing studies on organizational learning, the author reconceptualizes organizational learning and constructs an integrative model, which is corroborated and then supplemented by empirical research. Based on samples and materials from 3,000 managers and employees in organizations from all over China, the book further elaborates this integrative model covering the multilevel structure, trans-level functions and generative mechanisms that figure prominently in organizational learning in Chinese organizations. This framework helps enhance the organizational learning ability and the establishment of a learning culture, while offering possible directions for updating research methods and a stereoscopic theory of organizational learning.

The book will be a good reference for management practitioners, students and academics interested in organizational behaviour, human resource management, innovation management, and multilevel perspective.

Yu Haibo is Professor in the Department of Organization and Human Resource Management, School of Government, at Beijing Normal University, China. His research interests include organizational behaviour and human resource management such as leadership theory, organizational learning and innovation, career management, job crafting, career adaptability and employability.

China Perspectives

The *China Perspectives* series focuses on translating and publishing works by leading Chinese scholars, writing about both global topics and China-related themes. It covers Humanities & Social Sciences, Education, Media and Psychology, as well as many interdisciplinary themes.

This is the first time any of these books have been published in English for international readers. The series aims to put forward a Chinese perspective, give insights into cutting-edge academic thinking in China, and inspire researchers globally.

To submit proposals, please contact the Taylor & Francis Publisher for China Publishing Programme, Lian Sun (Lian.Sun@informa.com)

Titles in Business currently include:

Organizational Learning in China
Building a Multilevel Approach
Yu Haibo

Internationalisation of Chinese Enterprises
A Comparative Study of Cross-border Mergers and Acquisitions
JIA Zongda

For more information, please visit https://www.routledge.com/China-Perspectives/book-series/CPH

Organizational Learning in China

Building a Multilevel Approach

Yu Haibo

Routledge
Taylor & Francis Group

LONDON AND NEW YORK

First published 2021
by Routledge
2 Park Square, Milton Park, Abingdon, Oxon OX14 4RN

and by Routledge
52 Vanderbilt Avenue, New York, NY 10017

Routledge is an imprint of the Taylor & Francis Group, an informa business

British Library Cataloguing-in-Publication Data
A catalogue record for this book is available from the British Library

Library of Congress Cataloging-in-Publication Data
Names: Yu, Haibo, 1975- author.
Title: Organizational learning in China : building a multilevel approach Haibo Yu.
Description: 1 Edition. | New York : Routledge, 2021. | Series: China perspectives | Includes bibliographical references and index. | Identifiers: LCCN 2020052420 (print) | LCCN 2020052421 (ebook) | ISBN 9780367763398 (hardback) | ISBN 9780367763404 (paperback) | ISBN 9781003166542 (ebook)
Subjects: LCSH: Organizational learning--China. | Organizational learning--Research--China. Classification: LCC HD58.82 .Y84 2021 (print) | LCC HD58.82 (ebook) | DDC 658.3/1240951--dc23 LC record available at https://lccn.loc.gov/2020052420
LC ebook record available at https://lccn.loc.gov/2020052421

ISBN: 978-0-367-76339-8 (hbk)
ISBN: 978-0-367-76340-4 (pbk)
ISBN: 978-1-003-16654-2 (ebk)

Typeset in Times New Roman
by SPi Global, India

Contents

Figures

Tables

1 An integrated theoretical model of organizational learning

This chapter first defines organizational learning based on a review of its definitions in Chinese and international literature, and then provides our theoretical model of organizational learning on the basis of summarizing the literature so as to prepare the ground for later empirical research.

1.1 Meaning of organizational learning

1.1.1 Two preconditions of organizational learning

To define organizational learning entails the clarification of what "organizational" and "learning" mean in the phrase. Due to their various definitions of the two words, many theorists and practitioners have proposed different definitions of organizational learning.

Firstly, differences in interpretations of organizational learning reflect varying assumptions about "organization" (Crossan et al., 1999). If one views an organization as the sum of individual members, and that learning resides within individuals, then organizational learning will be viewed as predominantly individual learning. If one views an organization as something larger than the sum of individual members, and that learning resides within individuals, then organizational learning will be viewed as predominantly group-based learning (that is, collective learning). If an organization is defined as greater than the integration of its members, organizational learning becomes an organizationally based phenomenon. Finally, if one considers organizational boundaries as blurred, then organizational learning can be studied at an inter-organizational level. We support the multilevel theory proposed by Klein et al. (2000) that an organization includes its individuals and groups, as well as organizational characteristics such as strategies and structures at the organizational level. Against the backdrop of globalization, an organization is located in a globalized organizational network, where inter-organizational communication is inevitable. Inter-organizational level, therefore, is also an important aspect of an organization.

Secondly, conceptualizations of organizational learning will partly reflect differences of how "learning" is presented. Previous studies of organizational learning present "learning" in two ways: some view learning as an outcome; others discuss learning as a process (Edmondson, 1999). Levitt and March (1988) define organizational learning as "encoding inferences from history into routines that guide behavior," a typical view on organizational learning as an outcome. In contrast, Argyris and Schön (1978) define organizational learning as a process of detecting and correcting errors. Their view represents a process perspective. In this study, we define and investigate organizational learning as a process with a view to deepening the understanding of organizational learning.

1.1.2 Three perspectives on organizational learning

The definitions of organizational learning given by Chinese and international researchers, according to their fundamental perspectives, can be roughly classified into three categories. Table 1.1 summarizes some scholars' classifications.

1.1.2.1 Perspective of systems and behaviors

There are researchers investigating organizational learning from the perspective of overall organizational behavior. Argyris and Schön (1978), for instance, argue that organizational learning is the process by which members of the organization detect errors or anomalies, reconstruct organizational theory-in-use, and embed

Table 1.1 Summary of some scholars' classifications

Systems or behaviors perspective	Information processing perspective	Social interactions perspective
Argyris and Schön (1978)	Duncan and Weiss (1979)	Senge (1990)
Hedberg (1981)	Daft and Weick (1984)	Brown and Duguid (1991)
Levitt and March (1988)	Fiol and Lyles (1985)	Cook and Yanow (1993)
De Geus (1988)	Stata (1989)	Kim (1993)
Pedler et al. (1991)	Argote and Epple (1990)	Day (1994)
Lee et al. (1992)	Huber (1991)	Crossan et al. (1999)
Mills and Friesen (1992)	March (1991)	Cavaleri and Fearon (1996)
Marquardt (1996)	Garvin (1993)	Richter (1998)
Miller (1996)	Ulrich and Todd (1993)	Gherardi et al. (1998)
Chen and Ma (2000)	Levinthal and March (1993)	Fisher and White (2000)
Schwandt and Maruardt (2000)	Slater and Narver (1995)	Fox (2000)
Pawlowsky (2001)	DiBella and Nevis (1998)	Lahteenmarki et al. (2001)
Wang (2002)	Dixon (1999)	Berends et al. (2002)
	Templeton et al. (2002)	Akgun et al. (2003)
	Ellis and Shpielberg (2003)	Bogenrieder (2002)
	Gnyawali and Stewart (2003)	Bogenrieder and Nooteboom (2004)
	Tippins and Sohi (2003)	
	Jerez-Gómez et al. (2005a)	
	Jiang and Zhao (2006)	
	Wu (1995)	

the results of their inquiry in their cognition of organization so as to correct behaviors of the organization. Their emphasis is the double-loop learning through which organizational behaviors may be improved. Hedberg (1981) believes that organizational learning arises from adaptive and operational interactions between an organization and its environment, which includes both the process of an organization's passive adaptation to the environment and its active application of knowledge and its active adaptation to the environment. This definition conceptualizes organizational learning from a systematic and behavioral perspective. Pedler, a British researcher, defines the learning company (Pedler et al., 1991) as an organization that facilitates the learning of all its members and continuously transforms itself. From the perspective of systems theory, Marquardt (1996) claims that an organization with a strong collective learning ability will constantly transform itself so as to collect, manage, and apply knowledge. Chen and Ma (2000) argue that organizational learning refers to the process of an organization's continuous efforts to change or redesign itself to adapt to a changing environment and to a process of organizational innovation.

This definition assumes that the organization is a system and the organization's response to the environment is its learning behavior. This perspective focuses on the interaction between the organization as a whole and the environment, highlighting learning at the organizational level. However, this view to some extent blurs the distinction between organizational learning and organizational change by connecting the two concepts. And it fails to consider other levels of learning or micro-learning process inside the organization.

1.1.2.2 Perspective of information processing

This section discusses the view that deals with organizational learning from the perspective of organizational information processing. Huber (1991) believes that if an organization learns through information processing, the range of its potential behaviors is changed, and an organization learns if any of its units acquires knowledge that is potentially useful to it. In his model, he divides the organizational learning process into stages of generation, distribution, and application of knowledge. These three stages are widely cited by many researchers for studying organizational learning.

Huber's perspective investigates organizational learning as an organization's processing of information and as a process of knowledge generation, distribution, and application. This perspective pinpoints knowledge processing at the individual, group, and organizational levels, therefore facilitating in-depth examination of knowledge processing within an organization. However, this view to some extent borders on knowledge management, confusing organizational learning with it, and shifts the emphasis away from the subject of learning, i.e., people, onto the object of learning, i.e., knowledge.

1.1.2.3 Perspective of social interaction

This section summarizes research in which organizational learning is investigated from the perspective of interaction between individuals in an organization. According to Senge (1990), a learning organization refers to an organization where people continually expand their capacity to create the results they desire, where new and expansive patterns of thinking are nurtured, where collective aspiration is set free, and where people are continually learning how to learn together. These are the five disciplines he advocates, and he emphasizes the way an organization's members interact based on their transcendence over themselves. In particular, Cook and Yanow (1993) draw on a cultural perspective in which organizational learning is a formal or informal collective exploration and practice process between members in an organization. Their focus is the collective learning carried out by many people together within an organization.

This view interprets organizational learning from the perspective of interpersonal relationship as a collective exploration process at all levels of an organization, highlighting people, the subject of learning activity. But this perspective ignores the learning at the level of the entire organization and fails to explore the knowledge flow in organizational learning.

1.1.3 Concept of organizational learning

From the previous analysis, the three perspectives explore organizational learning from different angles, focusing on one or more aspects of organizational learning. Therefore, this study draws the following conclusion: organizational learning is a process, in which new knowledge is continuously generated and applied and organizational behavior is continuously improved through the interaction between an organization's members; in which organizational learning is carried out at multiple levels; in which organizational knowledge is continuously generated, distributed, and applied; in which everyone in the organization is involved in the collective learning and practice, suggesting a type of social learning (Örtenblad, 2002).

Therefore, from the perspective of managing organizational learning (Pawlowsky, 2001; Wang, 2002), this study defines organizational learning as follows (Yu et al., 2004, 2007):

> Organizational learning refers to a process of continuous change of organizational beliefs and behaviors caused by interpersonal social interaction at organizational and inter-organizational levels and based on individual learning; it is a cyclical process of collective exploration and practice in which new knowledge and behaviors are acquired or generated, and understood, integrated, and institutionalized; it intentionally or unintentionally affects the organization's performance.

There are generally three approaches to the study of organizational learning. The first is a **normative approach**, which highlights the study of learning organizations and assumes an organization will learn only under certain conditions. The researchers taking this approach, such as Senge (1990), attempt to explore certain characteristics that a learning organization should possess, focusing on the future state of the organization. The second is a **development approach**, which emphasizes that different stages of organizational development determine the continuous change of organizational learning style, and that organizational learning depends on the history of the organization. The theorists of this approach focus on changes in organizational learning styles and show a special interest in the history of an organization. The third is the **capacity approach**, which assumes that any organization consciously or unconsciously possesses organizational learning behavior but varies in capacity, stronger or weaker and that studying the so-called learning organization is meaningless. This approach focuses on how organizations learn and what they learn with a special interest in the current state of the organization.

In general, we mainly adopt the third approach—the capacity approach— and regard organizational learning as a sophisticated process. We do not think that learning organization is meaningless. Rather, we regard it as an aspect of organizational learning. This is because that from the perspective of Chinese corporate organizations, learning organization, as an endless process of constant exploration, is the direction for the majority of companies. Discussing the current learning state of companies outweighs merely setting a goal of being a learning organization.

1.2 Theoretical model of organizational learning

This section reviews and evaluates the literature basis from three aspects: the level of organizational learning, the two processes of information or knowledge flow in organizational learning, and the process of organizational learning to propose the integrated theoretical model of organizational learning.

1.2.1 Levels of organizational learning

No matter from what perspective, organizational learning is viewed to be taking place at certain levels. The views of many scholars are summarized in Table 1.2, which, in particular the summary, show that the individual level, collective (group) level, and organizational level have been widely recognized while inter-organizational learning is neglected by many scholars. Today, with economic globalization, the growing prosperity of business cooperation, strategic alliance and other forms of economic operation fully demonstrates the necessity and importance of inter-organizational learning. Therefore, in this study, we believe that organizational learning includes four levels: individual, collective (group), organizational and inter-organizational.

1.2.1.1 Individual learning

Within the purview of psychology, individual learning has been a research subject with a long history. Learning has been studied from the perspective of individuals according to classical, behaviorist, cognitive, constructivist and social learning theories. As stated by Simon (1991), all learning takes place inside individual human heads, thereby organizations learn only through learning of its members or ingesting new employees. Therefore, he focuses on personnel recruitment, training, development, and demission. March and Olsen (1975) as

Table 1.2 Summary of some scholars' interpretations of organizational learning level

Scholars	Organizational learning level			
	Individual	Collective (group)	Organizational	Inter-organizational
Argyris and Schön (1978)	√	√	√	
Duncan and Weiss (1979)		√	√	
Shrivastava (1983)	√	√		
Hedberg (1981)	√	√	√	
Daft and Weick (1984)	√	√	√	
Fiol and Lyles (1985)	√		√	
Levitt and March (1988)			√	√
Stata (1989)	√	√	√	
Senge (1990)	√	√	√	
Huber (1991)	√	√	√	
Garvin (1993)	√		√	
Kim (1993)	√		√	
Watkins and Marsick (1993)	√	√	√	
Crossan et al. (1995)				√
Nonaka and Takeuchi (1995)	√	√	√	√
Marquardt (1996)	√	√	√	√
DiBella and Nevis (1998)		√		
Crossan et al. (1999)	√	√	√	
Dixon (1999)	√		√	
Yeung et al. (1999)	√		√	
Chen (2007, 2016)	√	√	√	√
Pawlowsky (2001)	√	√	√	√
Moilanen (2001)	√	√	√	
Lahteenmarki et al. (2001)	√	√	√	

(*Continued*)

Table 1.2 (Continued)

Scholars	Organizational learning level			
	Individual	Collective (group)	Organizational	Inter-organizational
Argote and Ophir (2002)				√
Templeton et al. (2002)	√	√	√	
Bontis et al. (2002)	√	√	√	√
Wang (2002)	√	√	√	√
Knight (2002)				√
Ingram (2002)				√
Bogenrieder (2002)	√			
Gnyawali and Stewart (2003)			√	
Tippins and Sohi (2003)			√	
Ellis and Shpielberg (2003)			√	
Berends et al. (2002)	√		√	
Akgun et al. (2003)	√	√	√	
Salk and Simonin (2003)				√
Holmqvist (2003)	√	√	√	√
Jerez-Gómez et al. (2005a)	√	√	√	
Yang et al. (2004)	√	√	√	
Wu (1995)			√	
Jiang and Zhao (2006)			√	
Dai et al. (2006)	√	√	√	
Yang et al. (2010)			√	
Jiao et al. (2008)	√	√	√	
Yuan et al. (2006)	√	√	√	√
Yan and Guan (2006)				√

(*Continued*)

Table 1.2 (Continued)

Scholars	Organizational learning level			
	Individual	Collective (group)	Organizational	Inter-organizational
He and Tian (2008)			√	
Xie et al. (2006)			√	
Wei et al. (2014)			√	
Sun and Zhao (2017)			√	
Summary	30	28	√	15

well emphasize individual learning by situating at the central stage information exposure, memory, retrieval, learning incentives and belief structures. Senge's (1990) perspective suggests an emphasis on individual learning by highlighting the role of leaders in inspiring mental models, developing personal visions and applying systematic thinking. Garvin (1993) discusses problem solving, experimentation and learning from others, reflecting an emphasis on learning at an individual level. As Lahteenmarki et al. (2001) argue, too much emphasis is put on learning of individuals in the research of organizational learning. Therefore, any researcher who researches on learning does not avoid discussion of individual learning because individuals are the subjects of learning.

The general definition of learning (that is, learning at individual level) is continuous changes in human cognition and behavior caused by experience. Therefore, this study believes that individual-level learning in a company refers to the process in which individual employees, in the context of explicit work goals, continually summarize, explore and practice, thereby achieving improvement and development. The individual-level learning here includes not only the learning incentives of individual employees, but also their exploration and practical activities, especially activities that facilitate them to improve cognition and behaviors at work. Admittedly, from the perspective of knowledge and information, individual employees can acquire and generate, through intuition and their own work experience, new knowledge or behaviors, which are often the starting point or "fuse" of organizational learning.

1.2.1.2 Collective learning

Many researchers believe that organizational learning is incomplete if the knowledge generated by an individual is not shared by other members of the group, or not understood on common ground as collective knowledge, or not owned by the entire organization. Duncan and Weiss (1979) argue that organizational learning must be shared and integrated with other organization members for the organization to achieve its goals. Daft and Weick (1984) believe that organizational learning includes group learning, however, concentrating on learning of senior leadership groups. Weick's (1991) perspective reflects an emphasis on group learning by considering learning as a realistic social construction process. According to Pawlowsky (2001), group learning has the function of knowledge transformation in which individually acquired knowledge can be transformed into organizational knowledge, which can be shared by other members of the organization. Senge (1990) argues, "unless teams can learn, the organization cannot learn." Group learning integrates individual knowledge and concentrates individual learning capabilities, therefore serving as the smallest unit of organizational learning. Groups or teams play a significant role in the transformation of individual learning to organizational learning.

Many researchers often study team learning or group learning at the level of small collectives. This study treats the learning of all members within a division as collective learning so as to distinguish it from organizational-level learning. Therefore, this study defines collective learning as the process of collective members interacting at work to reach consensus on work and take collective action. That is to say, collective learning changes the cognition or behaviors of collective members, thereby reifying the social interaction process of organizational learning in which members of a division interact in order to improve interactions at work. Collective learning includes asking questions from each other, giving feedback, experimenting together, reflecting collectively on work and experimental results, and discussing errors or unexpected results (Edmondson, 1999). Collective members are required to test their underlying assumptions about work and problems and discuss their various perspectives openly.

1.2.1.3 Organizational-level learning

At the organizational level, many scholars provide their own understandings. Fiol and Lyles (1985) hold the opinion that organizational-level learning refers to the impact of organizational systems, structures and procedures on learning. Hedberg (1981) believes that organizational-level learning indicates that learning is preserved in organizational systems, structures and procedures. Argyris and Schön (1978) argue that only when knowledge is transferred from the individual to the organization will the organizational-level learning be possible; if an individual does not encode what he/she has learned into the organizational systems, structures and procedures, such learning fails to be organizational-level learning. The purpose of organizational-level learning, according to Shrivastava (1983), is to transform the individual knowledge to organizational knowledge in a system as the guidance for decision-making. Duncan and Weiss (1979) believe that the knowledge acquired by individuals will eventually be transferred to the organizational level as long as it is generated and preserved by individuals. Easterby-Smith et al. (2000) argue that an organization can benefit from past learning only when the newly acquired knowledge and behavior are penetrated into organizational systems, structures and procedures.

Based on the analysis presented, this study defines organizational-level learning as the integration of individual learning and collective learning, and their penetration into organizational systems, structures, strategies, procedures and culture, better accommodating the learning to both internal and external changes. Therefore, organizational learning can finally be reflected in changes and adjustments in structures, strategies, culture, etc., on the organizational level. This differs from collective learning—a people-oriented process of interaction, coordination and improvement among collective members; organizational-level learning shifts the focus from people to changes of the organizational characteristics on the organizational level. This shift, without doubt, demonstrates the further deepening process of collective learning, that is, a process of integration and institutionalization.

1.2.1.4 Inter-organizational learning

Previously, few studies have investigated learning on the inter-organizational level, as Lane (2001) points out that a majority of publications about organizational learning focus on intra-organizational learning instead of inter-organizational learning (or network learning, as they call it). Holmqvist (2003) adds support by arguing that inter-organizational learning has been emphasized only in the past few years, for many organization theories, with a hypothesis that differences exist between intra-organizational and inter-organizational relationships, pose a presumed either-or choice between intra-organizational and inter-organizational process in many studies.

In this study, we refer to inter-organizational learning as the process where an individual, a group and the whole organizational level in an organization transform cognition and behaviors by acquiring, generating, applying and distributing new knowledge through interaction with other organizations. This process involves exchanges of a huge amount of regular information, which benefits both parties in acquisition of knowledge and ability that they need. Pedler et al. (1991) describe inter-organizational learning as one of the features of learning companies. Crossan et al. (1995), amongst others, has studied inter-organizational learning in joint ventures and alliances. Nonaka and Takeuchi (1995), in their discussion on knowledge innovation, think that creative chaos may come from cooperation with clients, with suppliers and even with both; at the same time, they lay great emphasis to the promotion of knowledge innovation among organizations in their summary of the innovation. Pawlowsky (2001), in his discussion on the systematic level of organizational learning—where he advocates that organizational learning should include four levels—mentions inter-organizational learning (network learning, as he calls it), though he has not expounded on that. For Chinese enterprises which lag behind foreign companies in terms of industrialization and management, mutual learning from each other is indispensable, particularly from foreign-funded enterprises or joint ventures so as to enhance the learning and competitive capability.

March (1991) assumes there exists a conflict between exploration and exploitation of knowledge in organizational learning, both of which are essential to an organization but may compete with each other for limited resources in an organization. It is therefore advisable to view the whole process of organizational learning from the perspective of knowledge or information flow.

1.2.2 Two processes of information and knowledge flow in organizational learning

As for the information and knowledge flow in organizational learning, there are two processes: one flow from the higher level to the lower level, and the other from the lower level to a higher level. These are closely related to the concept of exploration and exploitation of knowledge by March (1991). The bi-directional flow reflects two different types of learning: Exploitative Learning and Explorative Learning (Crossan et al., 1999).

1.2.2.1 Exploitation

Exploitation features the flow of information or knowledge from organizational level to the group level and the individual level. It is the exploitation of information or knowledge, which transforms organizational knowledge into individual knowledge and gradually changes individuals' cognition and behaviors.

Actually, exploitation in nature is to put what an organization has acquired into practice (Holmqvist, 2003). The whole process is realized by primary organizational learning. Argyris and Schön (1978) believe that an organization detects and corrects errors through single-loop learning. Senge (1990) thinks that an organization accommodates itself to new situations through adaptive learning. Exploiting Learning emphasizes individuals' or groups' acceptance of knowledge that an organization has acquired so as to improve their behaviors. This is a lower-level learning (Fiol & Lyles, 1985), which is, however, necessary for any organization.

Meanwhile, to exploit the experience may bring singular perspective to an organization, depriving the possibility of exploiting new learning opportunities. What is effective in the short term may seem ineffective in the long term. In order to remedy the weakness, it is necessary for an organization to create diversity of experiences through innovation, experimentation and venturing. Such process of exploring new knowledge (March, 1991; Levinthal & March, 1993) is called Exploring Learning.

1.2.2.2 Exploration

Exploration, featuring the exploration of information or knowledge, is a flow of information or knowledge from the individual level to the organizational level, which integrates an individual's new knowledge and behavior and transforms them to organizational knowledge so as to gradually change organizational-level features such as organizational culture, strategy and procedure. The process is achieved through high-level organizational learning (Fiol & Lyles, 1985). Argyris and Schön (1978) think that an organization makes changes and adjustments in its basic action hypothesis through double-loop learning. Senge (1990) thinks an organization generates new knowledge and ideas through generative learning. Exploration emphasizes the process that an organization can sensitively capture the new knowledge and information so as to change the former action hypothesis and thinking mode. Such learning is what many organizations lack.

In fact, from the perspective of the flow of knowledge or information, inter-organizational learning also demonstrates both exploitation and exploration of knowledge. Inkpen (2000) puts forward a model of inter-organizational knowledge acquisition and describes how the inter-organizational knowledge is exploited. Lindholm (1997) summarizes three different learning procedures among international joint ventures: the transference of knowledge, the generation of knowledge, and the application of knowledge. It involves both exploitation and exploration of knowledge or information (Holmqvist, 2003).

In the previous studies concerning organizational learning, it is often emphasized that "maintaining an appropriate balance between exploration and exploitation is a primary factor in system survival and prosperity" (March, 1991); and that "strategic renewal requires that organizations explore and learn new ways while concurrently exploiting what they have already learned" (Crossan et al., 1999). They are interdependent on each other and co-exist, not the way of either-or alternative as many literatures claim (Holmqvist, 2003). It is the flow of knowledge or information that reflects that organizational learning is dynamic as a process of continuous cycling rise.

1.2.3 Process of organizational learning

In organizational learning, the level of learning is static, indicating the main occurrence place of learning subject; while the flow of knowledge or information in both Exploitative Learning and Explorative Learning is dynamic, reflecting the flow feature of the learning object (information or knowledge, and of course, new behavior as the carrier of new information and new knowledge). Through what mechanism can the two learning types be integrated into a process of organizational learning?

Many scholars have come up with their own model of organizational learning process based on their own understanding. According to their complexity, i.e., whether the model involves the four levels of learning and whether their relations have been explained, they can be categorized into three: primary, advanced and complex models of organizational learning process.

1.2.3.1 Primary model of the organizational learning process

The models of the organizational learning process in Table 1.3 divide the learning process into three or four steps. Step 1 is the input of organizational learning; Step 2 and Step 3 are the learning process; and Step 4 is the output of organizational learning. However, none of them regard individual and group learning as an important part of organizational learning.

Among all those models, Chen and Ma (2000) put forward a new model based on the one of Argyris and Schön (1978). They improved the linear model of learning process and make it a circular one, with emphasis on the role of knowledge base in organizational learning. The model, however, ignores the micro learning process as well as individual, group and inter-organizational learning levels.

Table 1.3 Primary models of organizational learning process

Researchers	Step 1	Step 2	Step 3	Step 4
Argyris and Schön (1978)	Discovery	Innovation	Implementation	Promotion
Chen and Ma (2000)	Discovery	Invention	Implementation	Promotion Feedback
Daft and Weick (1984)	Examination	Explanation	–	Learning
Carlsson (1995)	Specific experience	Reflective observation	Conceptualization	Active experiment
Nevis et al. (1995)	Acquisition	Sharing	–	Application

Table 1.4 Advanced model of organizational learning process

Researchers	Step 1	Step 2	Step 3	Step 4
March and Olsen (1975)	Individual belief	Individual action	Organizational action	Environmental reflection
Rosengarten (1999)	Individual learning	Discussion	Collective learning	Institutionalization and normalization
Dixon (1999)	Generation	Integration	Explanation	Action

Advanced model of organizational learning process makes up for the deficiency to some extent.

1.2.3.2 Advanced model of the organizational learning process

Most of the models in Table 1.4 consist of four different stages. March and Olsen (1975) pay great attention to the interaction among individuals, organizations and environments; Müller-Stewens and Pautzke (Rosengarten, 1999) to the transformation from individual-level learning to group-level learning, which the model of Dixon (1999) lacks because she separates two learnings into two independent circular processes. All the organizational learning process models include and regard individual-level learning as an important part of the organizational learning process, but none cover organizational-level knowledge, explain the transformation from individual-level learning to organizational-level learning or regard them as an important component of organizational learning. A complex model of the organizational learning process, however, describes the relations between different learning levels respectively.

1.2.3.3   Complex model of the organizational learning process

(1) Model of Organizational Learning Process by Müller-Stewens and Pautzke (Rosengarten, 1999)

The model that they put forward entails that an individual, through "action," generates some knowledge based on his/her own experience or understanding of the environment; that individual knowledge, through "group learning," can be transformed to organizational knowledge; that individual knowledge has to be transformed to organizational knowledge only through "institutionalization" so as to make individual knowledge available to the entire organization; and that the institutionalized and authoritative knowledge will in turn bring impact on individual action in the future so as to achieve the circle. The model depicts the relations between individual knowledge and organizational knowledge as well as the relations between organizational knowledge and individual action, though it has the obvious drawback that an organization cannot produce a certain kind of experience. The model of Nonaka and Takeuchi (1995) conducted more elaborate and in-depth description of knowledge generation at the individual, group and organizational levels.

(2) Model of the Five Stages of Organizational Knowledge Creation by Nonaka and Takeuchi (1995)

Nonaka and Takeuchi (1995) put forward Model of the Five Stages of Organizational Knowledge Creation from the perspective of the knowledge creation, which bases its epistemological and ontological dimensions on the spiral of knowledge creation. Epistemologically, they draw the distinction between implicit knowledge and explicit knowledge, as they emphasize the transformation between different knowledge models. The process starts with socialization (i.e., field building), followed by externalization (i.e., dialogue or collective reflection) and combination (i.e., connection with explicit knowledge), and ends with internalization (i.e., learning through action). Based on this, the circle can then start again. Ontologically, knowledge is generated on different levels: from individual level to group level and then to organizational level, or even to inter-organizational level. The combination of the two dimensions brings about five facilitating conditions: intention, autonomy, fluctuation/creative chaos, redundancy and requisite variety, from which the Model of the Five Stages of Organizational Knowledge Creation comes into being.

The model starts with sharing tacit knowledge (socialization) among individuals in a group, transforms the implicit knowledge to explicit knowledge (externalization)—which should be justified by verifying the concepts through externalization—then constructs an archetype (combination) and ends up with interactive knowledge dissemination from one unit to other units in the organization (transformation). The circle can re-start from any phase, and another process of learning can be restarted through the knowledge user's action (internalization).

However, Nonaka and Takeuchi emphasize only the double-loop learning of the team that explores new products. It is a limitation of the model because of its weakening of individual learning and single-loop learning, and its externalization as premise. In fact, externalization is only a sufficient, not a necessary condition for organizational learning. In this regard, organizational knowledge creation by improving existent products is therefore omitted, which is, on the contrary, an overall advantage of Japanese enterprises. In addition, the model lacks evaluation of model interruptions, for which Kim (1993) makes up in his circle model of organizational learning to some extent.

(3) The Integrated Model Put Forward by Kim (1993)

Based on the models of Argyris and Schön (1978) and Daft and Weick (1984), Kim (1993) put forward what he believed to be the integrated model. His circular model of organizational learning describes the transformation from individual learning to organizational learning. He divides the individual learning circle into two groups related to "frameworks" and "routines." The first group is "conceptual individual learning" (know why), which includes "evaluation" and "design," and they are influenced by the "framework" of the individual mental model. The other group is "operational individual learning" (know how), which includes "evaluation" and "observation," and they are influenced by the "routines" of the individual mental model.

Kim believes that the interplay between the individual and shared mental models associates individual learning with organizational learning. His so-called shared mental model is a mix of "world views," which is an organization's view of the world. That is, the individual mental model influences the shared mental model to realize the transformation from individual learning to organizational learning and vice versa to realize the transformation from organizational-level learning to individual learning.

Compared with the model of Nonaka and Takeuchi, Kim's model not only includes single-loop and double-loop learning but also depicts the transformation between individual learning and organizational learning. Yet, he overlooked the important role of groups in organizational learning. Later, he regarded groups as "micro organizations" or "extended individuals," but that didn't solve the problem. His model is too complex to follow, and he fails to pay attention to inter-organizational learning.

(4) Dynamic Model of Organizational Learning Proposed by Crossan et al.
(1999)

The dynamic model of organizational learning includes three learning levels (individual, group and organizational), four psychological and social interaction processes (intuition, interpretation, integration and institutionalization), and two processes of information flow (feedback and feed forward). This model obtains in-depth analysis of the different mechanisms of organizational learning at different levels, the relationship between different levels of learning and the knowledge flow in two different directions. However, this model excludes inter-organizational learning and puts too much emphasis on the potential intuitive and unconscious learning process in the organization, thus neglecting explicit regular learning process in the general sense.

1.2.3.4 The process view of organizational learning in this study

Based on the preceding review, this study holds the view that in terms of the stage of learning process, there are four psychological and social interaction processes (mainly the interaction process among people): acquisition and generation, interpreting, integrating and institutionalizing, of which acquisition and creation (new knowledge or behavior) refers to individuals acquiring some knowledge or new behaviors from the external world or their own experience, or creating some new knowledge through intuition; interpreting is the process of explaining an insight or idea to one's self and to others through words or deeds; integrating is the process of developing shared understanding amongst individuals and the taking of coordinated action through mutual adjustment; institutionalizing is the process of embedding learning that has occurred by individuals and groups into the institutions of the organization so as to ensure that routinized actions occur. Among them, the process of interpreting can refer to both individual self-interpretation and mutual interpretation among group members; the integrating process can occur at both the group level and the organizational level (Crossan et al., 1999). In this way, the three levels of learning are connected as a whole.

This study holds that, at the inter-organizational level, there are two psychological and social interaction processes (Holmqvist, 2003), namely extension and internalization. Extension is a process of increasing transparency of organizational experience and knowledge; and internalization is a process of an organization receiving knowledge or experience from other organizations. According to Lindholm (1997), the process of inter-organizational knowledge flow includes acquisition, generation and application of knowledge. The knowledge here includes technical-level knowledge, system-level knowledge and strategic-level knowledge (Child, 2001). Technical-level knowledge refers to the acquisition of skills, corresponding to single-loop learning; system-level knowledge refers to the knowledge about organizational characteristics such as organization system and organizational procedure, corresponding to double-loop learning; and strategic-level knowledge refers to the thoughts, concepts and ways of thinking of senior managers, and it requires a process of reflection. It can be seen that inter-organizational learning involves three levels: individual, group and organizational. Any of these levels can be engaged in inter-organizational learning. Therefore, extension and internalization can integrate intra-organizational learning and inter-organizational learning into a whole.

1.2.4 Comprehensive theoretical model of organizational learning

Based on the review and conceptualizations presented in this chapter, this study proposes a comprehensive theoretical model of organizational learning from the perspective of managing organizational learning, as shown in Figure 1.1 (Yu et al., 2004). The premise of this model is that all organizations have learning behaviors and that organizational learning is a process.

The organizational learning model proposed by this study follows the three principles and purposes, as follows.

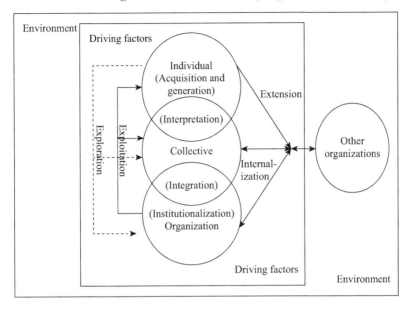

Figure 1.1 Comprehensive theoretical model of organizational learning

First, organizational learning occurs in all organizations. Learning capability is prerequisite for an organization to survive and thrive. For organizations, differences lie in the levels of learning and respective strengths.

Second, organizational learning is the unity of human and knowledge. Humans are the subject of learning, and the subject of organizational learning is also the individual and group in the organization. Individuals or groups are also the main carriers of learning behaviors at organizational levels and inter-organizational learning process. In addition, organizational learning process always takes knowledge as the carrier, and knowledge is the content and object of learning. Therefore, organizational learning always emphasizes the unity of human and knowledge.

Third, organizational learning is a process of social interactions. It is different from individual learning. Though individual learning is a key part of organizational learning, the latter focuses not on the learning ability of individual employees but that of the entire organization. The emphasis is placed on the sound interactions among individuals in an organization.

From the perspective of learning level, organizational learning includes four levels, namely individual, collective, organizational and inter-organizational. Each level is overlapping and mutually reinforcing with another, and thus the poor performance of a single level undermines the learning effects of the whole.

From the perspective of knowledge or information flow, organizational learning includes two processes: explorative learning (closely linked with exploration of knowledge) and exploitative learning (closely linked with exploitation of knowledge). The two processes demonstrate the dynamic circular characteristics of organizational learning process.

From the perspective of the organizational learning process, organizational learning includes four psychological and social interactive processes at the individual, collective and organizational levels: acquisition and generation, interpretation, integration and institutionalization. These four processes mainly reflect the dominant position of people in organizational learning, and human is the core of learning. It also shows that organizational learning emphasizes the collective learning process based on individuals. At the level of inter-organizational learning, organizational learning includes two processes: extension and internalization. What is emphasized here is that the four psychological and social interaction processes integrate individual, collective and organizational levels into one, while the interactions of the three levels with other organizations and the two processes (extension and internalization) of the three levels integrate the intra-organizational and inter-organizational learning into a whole.

At the same time, external facilitating factors are needed to maintain and retain organizational learning. This is a characteristic of learning organization that many scholars and practitioners have been studying.

The environment of organizational learning is also the external environment of the organization. Whether the external environment is turbulent or stable is an essential premise for organizational learning. In a turbulent environment, the external pressure of organizational learning will be large; while in a stable external environment, the external pressure of organizational learning will be small.

2 The multilevel construct of organizational learning

2.1 Literature review

2.1.1 Empirical studies on organizational learning abroad

Scholars abroad have conducted some empirical studies on organizational learning from different perspectives, but controversies abound in their research findings, which fall mainly into two categories. Lahteenmarki et al. (2001) argued that organizational learning can be divided into three steps: building the ability to learn, collaborative setting of missions and strategies, and building the future together. The study result of Templeton et al. (2002) demonstrates that organizational learning is composed of eight factors: awareness, communication, performance assessment, intellectual cultivation, environmental adaptability, social learning, intellectual capital management and organization grafting. Based on the dynamic model of Crossan et al. (1999), Bontis et al. (2002) studied the three levels of the organizational learning system and the relationship between feedback and feed forward. The research findings of Hult and Ferrell (1997) Hult et al. (2002) and Hult and David (2003) show that organizational learning ability includes team orientation, systems orientation, learning orientation and memory orientation. According to results of their research on 271 executives, Tippins and Sohi (2003) conclude that organizational learning includes information acquisition, information dissemination, shared interpretation, declarative memory and procedural memory. Ellis and Shpielberg's (2003) study on 395 project managers found that organizational learning mechanisms include formal learning processes, information dissemination, training, information gathering, information storage and retrieval. Jerez-Gómez et al. (2005a) conducted a study on 111 Spanish chemical companies to show that organizational learning includes management commitment, system perspective, openness and experimentation, and knowledge transfer and integration.

Second, there are studies on facilitating factors of organizational learning. A questionnaire famous abroad on the factors that facilitate organizational learning is based on Watkins and Marsick's (1993) and Marsick and Watkins's (1999) model. Building on various prior studies, Yang et al.'s (2004) exploratory and confirmatory factor analysis of 863 survey data participants (one person per company) validated the seven dimensions proposed in the model: create continuous learning opportunities, promote inquiry and dialogue, encourage collaboration and team learning, empower people toward a collective vision, connect the organization to its environment, establish a system to capture and share learning and provide strategic leadership for learning. The empirical research results of Goh and Richards (1997) proved that organizational learning capability comprises five factors: clarity of mission and purpose, leadership commitment, experimentation and rewards, transfer of knowledge, and teamwork and group problem solving.

In a word, these scholars study organizational learning process from the perspective of information processing, and often at a singular level (mostly at the organizational level). This explains why many studies often take only one subject to represent a company, which renders the in-depth exploration of the group members' interactive group learning in organizational learning impossible.

2.1.2   *Empirical research on organizational learning by chinese scholars*

Chinese scholars have obtained some results through theoretical analysis and empirical research, which falls into four main types.

The first type is general research based on system theory. Building on the organizational learning model of Argyris and Schön (1978), Chen and Ma (2000) studied the learning disability of Chinese companies from the perspective of organizational learning disability and developed an organizational learning self-test system. They also conducted case studies to discuss the types of organizational learning from the perspective of learning subjects (Chen & Zheng, 2005). Thanks to his long-term research, Chen Guoquan achieved a 6P-1B (6 processes, 1 knowledge base) model, which was revised into an organizational learning process model that encompasses nine aspects (Chen, 2007). Wang Runliang (2002) improved the organizational learning system model proposed by Marquardt (1996) and conducted an empirical organizational structure design.

The second type is the content construct of organizational learning. An empirical study conducted by Yu Wenzhao et al. (2002) on the continuous learning corporate culture came up with a corporate culture construct of learning with 10 dimensions: training and resource availability, tolerance of uncertainty, a reward system, interpersonal atmosphere, internal integrity of the organization, work autonomy, work cognition, responsibility attribution, environmental communication and future orientation. Based on the questionnaire of Tannenbaum (1997), Zhao Wenjin (2002) proposed the eight learning conditions that facilitate organizational learning, which are awareness of big picture, assigning to provide opportunities to learn, tolerating mistakes as part of learning, accountability/ high performance expectation, openness to ideas and change, policies and practices support training, supervisors support training, and coworkers supporting new ideas. Through the study of Chinese family companies, Yang Jianfeng et al. (2004) concluded that organizational learning of Chinese family companies includes eight learning factors representing three learning models, which are exploration, exploitation and regulatory learning, respectively. Case studies led Wei Jiang et al. (2014) to the findings that the order of organizational learning of companies is sowing type, solo type, consulting type and enhancing type. The research finding presents unique cultural characteristics.

The third type is the research based on March's study on exploration and exploitation. Many scholars in China are drawing from the basic theories of exploration and exploitation put forward by March (1991). Wu Xiaobo (1995) and others studied the interaction process of exploration and exploitation in companies' second round of entrepreneurship and reached the conclusion that latecomers evolve from small-scale, low member heterogeneity, weak strong alternating network to large scale and high member heterogeneity and dual network, and that the balance mode of organizational learning also shifts from intermittent type to dual type.

The fourth type is the research on the role of organizational learning. Jiang Chunyan and Zhao Shuming (2006) reached the conclusion that organizational learning plays a mediating role between social capital and corporate entrepreneurship and performance. Jiao Hao et al. (2008) found that organizational learning plays a mediating role between entrepreneurial orientation and dynamic capabilities. Yuan Xinwei et al. (2006) elaborated on the relationship between organizational learning and organizational performance. He Yuanqiong and Tian Zhilong (2008), Xie Hongming et al. (2007) and Sun Rui and Zhao Chen (2017) conducted empirical studies on the relationship between the two and the research findings show the positive value of organizational learning on organizational performance. In addition, they investigated the mediating variables of the relationship between organizational system and external environment. Dai Wanwen et al. (2006) summarized and studied the characteristics of cross-cultural organizational learning.

To sum up, while most researchers agree with the three levels of organizational learning (individual, collective and organizational levels), inter-organizational learning has not been widely recognized. Many researchers focus on information or knowledge in the process of organizational learning, confusing organizational learning with knowledge management. This study holds that learning is a human activity and that organizational learning contains a more complex knowledge and information flow. Therefore, when understanding the connotations of organizational learning, on the one hand, attention should be paid to the interactions among the subjects—human; on the other hand, it should be understood that organizational learning includes some changes with non-human characteristics at the organizational level. It should also be noted that although organizational learning cannot be simply attributed to knowledge processing, it remains to be verified by empirical research whether it definitely contains complex knowledge or information processing. Therefore, whether in theory or in practice, it is indeed necessary to study Chinese companies' organizational learning from the three perspectives of organizational learning based on the managing of organization learning.

2.2 Pilot study

2.2.1 Research purpose

This purpose of this book is to study the structure of organizational learning in Chinese companies through interviews and pre-test, and to compile and examine the organizational learning questionnaire to delve into further study.

2.2.2 Methodology

First, we determine the interview outline based on the literature analysis and definition of organizational learning; then we collect interview items related to organizational learning to form the organizational learning questionnaire; at last we proceed to explore the structure of organizational learning in Chinese companies through questionnaire survey and multivariate statistical analysis.

2.2.3 Research process

2.2.3.1 Interviews

The fact that organizational learning is still a new concept requires that this study conduct interviews to collect related items. The interviews are carried out in three steps. Firstly, we synthesize the definitions of organizational learning based on the above theoretical research, and present the synthesized concept of organizational learning to the respondents. Secondly, the respondents are told to have discussions on the concept of organizational learning and to share the organizational learning situation in their own companies according to their own understanding. Thirdly, after grasping the concept of organizational learning, the respondents asked questions according to the outline of interviews. We interviewed 10 middle- and senior-level managers from 9 companies (3 state-owned companies, 3 foreign-funded companies and 3 private companies, respectively). Each interview took about 1.5 hours.

2.2.3.2 Encoding and collecting items on organizational learning

The interview recordings were sorted into written materials for encoding carried out by two psychology PhD students who would have communications on the research plan, ideas and objectives before encoding. The terms in organizational learning theory and interview records went through a long period of in-depth discussions before being further explained. After reaching a consensus on the main issues, the codebook was compiled (Li, 2003). The compilation and encoding process is as follows. First, two interview records were extracted, and the two students independently extracted the learning behaviors from the interview records. Then, the two independent analysis results were combined and discussed to form the primary codebook. Based on the background in the interview record, they discussed the primary codebook, merged the statements with the same or similar meaning and modified the colloquial statements. Based on the primary codebook, the two students re-extracted the learning behaviors from the interview records; the extraction process follows the principle of detecting all the learning behaviors. Then the independent extraction of learning behavior went through discussions, combination, frequency statistics and analysis, and modification, and finally it was determined that the codebook would include 53 items. The two students discussed one of the interview records, and they communicated and understood each other's coding standards so as to make such standards consistent. According to the interview records, the assignment of each statement was discussed, which were "not mentioned (0)," "negative (1)," "neutral (2)" and "positive (3)." The two PhD students encoded independently, and the encoding consensus coefficient of the two encoders was 0.973. Therefore, the encoding process was one of constant modification and adjustment. Finally, four company practitioners (one employee from a foreign-funded company and three employees from a state-owned company) and six experts were invited to revise the rationale, meaning and wording of each item. In reference to relevant foreign scales, 53 items with clear and concise statements were selected to form the initial organizational learning questionnaire.

2.2.3.3 Preliminary test of organizational learning questionnaire

2.2.3.3.1 SUBJECTS

The pre-test was carried out in Jinan University, South China University of Technology and Central University of Finance and Economics. Two hundred questionnaires were distributed and 123 valid questionnaires were recovered, with an effective rate of 62%.

2.2.3.3.2 STATISTICAL METHODS

We adopted exploratory factor analysis and correlation analysis with the assistance of statistical software SPSS 10.0.

2.2.3.3.3 ANALYSIS OF PRE-TEST RESULTS

Given the small size of the pre-test sample, we focus on the analysis of the item quality. First, we carried out exploratory factor analysis on the data of 53 preliminary items. We used the principal component analysis method to extract factors and the orthogonal variance maximum method for rotation axis. The factor structure was obtained after multiple explorations. Then, we calculated the correlation coefficient between the score of each item and the total score, the kurtosis value of each item, and the internal consistency coefficient of the dimension after excluding the items to identify the quality of each item. In light of the results of factor analysis and the quality of each item determined by the analysis, 37 items were finalized as the questionnaire items for the ensuing investigation.

2.3 Construct of organizational learning structure model

2.3.1 Research purpose

To further explore the structure of organizational learning of Chinese companies, we conducted a large-scale survey with the 37-item questionnaire finalized after the pre-test, and we analyzed the survey data through multivariate statistical analysis.

2.3.2 Methodology

2.3.2.1 Subjects

A total of 1800 questionnaires were distributed to 43 companies in nine cities (Beijing, Guangzhou, Qingdao, Shanghai, Jinan, Yantai, Chengdu, Shijiazhuang and Tangshan), and 982 valid questionnaires were recovered, with an effective rate of 55%. A total of 614 questionnaires from 80% of the top 33 companies were randomly selected for exploratory factor analysis. The basic information of the subjects is shown in Table 2.1.

Table 2.1 Basic information of the subjects (*N* = 614)

Variable	Category	Number	Percentage
Nature of company	State-owned companies	375	61.1
	Private companies	117	19.1
	Companies in three forms of ventures—Sino-foreign joint ventures, cooperative business and exclusively foreign-funded company	63	10.3
	Other	59	9.6
Scale of company	50–99	43	7.0
	100–499	190	30.9
	500–999	56	9.1
	1000–1999	127	20.7
	2000–4999	62	10.1
	Above 5000	136	22.1
Development stage of company	Start-up	38	6.2
	Growing	225	36.6
	Mature	123	20.0
	Re-innovation	228	37.1
Position	General staff	386	62.9
	Front-line managers	136	22.1
	Middle-level management	68	11.1
	Senior management	11	1.8
	None	13	2.1
Level of literacy	Middle school	44	7.2
	Junior college	202	32.9
	Undergraduate college	304	49.5
	Master	48	7.8
	Doctor	2	0.3
	None	14	2.3

2.3.2.2 Measure

The 37-item organizational learning questionnaire was put into use. We use the Likert five-point scale to measure and evaluate the learning behaviors of different levels of companies from "1—completely inconsistent" to "5—completely consistent" in ascending order, which are: "completely inconsistent," "relatively inconsistent," "not sure," "relatively consistent" and "completely consistent" respectively.

2.3.2.3 Statistical method

We adopted SPSS 10.0 for the explorative factor analysis and other analysis.

2.3.2.4 Research procedure

All investigations were completed in a relatively concentrated period of time. In some of the investigations, investigators answered specific questions on the spot; proxy investigators were also hired to conduct some investigations, and the procedures and precautions were made clear to them beforehand. It was required that the investigated employees should come from multiple departments at all levels of a company, and an average of 40 employees in each company were interviewed. The respondents did not need to provide their names and company, and only the investigators needed to know the name of the company.

2.3.3 Research results

The data of 614 questionnaires were analyzed by exploratory factor analysis. We adopted the principal component analysis method to extract the factors, and the orthogonal maximum variance method to carry out the rotation axis. The principle of factor extraction was that the eigenvalues were greater than 1, and the scree plot was used to determine the items and factors. At the same time, item analysis was carried out, which covers the change of internal consistency coefficient after excluding each item, the correlation between item score and total score, and the kurtosis value of the items. After comprehensive analysis, 8 items were deleted, with 29 items remaining. Factor analysis was carried out on these 29 items. Varimax in principal component analysis was adopted. The results are shown in Table 2.2.

The research finding shows that the structure of Chinese companies' organizational learning includes six factors, which altogether can explain 54.25% of the total variance. The name and content of each factor is presented as follows.

Factor 1: inter-organizational learning, which involves six items. The main content includes searching for and retaining the experience of other companies, exchanging experience and personnel with other companies, discussing future development with customers, and learning from good practices of other companies.

Factor 2: exploitative learning, which involves four items. The main content includes company policy communication, strategy publicity to employees, company planning to point out the work direction for employees, company belief and regulations training.

Table 2.2 Results of exploratory factor analysis of organizational learning questionnaire ($N = 614$)

Factors	Inter-organizational learning	Exploitative learning	Explorative learning	Organizational-level learning	Collective learning	Individual learning
25. Our company searches for and retains the experience and lessons of other companies.	**0.639**	0.254	0.308	0.085	0.217	0.009
29. Our company often cooperates with other companies for common development.	**0.628**	0.013	0.137	0.228	0.176	0.221
5. Our company often exchanges work experience with cooperative companies.	**0.596**	0.175	0.113	0.113	−0.083	0.255
17. Our company engages in exchanges and training with other companies.	**0.556**	0.106	0.171	0.073	0.092	0.180
37. Our company discusses future development with customers.	**0.527**	0.134	0.261	0.275	0.093	0.071
23. Our company often learns from the good practices of other companies.	**0.479**	0.340	0.220	0.158	0.217	0.083
9. Our company can convey its policy to every employee.	0.074	**0.770**	0.073	0.168	0.141	0.141
7. Our company publicizes the established strategy to employees in various forms.	0.280	**0.675**	0.026	0.094	0.059	0.222
10. Our company planning points out the work direction for the staff.	0.036	**0.636**	0.403	0.169	0.044	0.149
19. Our company carries out trainings on beliefs and rules and regulations.	0.296	**0.627**	0.225	0.162	0.142	0.081

35. Both general staff and managers have an impact on corporate strategy.	0.238	−0.010	**0.707**	0.108	−0.046	0.043
24. Employees often participate in collective decision-making.	0.231	0.182	**0.706**	0.114	0.116	0.127
20. The personal opinions of employees can be taken into account when making decisions.	0.295	0.274	**0.687**	0.056	0.105	−0.006
34. The company planning often adopts the department's work suggestions.	0.170	0.104	**0.402**	0.387	0.237	0.072
12. The organizational structure of the company constantly adjusts according to business needs.	−0.023	0.192	0.106	**0.742**	0.071	0.191
15. The company planning constantly adjusts according to the internal and external changes.	0.142	0.098	0.095	**0.698**	0.083	0.067
33. The company's business process is constantly adjusted.	0.291	0.328	0.053	**0.560**	0.259	−0.102
27. The company will adjust strategy to adapt to the change of external environment.	0.223	0.014	0.118	**0.555**	0.099	0.093
4. The organizational structure of the company changes appropriately to adapt to the strategic changes.	0.165	0.466	−0.029	**0.515**	−0.042	0.211

(Continued)

Table 2.2 (Continued)

Factors	Inter-organizational learning	Exploitative learning	Explorative learning	Organizational-level learning	Collective learning	Individual learning
30. Colleagues often cooperate and help each other in their work.	0.100	0.111	−0.002	0.041	**0.770**	0.141
21. Colleagues often exchange freely work-related information.	−0.020	0.124	0.188	0.115	**0.671**	0.126
13. Communication between colleagues is smooth.	0.156	0.172	−0.018	0.088	**0.622**	0.239
28. Colleagues often solve the disagreement in their work through discussions and consultations.	0.174	−0.113	0.157	0.203	**0.604**	0.195
3. My colleagues sum up their work experience in time.	0.098	0.227	0.246	0.048	0.161	**0.656**
8. My colleagues will have a lot of new ideas in their work.	0.207	0.056	−0.027	0.142	0.128	**0.614**
16. My colleagues can break old thinking habits and look at problems from a new perspective.	0.023	0.083	0.349	0.190	0.235	**0.567**
1. My colleagues have clear work goals.	0.287	0.267	−0.163	0.066	0.119	**0.552**
11. My colleagues often try and test new ideas.	0.066	0.105	0.374	0.144	0.290	**0.541**
6. My colleagues actively seek help from others to solve problems.	0.247	0.095	−0.169	−0.008	0.387	**0.490**
Eigenvalue	8.412	2.062	1.610	1.383	1.188	1.075
Explained variance	9.73%	9.66%	8.96%	8.69%	8.65%	8.56%

Factor 3: explorative learning, which involves four items. The main content includes employee engagement in collective decision-making, employee influence strategy, consideration of personal opinions in company decision-making, and adoption of department opinions in company planning.

Factor 4: organizational-level learning, which involves five items. The main content includes the following: the organizational structure is adjusted in tempo with the business, the company planning is adjusted according to the conditions, the company strategy adapts to the changes of the external environment, and the company process is adjusted.

Factor 5: collective learning, which involves four items. The main content includes cooperation among colleagues, free exchange of work information, smooth communication among colleagues and coordination and conflict among colleagues.

Factor 6: individual learning, which involves six items. The main content includes new ideas, reflection on work, breaking out of traditional mind-sets, clear working goals, trying new ideas in work, and seeking help from others.

It can be seen from these results that the organizational learning of Chinese companies includes six factors, including four learning levels and two processes of knowledge and information flow. The learning at individual, collective and organizational levels has been widely recognized (Easterby-Smith et al., 2000), while there were few theoretical discussions on inter-organizational learning. Pedler et al. (1991), Nonaka and Takeuchi (1995), Pawlowsky (2001) and Holmqvist (2003) have held theoretical discussions on inter-organizational learning, and their views are justified by the results of this study. There have been many discussions about two processes of information or knowledge flow in organizational learning, namely exploitative learning and explorative learning in theoretical circles (such as the March school). The results of this study verify the views of these scholars to a certain extent.

Therefore, these six factors indicate that organizational learning is trans-level in nature. It is not only a phenomenon on a singular organizational level but also a complicated process that involves the entire organization and beyond. The four levels demonstrate where the organizational learning takes place; the two processes of information or knowledge flow indicate that the information or knowledge, as the learning content in organizational learning, has the flow characteristics. These two aspects combine to reflect the dynamic cycling of organizational learning.

2.4 Verification of organizational learning structure model

2.4.1 Research process

We used the data of another sample to verify whether the six-factor organizational learning structure model obtained through exploratory factor analysis is the optimal model.

2.4.2 Methodology

2.4.2.1 Subjects

With another 20% of questionnaires from the top 33 companies and the last 10 companies, and a small number of questionnaires whose companies cannot be identified, we obtained 368 questionnaires in total. The basic information of the subjects is shown in Table 2.3.

Table 2.3 Basic information of subjects (*N* = 368)

Variable	Type	Number of people	Percentage
Nature of companies	State-owned	191	51.9
	Private	69	18.8
	Three-capital	49	13.3
	Other	58	15.8
	Not filled in	1	0.3
Scale of companies	1–49	16	4.3
	50–99	11	3.0
	100–499	142	38.6
	500–999	30	8.2
	1000–1999	80	21.7
	2000–4999	43	11.7
	Above 5000	45	12.2
	Not filled in	1	0.3
Development stage of development	Start-up	24	6.5
	Growing	150	40.8
	Mature	59	16.0
	Re-innovation	130	35.3
	Other	4	1.1
	Not filled in	1	0.3
Position	General staff	227	61.7
	First-line managers	75	20.4
	Middle-level managers	50	13.6
	Senior management	8	2.2
	Top management	2	0.5
	Not filled in	6	1.6
Level of education	Middle school	33	9.0
	Junior college	147	39.9
	Undergraduate college	165	44.8
	Master	16	4.3
	Not filled in	7	1.9

2.4.2.2 Measure

We used the 29-item organizational learning questionnaire of Chinese companies. The Likert five-point scale is employed to evaluate the learning behaviors at various levels in companies. Ranging from "1—completely inconsistent" to "5—completely consistent," they are: "completely inconsistent," "relatively inconsistent," "not sure," "relatively consistent" and "completely consistent."

2.4.2.3 Statistical method

The confirmatory factor analysis was adopted using software Amos4.0.

2.4.3 Hypothetical model and measurement model

This chapter has shown that the organizational learning of Chinese companies can be explained by the six-factor structure model. We adopted confirmatory factor analysis (CFA) to compare the six-factor model with several potential models to test whether the six-factor model is the optimal model.

First, is organizational learning per se a single-factor structure? Figure 2.1 shows a single-factor model.

Second, inter-organizational learning is the most prominent feature that distinguishes this study from the prior empirical studies. So, do inter-organizational learning and the other five factors form the two aspects that constitute organizational learning? If so, we can build a two-factor model consisting of these two aspects, as shown in Figure 2.2.

The literature review also shows that up to now, most empirical studies on organizational learning were conducted from the perspective of the object or content of organizational learning—information or knowledge processing (e.g., Templeton et al., 2002; Tippins & Sohi, 2003; Ellis & Shpielberg, 2003). However, more and more theoretical discussions have advised that organizational learning should be understood from the interaction of the subject in the organization—human (e.g., Bogenrieder, 2002; Bogenrieder & Nooteboom, 2004; Akgun et al., 2003; Berends et al., 2002). Therefore, understanding of organizational learning includes the third and fourth perspectives (Models 3 and 4), described next.

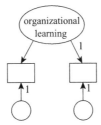

Figure 2.1 Single-factor model

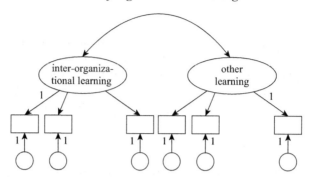

Figure 2.2 Model 2: a two-factor model consisting of inter-organizational learning and other learning

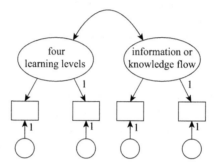

Figure 2.3 Model 3: a two-factor model composed of learning level and information or knowledge flow

Third, organizational learning can be understood from two aspects, namely level of organizational learning and information or knowledge flow, which means that it is a two-dimensional structure that mainly includes these two aspects, as shown in Figure 2.3.

Fourth, organizational learning can also be a three-dimensional structure interpreted from the three levels within the learning organization, inter-organizational learning and the process of information or knowledge flow in learning, as shown in Figure 2.4.

Fifthly, in the literature of organizational learning, the relationship between individual learning and organizational learning has always been the focus of debate among scholars. Many scholars (such as Argyris & Schön, 1978; Senge, 1990) believe that individual learning is a necessary condition of organizational learning. However, other scholars (who understand organizational learning only from the collective level, particularly the system and behaviorial perspectives) exclude individual learning from organizational learning and contend that the two are different. Therefore, organizational learning is a two-dimensional structure that includes individual learning and collective level learning. This can constitute hypothetical Model 5, as shown in Figure 2.5.

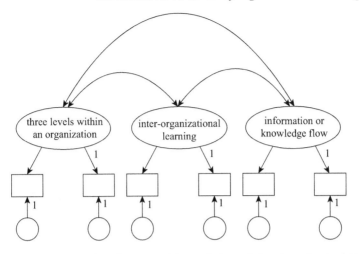

Figure 2.4 Model 4: a three-factor model consisting of the three levels within an organization, inter-organizational learning, and information or knowledge flow

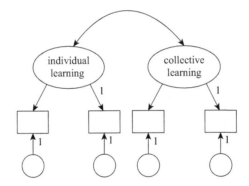

Figure 2.5 Model 5: a two-factor model composed of individual learning and collective level learning

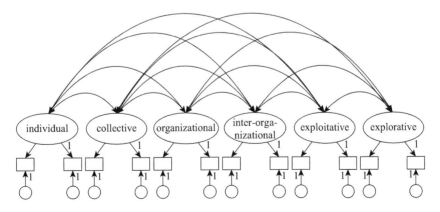

Figure 2.6 Model 6: a six-factor model

Sixth, the results of our studies show that organizational learning is a six-factor structure. The measurement model obtained in this study is shown in Figure 2.6.

2.4.4 Results and analysis

2.4.4.1 Results of confirmatory factor analysis

The x^2/df and RMSEA indexes in Table 2.4 render Model 1, which views organizational learning as a single-factor structure, and Model 2, which distinguishes inter-organizational learning from other learning, unacceptable. Models 3, 4, 5 and 6 are acceptable, and the measurement indexes x^2/df, NFI, IFI, TLI, CFI and RMSEA increase gradually. In addition, it can be seen from Table 2.5 that Models 3, 4 and 5 represent different perspectives and standards, but from the data fit point of view, the six-factor model is the optimal model, and this conclusion dovetails with the theoretical hypotheses of this study.

In addition, the evaluation index of measurement model also includes the loading of each explicit variable on latent variable and the loading on error. The results of the six-factor model are shown in Table 2.6. It can be seen that the loading of each item and factor is higher, and the loading on error (error loading) is lower, which indicates that the interpretation rate of each item to the corresponding latent variable is relatively high with small error.

The preceding has proven that through explorative factor analysis, this study obtained a six-factor structure model for the organizational learning of Chinese companies. Building on this, we verified the six-factor model through confirmatory factor analysis and reached the conclusion that six-factor model is indeed the ideal model for Chinese companies' organizational learning.

Table 2.4 Comparison of various models

	x	df	x^2/df	NFI	IFI	TLI	CFI	PNFI	RMSEA
Model 0	26,412.6	435	60.72						
Model 1	32,309.7	435	74.28	0.960	0.971	0.967	0.971	0.832	0.081
Model 2	32,309.7	435	74.28	0.961	0.955	0.968	0.973	0.831	0.080
Model 3	1067.7	376	2.84	0.960	0.973	0.969	0.973	0.829	0.078
Model 4	1001.5	374	2.68	0.962	0.976	0.972	0.976	0.827	0.075
Model 5	951.2	376	2.53	0.964	0.978	0.974	0.978	0.833	0.072
Model 6	651.2	362	1.79	0.975	0.989	0.987	0.989	0.812	0.052

Note: Model 1 refers to a single-factor model; Model 2 is a two-factor model composed of inter-organizational learning and other learning; Model 3 refers to a two-factor model composed of learning levels and information or knowledge flow; Model 4 refers to a three-factor model composed of three levels within an organization, inter-organizational learning and information or knowledge flow; Model 5 refers to a two-factor model composed of individual learning and collective level learning; and Model 6 refers to the six-factor model.

Table 2.5 Test of the model fitting difference

Comparing model	$\triangle x^2$	$\triangle df$	$\triangle (x^2/df)$
Model 6–Model 3	−416.5	−14	29.75**
Model 6–Model 4	−350.3	−12	29.19**
Model 6–Model 5	−300	−14	21.43**

** $p < 0.01$
Note: When $df = 12$, the critical value of $p < 0.01$ is $x^2 = 26.2$; When $df = 14$, the critical value of $p < 0.01$ is $x^2 = 29.1$.

Table 2.6 Loading of latent variables on explicit variables and error variables of six-factor model

Individual learning			Collective learning			Organizational learning		
Item	Load	Error load	Item	Load	Error load	Item	Load	Error load
3	0.631	0.1398	30	0.534	0.285	12	0.629	0.396
8	0.704	0.495	21	0.562	0.315	15	0.724	0.524
16	0.621	0.386	13	0.624	0.389	33	0.613	0.376
1	0.531	0.282	28	0.554	0.307	27	0.684	0.468
11	0.740	0.548				4	0.590	0.348
6	0.493	0.243						
25	0.643	0.413	9	0.759	0.576	35	0.612	0.374
29	0.637	0.406	7	0.716	0.512	24	0.739	0.546
5	0.527	0.278	10	0.710	0.505	20	0.740	0.547
17	0.497	0.247	19	0.613	0.375	34	0.598	0.357
37	0.582	0.338						
23	0.661	0.437						

2.4.4.2 Reliability and validity of the organizational learning questionnaire

2.4.4.2.1 RELIABILITY ANALYSIS

The internal consistency coefficient of each dimension and the total can be found in Table 2.7, which shows that the internal consistency coefficient of each dimension is higher than 0.70, while that of the total table reaches 0.91, signifying that the reliability of the questionnaire meets the requirements of psychometrics.

2.4.4.2.2 VALIDITY ANALYSIS

First, the results of exploratory factor analysis and confirmatory factor analysis can be used as proof of the structure validity of the questionnaire. The results show that the factor structure is clear and the indicators meet the requirements of

Table 2.7 Internal consistency coefficient of each dimension and total (*N* = 982)

Factor	Total scale	Inter-organizational learning	Exploitative learning	Explorative learning	Organizational level learning	Collective level learning	Individual learning
Coefficient α	0.91	0.77	0.78	0.75	0.73	0.71	0.76

Table 2.8 Correlation between items and total score of each dimension ($N = 982$)

Factor	Total scale	Inter-organizational learning	Exploitative learning	Explorative learning	Organizational level learning	Collective learning
Item 1	0.657***	0.777*	0.808***	0.704***	0.723***	0.632***
Item 2	0.652***	0.814*	0.805***	0.746***	0.721***	0.684***
Item 3	0.680***	0.751*	0.668***	0.728***	0.705***	0.628***
Item 4	0.727***	0.780*	0.752***	0.719***	0.733***	0.736***
Item 5	0.713***			0.665***		0.726***
Item 6	0.680***					0.693***

*** $p < 0.001$.

Notes: Item 1 represents the first item in the corresponding dimension; Item 2 represents the second item and so on. The relationship with effect variables: the positive effects of organizational learning on individual-level variables and collective-level variables (organizational innovation ability and corporate financial performance) in Chapter 3 can also explain the criterion-related validity of this questionnaire. The specific results are shown in Chapter 3.

psychometrics. In addition, the results of confirmatory factor analysis are consistent with the theoretical concept of the study.

Second, the correlation between the items of the six subscales and the total score of each dimension can prove the structure validity of the questionnaire. The results in Table 2.8 show that the correlation between each item and the total score of each dimension is in the range of 0.628–0.808, all at a very significant level. This shows that the questionnaire has good structural validity.

2.5 Analysis and discussion

This study got a six-factor measurement model of organizational learning in companies from the perspective of management learning. The individual, collective and organizational levels are widely recognized. The theoretical views of Pedler et al. (1991), Nonaka and Takeuchi (1995) and Holmqvist (2003) are verified by inter-organizational learning, which is rarely mentioned in empirical studies abroad. The development process of China's well-known domestic companies such as Haier and Lenovo provides the best practical evidence for inter-organizational learning. The two processes of information or knowledge flow in organizational learning are exploration and exploitation. This study also verifies the ideas of scholars such as March. The results of confirmatory factor analysis show that each factor in organizational learning is an integral part of organizational learning, and its status in organizational learning is not affected by the different classification criteria (five hypothetical models). This six-factor measurement model also verifies the four learning levels and two processes of knowledge or information flow in the definition of organizational learning.

These six factors reflect the features of the combination of human and knowledge, human and non-human organization, internal and external organization, static and dynamic characteristics. In this six-factor model, on the one hand, the four levels reflect where organizational learning takes place, indicating the trans-level nature of organizational learning, and that it is not only a phenomenon at a single level of the organization, but also involves the interactions of a complex learning network within an organization and between organizations. On the other hand, the two processes of information or knowledge flow reflect the flow characteristics of information or knowledge as learning content in organizational learning, and the information or knowledge flow happens at four levels. The four levels reflect the static characteristics of organizational learning, while two processes of information or knowledge processing reflect the dynamic characteristics. The combination of these two aspects reflects the characteristics of the dynamic cycle of organizational learning and verifies the integration of social interaction, information processing and system.

The six-factor model can achieve a relatively holistic measurement of the learning of an organization and thus provide a reference index and framework for companies to better manage their organizational learning, as well as a framework for better understanding the internal mechanism of organizational learning. This model makes us realize that in order to measure the organizational learning status of companies, we need to investigate the following four aspects: (1) the learning status of people in the organization, including individual learning and collective learning; (2) the processes of knowledge or information flow, namely explorative learning and exploitative learning; (3) continuous adjustment of organizational strategy and organizational structure at the organizational level; (4) mutual learning and communication between organizations. This model also suggests that we must grasp these six factors and their complex interactive relationship to realize deeper understanding of organizational learning.

Different from some studies on learning organizations, this study's six-factor model is based on the understanding of the organizational learning process, and it describes how organizations learn. Learning organizations are often discussed only from the perspective of the conditions and characteristics of organizational learning (or the facilitating factors of organizational learning). In contrast, the six factors in this study can be used as six indicators to promote and measure the learning organization so as to provide operational reference for the establishment of the learning organization.

3 The trans-level effectiveness of organizational learning

3.1 The effect of organizational learning on individuals

3.1.1 Research hypothesis

This chapter investigates the relationship between organizational learning and employee satisfaction, affective commitment, turnover intention, task performance, the role of individual learning in influencing individual variables on collective-level learning and the role of organizational learning in the relationship between individual variables.

3.1.1.1 Related theories and hypotheses

3.1.1.1.1 ORGANIZATIONAL LEARNING AND EMPLOYEE SATISFACTION

Organizational learning, as a long-term strategy to improve the core competitiveness of the organization, is closely related to the working attitude of employees. There are some related studies in the literature. Goh and Rhan (2002) analyzed the survey data of 89 companies and found that there was a strong and significant positive correlation between the five kinds of organizational learning capability and job satisfaction, and the correlation coefficient reached 0.66 ($p < 0.001$). The study of Yu Wenzhao et al. (2002) on organizational culture of continuous learning shows a significant positive correlation between organizational culture of continuous learning and satisfaction, and the correlation coefficient reaches a medium level. Although the aforementioned studies are not direct research on organizational learning and employee satisfaction, the findings do suggest that there may be a positive relationship between them. Therefore, the following theoretical hypothesis is set forth:

Hypothesis 1:

The higher the level of organizational learning, the higher the employee satisfaction.

3.1.1.1.2 ORGANIZATIONAL LEARNING AND ORGANIZATIONAL COMMITMENT

Organizational learning is also closely related to organizational commitment, another work attitude of employees. Similarly, there have been some related studies. Howard (2003), for example, proved a significant positive correlation between organizational learning culture and organizational commitment. Yu Wenzhao et al. (2002) found that there is a significant positive correlation between organizational culture of continuous learning and organizational commitment, and the correlation coefficient reached a medium level. Given that the organizational commitment questionnaire is lengthy, this study chooses some commonly used items on affective commitment and posits the following theoretical hypothesis:

Hypothesis 2:

The higher the level of organizational learning, the stronger the affective commitment of employees.

3.1.1.1.3 ORGANIZATIONAL LEARNING AND TURNOVER INTENTION

The point of organizational learning is to give full play to the potentials and ability of each member of the organization to maximize the effect, and one of the goals of the organization is to attain the learning ability independent of the influence of personnel turnover; that is, even when there is turnover, the organization can maintain its learning ability and keep improving. Crossan and Berdrow (2003) found in their case studies that when Canada Post implemented top-down restructuring, it led to the resignation of senior managers. Based on our understanding, we propose the following theoretical hypothesis:

Hypothesis 3:

The higher the level of organizational learning, the lower the turnover intention of employees.

3.1.1.1.4 ORGANIZATIONAL LEARNING AND TASK PERFORMANCE

Organizational learning is a long-term strategy characterized by high cost. Every single organization hopes that the measures taken will have positive influence on employees' performance. Organizational learning changes the behavior and concept of the individual and the entire organization. Of course, the direct purpose of this change is to improve the work performance of employees. Therefore, the following theoretical hypothesis is set forth:

Hypothesis 4:

The higher the level of organizational learning, the higher the task performance of employees.

3.1.1.1.5 THE ROLE OF ORGANIZATIONAL LEARNING

3.1.1.1.5.1 Research hypothesis on the role of organizational learning
It has been indicated in the prior literature review and empirical research that organizational learning is a phenomenon that crosses both individual and collective levels, but there is not sufficient research on the role of organizational

learning. Scholars generally believe that what happens at one level affects the phenomena at other levels (O'Reilly, 1990). The limited empirical studies on organizational learning are often conducted at the collective level. Templeton et al. (2002) pinpointed that trans-level research is still insufficient in the research on organizational learning.

In order to explore the mechanism of action of organizational learning, we must identify the level of its mechanism of action according to the multilevel theory. Among the six factors in organizational learning, only individual learning is at the individual level; the others are of collective-level structure. For the individual-level learning dimension, the relationship between learning and employee satisfaction, affective commitment, turnover intention and task performance is a relationship among individual-level variables; to analyze the relationship between the other five collective-level learning dimensions and these individual-level variables, we need to consider the difference between the levels of variables.

First, do the six dimensions of organizational learning have direct effects on individual variables? Does the impact of collective-level structure on individual variables need to be generated through one mediated variable? Is this mediated variable individual learning? In organizational learning, individual learning is just the structure of the individual level and a dimension of organizational learning. Therefore, this study puts forward the following theoretical hypotheses:

Hypothesis 5:

Individual learning is the mediator between the collective level learning dimensions and employee satisfaction.

Hypothesis 6:

Individual learning is the mediator between the collective level learning dimensions and affective commitment.

Hypothesis 7:

Individual learning is the mediator between the collective level learning dimensions and turnover intention.

Hypothesis 8:

Individual learning is the mediator between the collective level learning dimensions and task performance.

Second, in the organizational context, the structure of the collective level is often the background or condition of the relationship between individual-level variables; that is, the structure of the collective level can be used as the moderator variable of the structural interaction at the individual level. In the study of Choe (2004), facilitating factors of organizational learning significantly moderated the relationship between provision of information and improvement of performance; that is, the higher the level of organizational learning facilitators, the more information provision can lead to improvement of performance. This inspires us to set forth the following theoretical hypotheses:

Hypothesis 9:

Employee satisfaction has a negative effect on turnover intention.

Hypothesis 10:

Organizational learning is a moderator variable between employee satisfaction and turnover intention.

Hypothesis 11:

Affective commitment has a negative effect on turnover intention.

Hypothesis 12:

The relationship between affective commitment and turnover intention is moderated by organizational learning.

Hypothesis 13:

Employee satisfaction has a positive effect on task performance.

Hypothesis 14:

The relationship between employee satisfaction and task performance is moderated by organizational learning.

Hypothesis 15:

Affective commitment has a positive effect on task performance.

Hypothesis 16:

The relationship between affective commitment and task performance is moderated by organizational learning.

3.1.1.1.5.2 MEDIATOR VARIABLE AND MODERATOR VARIABLE

Baron and Kenny (1986) explicated the moderator and mediator variables. According to the requirements of these two variables, this study will explore the mediating role of individual learning and the moderating role of collective level learning dimensions, as shown in Figures 3.1 and 3.2 (Baron and Kenny, 1986).

3.1.1.2 Research framework

The research frameworks of this section, as shown in Figures 3.3, 3.4 and 3.5, discuss the direct effect of organizational learning, the mediating effect of individual learning between collective-level learning dimension and individual-level variables, and the moderating effect of organizational learning in the relationship among individual-level variables.

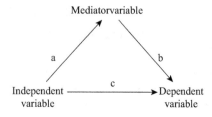

Figure 3.1 Diagram of mediator variable

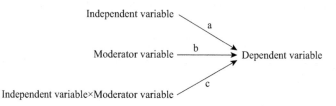

Figure 3.2 Diagram of moderator variable

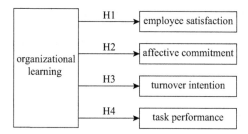

Figure 3.3 Research framework 1: direct effect of organizational learning on individual-level variables

3.1.2 Methodology and procedure

3.1.2.1 Measures

The adopted organizational learning questionnaire is the 29-item questionnaire that has been studied and confirmed. The Likert five-point scale is employed to evaluate the learning behaviors atvarious levels in companies. Ranging from "1—completely inconsistent" to "5—completely consistent". The overall employee satisfaction questionnaire uses the six-item questionnaire by Tsui et al. (1992). The affective commitment questionnaire is the six-item questionnaire by Meyer et al. (1993) that originally contained three negative and positive items, respectively. All the items in this study are positive. The three-item turnover intention questionnaire by Konovsky and Cropanzano (1991) was adopted as the turnover intention questionnaire. All the above three questionnaires evaluate by using the Likert five-point scale, from "1" to "5," "totally disagree," "relatively disagree," "uncertain," "relatively agree" and "totally agree."

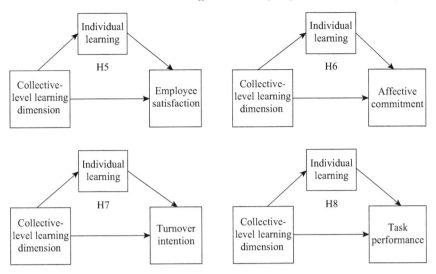

Figure 3.4 Research framework 2: mediating effect of individual learning between collective-level learning dimensions and individual-level variables

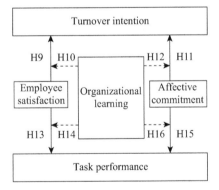

Figure 3.5 Research framework 3: moderating effect of organizational learning on the relationship among individual-level variables

The three-item overall task performance questionnaire by Motowidlo and Scotter (1994) was used as the task performance questionnaire. The questionnaire uses a six-point scale in ascending order from low to high for evaluation. These three items evaluate respectively: individual work performance compared with colleagues, individual contribution to the department compared with colleagues and the comparison with the work standards of the unit.

3.1.2.2 Subjects

A total of 908 valid questionnaires were obtained from 43 companies. The basic information of the subjects is shown in Table 3.1, with an average of 21 people in each company.

3.1.2.3 Statistical analysis methods

This study adopts the statistical analysis methods, such as explorative factor analysis, HLM (hierarchical linear modeling) analysis, hierarchical regression analysis, and uses the statistical software HLM 5.04 and SPSS 10.0.

Table 3.1 Basic information of subjects (*N* = 908)

Variable	Type	Number of people	Percentage
Nature of enterprise	State-owned companies	517	56.9
	Private companies	178	19.6
	Companies in three forms of ventures—Sino-foreign joint ventures, cooperative businesses and exclusively foreign-funded companies	110	12.1
	Other	103	11.3
Scale	50–99	48	5.3
	100–499	318	35.0
	500–999	78	8.6
	1000–1999	196	21.6
	2000–4999	95	10.5
	Over 5000	173	19.1
Development stage	Startup	56	6.2
	Growing	357	39.3
	Mature	157	17.3
	Re-innovation	338	37.2
Position	General staff	576	64.6
	Front line managers	201	22.5
	Middle-level management	100	11.2
	Senior management	15	1.7
	None	16	1.8
Level of literacy	Middle school	76	8.5
	Junior college	310	34.6
	Undergraduate college	438	48.9
	Master	63	7.0
	Doctor	2	0.2
	None	19	1.3

3.1.2.3.1 COLLECTIVE-LEVEL CONSTRUCTS

The following three aspects should be determined when the study involves the multilevel of the organization: the type of the collective-level construct, the compositional model of collective-level construct and the level of data source, measurement and analysis (Kozlowski & Klein, 2000; Hofmann, 2002).

3.1.2.3.1.1 DETERMINING THE TYPE OF COLLECTIVE-LEVEL CONSTRUCT

The structure of collective level can be generally divided into three types: global construct, shared construct and configural construct (Kozlowski & Klein, 2000). In this study, collective learning, exploration, exploitation[1], organizational learning and inter-organizational learning are all shared constructs. After the type of collective level is determined, how does one measure different types? This rests on the determination of the compositional model of collective level.

3.1.2.3.1.2 DETERMINING THE COMPOSITIONAL MODEL OF COLLECTIVE-LEVEL CONSTRUCT

Chan (1998) established five models, which are additive model, direct consensus model, referent-shift consensus model, dispersion model and process model. In this study, the compositional model of collective learning is the direct consensus model[2] because it can be called so only when collective members are involved in the interactions. In this case, intra-group consensus needs to be calculated to verify the existence of the structure. In the research on explorative learning, exploitative learning, organizational level learning and inter-organizational learning, the reference-shift consensus model[3] is adopted to locate the reference point at the collective level to which the structure belongs (for example, when measuring organizational-level learning, the subject of the item is "company"; that is, the measurement is conducted at the collective level).

3.1.2.3.1.3 DETERMINING THE LEVEL OF DATA SOURCE, MEASUREMENT AND ANALYSIS

In this study, the measurement item of collective level learning dimension (such as the regular free exchange of work-related information among colleagues) measures at the collective level. Since explorative learning, exploitative learning, organizational level learning and inter-organizational learning use the referent-shift consensus model, the measurement is also at the collective level. This requires that data at the individual level should be aggregated at the collective level so as to conduct research on relationship among variables at the collective level.

3.1.2.3.2 DEMONSTRATION OF COLLECTIVE-LEVEL CONSTRUCT

In order to use the mean of person perception to represent the variables at the collective level, it is necessary to demonstrate the effectiveness of the mean from two aspects: intra-group homogeneity and inter-group difference (Kozlowski and Klein, 2000; Zohar, 2000).

(a) *Index r_{wg}*. The test of intra-group homogeneity of collective level construct is generally tested by r_{wg} (James et al., 1984, 1993). In order to more comprehensively test the each collective level construct, this study adopts two kinds of desirable distributions, uniform distribution and partial distribution, and calculates two r_{wg} values for each scale of each company. The mean and median of r_{wg} of each collective construct on the two distributions are shown in Table 3.2. The results are far greater than the empirical 0.70 (Klein et al., 2000), which indicates that the scales have sufficient internal homogeneity in each company to aggregate the data of individual perception (Campion et al., 1993; Hofmann & Stetzer, 1996; Bunderson, 2003).

(b) *Intra-class correlation*. Intra-class correlation ICC (1) and ICC (2) (Bartko, 1976; James, 1982; Zohar, 2000) can also be used to test the intra-group homogeneity of collective-level structure. Table 3.3 shows the results of these two indicators of the collective level constructs. James (1982) concluded that ICC (1) was between 0 and 0.5, and all the results of this study fall within this range. The ICC (2) is higher than the empirical standard of 0.70 (Klein et al., 2000), except for the collective learning, whose ICC(2) is 0.68. ICC (1) proves from another perspective that the intra-group homogeneity is high; ICC (2) shows that the mean of various collective-level constructs of each company has high credibility.

Interclass difference is tested by the ANOVA (analysis of variance) (Chen & Bliese, 2002; Zohar, 2000; Hofmann, 2002), which takes the research variable as the dependent variable and the second-level unit identifier as the independent variable. Table 3.4 shows the results of ANOVA of interclass differences of collective-level constructs in this study. The differences among groups of the six collective-level constructs are extremely significant, indicating that there are significant differences among different companies.

In conclusion, sufficient intra-group homogeneity and significant intergroup differences are good evidence to aggregate individual data into a collective-level construct. Therefore, the mean variable of individual data in a company can be used as observations of the collective-level construct.

This study explores the relationship between organizational learning and individual attitudes and behaviors, which are variables at the individual level. Organizational learning includes both individual learning at the individual level and the other five collective level dimensions. Therefore, the relationship between organizational learning and individual attitudes and behaviors is a trans-level relationship. The traditional regression analysis method does not apply, but we

Table 3.2 Mean and median of r_{wg} indicator of the various collective-level constructs ($N = 908$)

	Hypothetical distribution	Collective learning	Organizational level leaning	Inter-organizational learning	Exploitative learning	Explorative learning
Mean	Uniform distribution	0.88	0.90	0.89	0.85	0.82
	Negative skew distribution	0.90	0.92	0.91	0.82	0.85
Median	Uniform distribution	0.89	0.91	0.89	0.87	0.84
	Negative skew distribution	0.91	0.92	0.91	0.84	0.87

Table 3.3 ICC (1) and ICC (2) of each collective-level construct (average $N = 21$)

	Collective learning	Organizational level leaning	Inter-organizational learning	Exploitative learning	Explorative learning
ICC (1)	0.09	0.23	0.21	0.25	0.12
ICC (2)	0.68	0.86	0.85	0.87	0.74

Table 3.4 Variance analysis results of intergroup differences of each collective-level construct

	Intergroup mean square	Intra-group mean square	DF	F
Collective learning	1.075	0.342	42/863	3.14***
Organizational level learning	2.189	0.305	42/863	7.19***
Inter-organizational learning	2.318	0.353	42/863	6.57***
Exploitative learning	3.849	0.486	42/863	7.91***
Explorative learning	1.874	0.495	42/863	3.79***

*** $p < 0.001$.

can use hierarchical linear modeling (HLM) (Bryk & Raudenbush, 1992; Zhang et al., 2003).

3.1.3 Research results

3.1.3.1 Test of the research variable questionnaire

We adopt the principal component analysis to analyze the employee satisfaction questionnaire, affective commitment questionnaire, turnover intention questionnaire and task performance questionnaire to determine the number of factors extracted from the project based on the eigenvalues greater than 1 and the scree plot. The results of exploratory factor analysis showed that the factor loadings and internal consensus reliability coefficient of the four scales met the basic requirements of psychometrology. See Tables 3.5, 3.6, 3.7 and 3.8 for details.

3.1.3.2 Descriptive statistics of research variables

Table 3.9 shows the means, standard deviations and correlations for research variables. The result is calculated after assigning the mean of the company to each employee in the company. Therefore, for the collective-level structure, the sample number is 43. Table 3.9 can provide preconditions for the latter test as the correlation coefficients among variables are required to be tested when testing mediator variables and moderator variables.

Table 3.5 Exploratory factor analysis results of employee satisfaction questionnaire (*N* = 806)

Item	V50	V45	V49	V46	V48	V47	Eigen value	Explained variance	α coefficient
Load	0.80	0.69	0.68	0.66	0.65	0.44	2.62	43.70%	0.74

Table 3.6 Results of exploratory factor analysis of affective commitment questionnaire (*N* = 742)

Item	V54	V55	V56	V53	V52	V51	Eigen value	Explained variance	α coefficient
Load	0.81	0.78	0.78	0.77	0.76	0.72	3.55	59.15%	0.86

Table 3.7 Results of exploratory factor analysis of turnover intention questionnaire (*N* = 812)

Item	V63	V64	V65	Eigen value	Explained variance	α coefficient
Load	0.86	0.86	0.78	2.09	69.70%	0.78

Table 3.8 Exploratory factor analysis results of task performance questionnaire (*N* = 666)

Item	V67	V66	V68	Eigen value	Explained variance	α coefficient
Load	0.88	0.87	0.79	2.17	72.33%	0.81

3.1.3.3 Direct influence of organizational learning on individual variables

Table 3.10 shows the results of hierarchical linear model analysis of the effectiveness of organizational learning on four individual variables. The significance of the coefficients shows that in terms of employee satisfaction, apart from exploitative learning, all the other five dimensions, namely individual learning ($\gamma = 0.41$, $p < 0.001$), collective learning ($\gamma = 0.42$, $p < 0.05$), organizational level learning ($\gamma = 0.40$, $p < 0.01$), inter-organizational learning ($\gamma = 0.45$, $p < 0.01$) and explorative learning ($\gamma = 0.44$, $p < 0.01$), have significant positive impact on employee satisfaction, which confirms Hypothesis 1.

In terms of affective commitment, except for collective learning, all the other five dimensions, namely individual learning ($\gamma = 0.33$, $p < 0.001$), organizational level learning ($\gamma = 0.45$, $p < 0.05$), inter-organizational learning ($\gamma = 0.55$, $p < 0.001$), exploitative learning ($\gamma = 0.37, p < 0.01$) and explorative learning ($\gamma = 0.59, p < 0.001$),

Table 3.9 Means, standard deviations and correlations for study variables

Variable	Mean	Standard deviation	1	2	3	4	5	6	7	8	9
1. Individual learning	3.56	0.59									
2. Collective learning	3.73	0.22	0.30**								
3. Organizational level learning	3.65	0.32	0.31**	0.51**							
4. Inter-Organizational learning	3.36	0.33	0.31**	0.43**	0.75**						
5. Exploitative learning	3.53	0.42	0.24**	0.32**	0.80**	0.65**					
6. Explorative learning	2.94	0.29	0.23**	0.17**	0.61**	0.81**	0.58**				
7. Employee satisfaction	3.27	0.64	0.37**	0.14**	0.18**	0.21**	0.12**	0.19**			
8. Emotional commitment	3.37	0.76	0.28**	0.11**	0.23**	0.23**	0.21**	0.24**	0.62**		
9. Turnover intention	2.79	0.87	-0.15**	-0.09*	-0.08*	-0.11**	-0.03	-0.08*	-0.38**	-0.46**	
10. Task performance	4.22	0.82	0.00	-0.08*	-0.07	-0.07	-0.01	-0.01	-0.04	0.07	0.05

$** p < 0.01.$
$* p < 0.05$

Table 3.10 Impact of organizational learning on employee satisfaction, affective commitment, turnover intention and task performance

Independent variables	Coefficient	Standard deviation	T	P
Employee satisfaction				
Individual learning	0.41***	0.04	10.04	0.000
Collective learning	0.42*	0.18	2.37	0.023
Organizational level learning	0.40**	0.12	3.09	0.004
Inter-organizational learning	0.45**	0.12	3.73	0.001
Exploitative learning	0.19	0.11	1.79	0.080
Explorative learning	0.44**	0.14	3.21	0.003
Affective commitment				
Individual learning	0.33***	0.05	7.18	0.000
Collective learning	0.42	0.28	1.52	0.135
Organizational level learning	0.45*	0.17	2.69	0.011
Inter-organizational learning	0.55***	0.13	4.32	0.000
Exploitative learning	0.37**	0.11	3.46	0.002
Explorative learning	0.59***	0.12	4.97	0.000
Turnover intension				
Individual learning	−0.19*	0.08	−2.47	0.018
Collective learning	−0.33	0.27	−1.20	0.238
Organizational level learning	−0.21	0.20	−1.05	0.301
Inter-organizational learning	−0.30	0.17	−1.82	0.075
Exploitative learning	−0.06	0.14	−0.43	0.668
Explorative learning	−0.16	0.22	−0.75	0.456
Task performance				
Individual learning	0.01	0.06	0.23	0.816
Collective learning	−0.21	0.15	−1.47	0.150
Organizational level learning	−0.10	0.14	−0.71	0.485
Inter-organizational learning	−0.09	0.18	−0.49	0.629
Exploitative learning	0.10	0.12	0.79	0.435
Explorative learning	0.03	0.18	0.17	0.862

*** $p < 0.001$.
** $p < 0.01$.
* $p < 0.05$

have a significant positive effect on employees' affective commitment, which verifies Hypothesis 2.

In terms of turnover intention, individual learning has a significant negative effect on employee turnover intention ($\gamma = -0.19$, $p < 0.05$), while other dimensions have no significant effect on turnover intention, which partially supports Hypothesis 3.

In terms of task performance, none of the dimensions of organizational learning has any significant effect on individual task performance, and Hypothesis 4 is not supported.

3.1.3.4 The mediating role of individual learning between the collective level learning dimensions and individual variables

The results of direct effect can serve as the premise of this study for testing the mediating role of individual learning. The aforementioned results (see Table 3.10) show that collective level learning dimension has no significant impact on turnover intention or task performance. According to Baron and Kenny (1986), there exists no relationship between independent variable and dependent variable, so there is no mediating role of individual learning in it. Therefore, Hypotheses 7 and 8 are not supported.

For Hypotheses 5 and 6 with employee satisfaction and affective commitment as dependent variables, similarly, according to Baron and Kenny (1986), exploitative learning does not have a main effect on employee satisfaction, while collective learning has no significant main effect on affective commitment, so it is unnecessary to analyze the mediating role of individual learning and in terms of employee satisfaction. We need only to analyze the mediating role of individual learning in the role of collective learning, organizational level learning, inter-organizational learning and explorative learning on employee satisfaction; for affective commitment, we need only to analyze the mediating role of individual learning in how organizational level learning, inter-organizational learning, exploitative learning and explorative learning influence affective commitment.

3.1.3.4.1 THE MEDIATING ROLE OF INDIVIDUAL LEARNING BETWEEN COLLECTIVE LEVEL LEARNING DIMENSION AND EMPLOYEE SATISFACTION

3.1.3.4.1.1 The mediating role of individual learning between collective learning and employee satisfaction   According to Baron and Kenny (1986), the results of Models M2, M3 and M4 in Table 3.11 show that the relationship a ($\gamma_{01} = 0.75$, $p < 0.001$) between the independent variable (collective learning) and the mediator variable (individual learning), the relationship b ($\gamma_{01} = 0.41$, $p < 0.01$) between the mediator variable (individual learning) and the dependent variable (employee satisfaction) and relationship c ($\gamma_{01} = 0.42$), $p < 0.05$) between independent variable (collective learning) and dependent variable (employee satisfaction) are all significant. However, through the comparison between Models M4 and M5, we can see that the main effect of collective learning on employee satisfaction will change from significant in Model M4 to insignificant in Model M5 ($\gamma_{01} = 0.12$), indicating that individual learning is a full mediator between collective learning and employee satisfaction. From Model M5, individual learning can explain 15% variance ($[0.40 - 0.34]/0.40$). Figure 3.6 shows more clearly the role of individual learning as a mediator variable between collective learning and employee satisfaction. The coefficient 0.40 between individual learning and employee satisfaction is the result of γ_{01} in Model M5.

3.1.3.4.1.2 The mediating role of individual learning between organizational level learning and employee satisfaction   In the same vein, the HLM analysis results in Table 3.12 show that the main effect of organizational learning on employee satisfaction changes from significant in Model M4 to insignificant in

Table 3.11 Mediating role of individual learning between collective learning and employee satisfaction

Model	Parameter estimate						
	γ_{00}	γ_{01}	γ_{10}	σ^2	τ_{00}	τ_{11}	*Effect*
M1: null model							
L1: $SA_{ij} = \beta_{0j} + \Gamma_{ij}$	3.23**			0.39	0.037**		
L2: $\beta_{0j} = \gamma_{00} + U_{0j}$							
M2: the relationship between independent variable and mediator variable							
L1: $I_{ij} = \beta_{0j} + \Gamma_{ij}$	0.73	**0.75*****		0.30	0.022***		
L2: $\beta_{0j} = \gamma_{00} + \gamma_{01}(G_{ij}) + U_{0j}$							
M3: the relationship between mediator variable and dependent variable							
L1: $SA_{ij} = \beta_{0j} + \beta_{ij} + \Gamma_{ij}$							
L2: $\beta_{0j} = \gamma_{00} + U_{0j}$	3.23**		**0.41****	0.34	0.027**	0.002	0.13
$\beta_{1j} = \gamma_{10} + U_{0j}$							
M4: the relationship between independent variable and dependent variable							
L1: $SA_{ij} = \beta_{0j} + \Gamma_{ij}$	1.68*	**0.42***		**0.40**	0.032**		0.14
L2: $\beta = \gamma_{00} + \gamma_{01}(G_{ij}) + U_{0j}$							
M5: test model of mediator variable							
L1: $SA_{ij} = \beta_{0j} + \beta_{0j}(I_{ij}) + \Gamma_{ij}$							
L2: $\beta_{0j} = \gamma_{00} + \gamma_{01}(G_{ij}) + U_{0j}$	2.78**	**0.12**	0.40**	0.34	0.029**	0.003	**0.15**
$\beta_{0j} = \gamma_{10} + U_{1j}$							

*** $p < 0.001$.
** $p < 0.01$.
* $p < 0.05$.

Notes: σ^2 is the horizontal residual, τ_{00} is the intercept residual, namely U_{0j}; τ_{11} is the slope residual, namely U_{1j}.
"Effect" refers to the effect of independent variable on dependent variable, here, effect = (baseline model residual − research model residual)/benchmark model residual.
I refers to individual learning, G refers to collective learning, and SA refers to employee satisfaction.

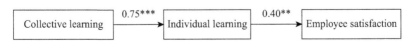

Figure 3.6 Full mediating role of individual learning between collective learning and employee satisfaction

Table 3.12 Mediating role of individual learning between organizational learning and employee satisfaction

Model	Parameter estimate						
	γ_{00}	γ_{01}	γ_{10}	σ^2	τ_{00}	τ_{11}	Effect
M1: null model							
L1: $SA_{ij} = \beta_{0j} + \Gamma_{ij}$	3.23**			0.39	0.037**		
L2: $\beta_{0j} = \gamma_{00} + U_{0j}$							
M2: the relationship between independent variable and mediator variable							
L1: $I_{ij} = \beta_{0j} + \Gamma_{ij}$	1.40	**0.59***		0.55	0.135**		
L2: $\beta_{0j} = \gamma_{00} + \gamma_{01}(O_{ij}) + U_{0j}$							
M3: the relationship between mediator variable and dependent variable							
L1: $SA_{ij} = \beta_{0j} + \beta_{1j}(I_{ij}) + \Gamma_{ij}$							
L2: $\beta_{0j} = \gamma_{00} + U_{0j}$	3.23**		**0.41**	0.34	0.027**	0.002	0.13
$\beta_{1j} = \gamma_{10} + U_{1j}$							
M4: the relationship between independent variable and dependent variable							
L1: $SA_{ij} = \beta_{0j} + \Gamma_{ij}$	1.92**	**0.36**		**0.40**	0.024**		0.41
L2: $\beta_{0j} = \gamma_{00} + \gamma_{01}(O_{ij}) + U_{0j}$							
M5: test model of mediator variable							
L1: $SA_{ij} = \beta_{0j} + \beta_{1j}(I_{ij}) + \Gamma_{ij}$							
L2: $\beta_{0j} = \gamma_{00} + \gamma_{01}(O_{ij}) + U_{0j}$	2.69**	**0.15**		0.39**	**0.34**	0.027**	0.004	**0.15**
$\beta_{1j} = \gamma_{10} + U_{1j}$							

*** $p < 0.001$.
** $p < 0.01$.

Notes: σ^2 is the horizontal residual, τ_{00} is the intercept residual, namely U_{0j}; τ_{11} is the slope residual, namely U_{1j}.
"Effect" refers to the effect of independent variable on dependent variable. Here, effect = (baseline model residual − research model residual)/benchmark model residual.
I refers to individual learning, *O* refers to organizational-level learning and *SA* refers to employee satisfaction.

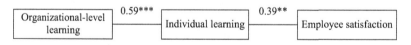

Figure 3.7 Full mediating role of individual learning between organizational-level learning and employee satisfaction

Model M5. ($\gamma_{01} = 0.15$), indicating that individual learning is a full mediator between organizational learning and employee satisfaction. Model M5 shows that individual learning can explain 15% variance ([0.40 − 0.34]/0.40), and the full mediation effect is shown in Figure 3.7.

3.1.3.4.1.3 The mediating role of individual learning between inter-organizational learning and employee satisfaction In the same way, the HLM analysis results in Table 3.13 show that the main effect of inter-organizational learning on employee satisfaction changes from significant in Model M4 to insignificant in

Table 3.13 The mediating role of individual learning between inter-organizational learning and employee satisfaction

Model	Parameter estimate						
	γ_{00}	γ_{01}	γ_{10}	σ^2	τ_{00}	τ_{11}	*Effect*
M1: null model							
L1: $SA_{ij} = \beta_{0j} + \Gamma_{ij}$	3.23**			0.39	0.037**		
L2: $\beta_{0j} = \gamma_{00} + U_{0j}$							
M2: the relationship between independent variable and mediator variable							
L1: $I_{ij} = \beta_{0j} + \Gamma_{ij}$	1.69***	**0.55***		0.30	0.018**		
L2: $\beta_{0j} = \gamma_{00} + \gamma_{01}(BE_{ij}) + U_{0j}$							
M3: the relationship between mediator variable and dependent variable							
L1: $SA_{ij} = \beta_{0j} + \beta_{1j}(I_{ij}) + \Gamma_{ij}$							
L2: $\beta_{0j} = \gamma_{00} + U_{0j}$	3.23**		**0.41**	0.34	0.027**	0.002	0.13
$\beta_{1j} = \gamma_{10} + U_{1j}$							
M4: the relationship between independent variable and dependent variable							
L1: $SA_{ij} = \beta_{0j} + \Gamma_{ij}$	1.71**	**0.45**		**0.38**	0.021**		0.43
L2: $\beta_{0j} = \gamma_{00} + \gamma_{01}(BE_{ij}) + U_{0j}$							
M5: test model of mediator variable							
L1: $SA_{ij} = \beta_{0j} + \beta_{1j}(I_{ij}) + \Gamma_{ij}$							
L2: $\beta_{0j} = \gamma_{00} + \gamma_{01}(BE_{ij}) + U_{0j}$	2.38**	**0.25**	**0.38**	0.34	0.024**	0.003	**0.11**
$\beta_{1j} = \gamma_{10} + U_{1j}$							

*** $p < 0.001$.
** $p < 0.01$.

Notes: σ^2 is the horizontal residual, τ_{00} is the intercept residual, namely U_{0j}; τ_{11} is the slope residual, namely U_{1j}.
"Effect" refers to the effect of independent variable on dependent variable. Here, effect = (baseline model residual − research model residual)/benchmark model residual.
I refers to individual learning, *BE* refers to inter-organizational learning and *SA* refers to employee satisfaction.

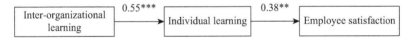

Figure 3.8 Full mediating role of individual learning between inter-organizational learning and employee satisfaction

Model M5 ($\gamma_{01} = 0.25$), indicating that individual learning is a full mediator variable between inter-organizational learning and employee satisfaction, and Model M5 shows that individual learning can explain 11% variance ([0 38 − 0.34]/0.38), as shown in Figure 3.8.

3.1.3.4.1.4 The mediating role of individual learning between explorative learning and employee satisfaction In the same way, according to Baron and Kenny (1986), the results of Models M2, M3 and M4 in Table 3.14 respectively show that the relationship between independent variable (explorative learning) and

Table 3.14 The mediating role of individual learning between explorative learning and employee satisfaction

Model	γ_{00}	γ_{01}	γ_{10}	σ^2	τ_{00}	τ_{11}	Effect
	Parameter estimate						
M1: null model							
L1: $SA_{ij} = \beta_{0j} + \Gamma_{ij}$	3.23**			0.39	0.037**		
L2: $\beta_{0j} = \gamma_{00} + U_{0j}$							
M2: the relationship between independent variable and mediator variable							
L1: $I_{ij} = \beta_{0j} + \Gamma_{ij}$	2.16***	**0.47*****		0.30	0.033**		
L2: $\beta_{0j} = \gamma_{00} + \gamma_{01}(FF_{ij}) + U_{0j}$							
M3: the relationship between mediator variable and dependent variable							
L1: $SA_{ij} = \beta_{0j} + \beta_{1j}(I_{ij}) + \Gamma_{ij}$							
L2: $\beta_{0j} = \gamma_{00} + U_{0j}$	3.23**		**0.41****	0.34	0.027**	0.002	0.13
$\beta_{1j} = \gamma_{10} + U_{1j}$							
M4: the relationship between independent variable and dependent variable							
L1: $SA_{ij} = \beta_{0j} + \Gamma_{ij}$	1.93**	**0.44****		0.38	0.024**		0.35
L2: $\beta_{0j} = \gamma_{00} + \gamma_{01}(FF_{ij}) + U_{0j}$							
M5: test model of mediator variable							
L1: $SA_{ij} = \beta_{0j} + \beta_{1j}(I_{ij}) + \Gamma_{ij}$							
L2: $\beta_{0j} = \gamma_{00} + \gamma_{01}(FF_{ij}) + U_{0j}$	2.45**	**0.27**	**0.39****	**0.34**	0.023**	0.003	**0.11**
$\beta_{1j} = \Gamma_{10} + U_{1j}$							

*** $p < 0.001$.
** $p < 0.01$.

Notes: σ^2 is the horizontal residual, τ_{00} is the intercept residual, namely U_{0j}; τ_{11} is the slope residual, namely U_{1j}.
"Effect" refers to the effect of independent variable on dependent variable. Here, effect = (baseline model residual − research model residual)/benchmark model residual.
I refers to individual learning, *FF* refers to explorative learning and *SA* refers to employee satisfaction.

mediator variable (individual learning) verifies that the conditions of individual learning mediator variable are all valid. HLM analysis results show that the main effect of explorative learning on employee satisfaction changes from significant in Model M4 to insignificant in Model M5 ($\gamma_{01} = 0.27$), indicating that individual learning is a complete mediator between explorative learning and employee satisfaction. The results of Model M5 show that individual learning can explain 11% variance ([0.38 – 0.34]/0.38), and the full mediating effect is shown in Figure 3.9.

The above results in Tables 3.1 through 3.14 show that individual learning plays a full mediating role in the relationship between collective learning, organizational level learning, inter-organizational learning, explorative learning and employee satisfaction, validating Hypothesis 5.

Figure 3.9 Full mediating effect of individual learning between explorative learning and affective commitment

3.1.3.4.2 THE MEDIATING EFFECT OF INDIVIDUAL LEARNING BETWEEN
COLLECTIVE LEARNING DIMENSION AND AFFECTIVE COMMITMENT

3.1.3.4.2.1 The mediating effect of individual learning between organizational level learning and affective commitment   According to the same procedure, the HLM analysis results in Table 3.15 show that the main effect of organizational level learning on affective commitment changes from significant in Model M4 to insignificant in Model M5 ($\gamma_{01} = 0.25$), indicating that individual learning is a full mediator between organizational level learning and affective commitment. The results of Model M5 show that individual learning can explain 6% variance ($[0.51 - 0.48]/0.51$), and the full mediating role is shown in Figure 3.10.

Table 3.15 Mediating effect of individual learning between organizational-level learning and affective commitment

Model	Parameter estimate						
	Γ_{00}	Γ_{01}	Γ_{10}	σ^2	τ_{00}	τ_{11}	Effect
M1: Null Model							
L1: $OC_{ij} = \beta_{0j} + \Gamma_{ij}$	3.36**			0.51	0.057***		
L2: $\beta_{0j} = \Gamma_{00} + U_{0j}$							
M2: the relationship between independent variable and mediator variable							
L1: $I_{ij} = \beta_{0j} + \Gamma_{ij}$	1.40**	**0.59*****		0.55	0.135**		
L2: $\beta_{0j} = \Gamma_{00} + \Gamma_{01}(O_{ij}) + U_{0j}$							
M3: the relationship between mediator variable and dependent variable							
L1: $OC_{ij} = \beta_{0j} + \beta_{1j}(I_{ij}) + \Gamma_{ij}$							
L2: $\beta_{0j} = \Gamma_{00} + U_{0j}$	3.36**		**0.33*****	0.48	0.039**	0.002	0.06
$\beta_{1j} = \Gamma_{10} + U_{1j}$							
M4: the relationship between independent variable and dependent variable							
L1: $OC_{ij} = \beta_{0j} + \Gamma_{ij}$	1.71**	**0.45****		**0.51**	0.039***		0.32
L2: $\beta_{0j} = \Gamma_{00} + \Gamma_{01}(O_{ij}) + U_{0j}$							
M5: test model of mediator variable							
L1: $OC_{ij} = \beta_{0j} + \beta_{1j}(I_{ij}) + \Gamma_{ij}$							
L2: $\beta_{0j} = \Gamma_{00} + \Gamma_{01}(O_{ij}) + U_{0j}$	2.45**	**0.25**	0.39**	**0.48**	0.035**	0.011	**0.06**
$\beta_{1j} = \Gamma_{10} + U_{1j}$							

*** $p < 0.001$.
** $p < 0.01$.

Notes: σ^2 is the horizontal residual, τ_{00} is the intercept residual, namely U_{0j}; τ_{11} is the slope residual, namely U_{1j}.
"Effect" refers to the effect of independent variable on dependent variable, here, effect = (baseline model residual - research model residual) / benchmark model residual.
I refers to individual learning, *O* refers to organizational level learning, and *OC* refers to affective commitment.

Figure 3.10 Mediating effect of individual learning between organizational-level learning and affective commitment

3.1.3.4.2.2 The mediating effect of individual learning between inter-organizational learning and affective commitment   According to the same procedure, the HLM analysis result of Table 3.16 shows that the main effect of inter-organizational learning on affective commitment will be lowered from $\gamma_{01} = 0.55$ ($p < 0.01$) in Model M4 to $\gamma_{01} = 0.35$ ($p < 0.05$) in Model M5. This signifies that individual learning has partial mediating effect between inter-organizational learning and affective commitment. Model M5 shows that individual learning can explain 6% variance ([0.51 − 0.48/0.51]). The partial mediating effect is shown in Figure 3.11.

3.1.3.4.2.3 The mediating role of individual learning between exploitative learning and affective commitment   Likewise, the HLM analysis results in Table 3.17 show that the main effect of exploitative learning on affective commitment will

Table 3.16 The mediating role of individual learning between inter-organizational learning and affective commitment

Model	Parameter estimate						
	γ_{00}	γ_{01}	γ_{10}	σ^2	τ_{00}	τ_{11}	Effect
M1: null model							
L1: $OC_{ij} = \beta_{0j} + \Gamma_{ij}$	3.36**				0.51	0.057**	
L2: $\beta_{0j} = \gamma_{00} + U_{0j}$							
M2: the relationship between independent variable and mediator variable							
L1: $I_{ij} = \beta_{0j} + \Gamma_{ij}$	1.69***	**0.55****			0.30	0.018**	
L2: $\beta_{0j} = \gamma_{00} + \gamma_{01} (BE_{ij}) + U_{0j}$							
M3: the relationship between mediator variable and dependent variable							
L1: $OC_{ij} = \beta_{0j} + \beta_{1j} (I_{ij}) + \Gamma_{ij}$							
L2: $\beta_{0j} = \gamma_{00} + U_{0j}$	3.36**		**0.33*****	0.48	0.03	0.012	0.06
$\beta_{1j} = \gamma_{10} + U_{1j}$							
M4: the relationship between independent variable and dependent variable							
L1: $OC_{ij} = \beta_{0j} + \Gamma_{ij}$	1.51**	**0.55***		**0.51**	0.030*		0.47
L2: $\beta_{0j} = \gamma_{00} + \gamma_{01} (BE_{ij}) + U_{0j}$							
M5: test model of mediator variable							
L1: $OC_{ij} = \beta_{0j} + \beta_{1j} (I_{ij}) + \Gamma_{ij}$							
L2: $\beta_{0j} = \gamma_{00} + \Gamma_{01} (BE_{ij}) + U_{0j}$	2.19**	**0.35***	0.29**	**0.48**	0.031*	0.008	**0.06**
$\beta_{1j} = \gamma_{10} + U_{1j}$							

*** $p < 0.001$.
** $p < 0.01$.
* $p < 0.05$

Notes: σ^2 is the horizontal residual; τ_{00} is the intercept residual, namely U_{0j}; τ_{11} is the slope residual, namely U_{1j}.
"Effect" refers to the effect of independent variable on dependent variable. Here, effect = (baseline model residual − research model residual)/benchmark model residual.
I refers to individual learning, *BE* refers to inter-organizational learning and *OC* refers to affective commitment.

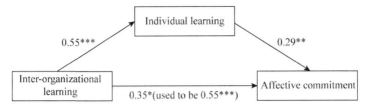

Figure 3.11 Mediating role of individual learning between inter-organizational learning and affective commitment

Table 3.17 Mediating effect of individual learning between exploitative learning and affective commitment

Model	Parameter estimate						
	γ_{00}	γ_{01}	γ_{10}	σ^2	τ_{00}	τ_{11}	Effect
M1: null model							
L1: $OC_{ij} = \beta_{0j} + \Gamma_{ij}$	3.36**			0.51	0.057**		
L2: $\beta_{0j} = \gamma_{00} + U_{0j}$							
M2: the relationship between independent variable and mediator variable							
L1: $I_{ij} = \beta_{0j} + \Gamma_{ij}$	2.42***	**0.32****		0.30	0.033***		
L2: $\beta_{0j} = \gamma_{00} + \gamma_{01}(FB_{ij}) + U_{0j}$							
M3: the relationship between mediator variable and dependent variable							
L1: $OC_{ij} = \beta_{0j} + \beta_{1j}(I_{ij}) + \Gamma_{ij}$							
L2: $\beta_{0j} = \gamma_{00} + U_{0j}$	3.36**		**0.33*****	0.48	0.039**	0.012	0.06
$\beta_{1j} = \gamma_{10} + U_{1j}$							
M4: the relationship between independent variable and dependent variable							
L1: $OC_{ij} = \beta_{0j} + \Gamma_{ij}$	2.04**	**0.37****		0.51	0.035**		0.39
L2: $\beta_{0j} = \gamma_{00} + \gamma_{01}(FB_{ij}) + U_{0j}$							
M5: test model of mediator variable							
L1: $OC_{ij} = \beta_{0j} + \beta_{1j}(I_{ij}) + \Gamma_{ij}$							
L2: $\beta_{0j} = \gamma_{00} + \gamma_{01}(BE_{ij}) + U_{0j}$	2.48**	**0.25***	0.31**	**0.48**	0.029*	0.008	**0.06**
$\beta_{1j} = \gamma_{10} + U_{1j}$							

*** $p < 0.001$.
** $p < 0.01$.
* $p < 0.05$.

Notes: σ^2 is the horizontal residual; τ_{00} is the intercept residual, namely U_{0j}; τ_{11} is the slope residual, namely U_{1j}.
"Effect" refers to the effect of independent variable on dependent variable. Here, effect = (baseline model residual − research model residual)/benchmark model residual.
I refers to individual learning, *FB* refers to exploitative learning and *OC* refers to affective commitment.

be reduced from $\gamma_{01} = 0.37$ ($p < 0.01$) in Model M4 to $\gamma_{01} = 0.25$ ($p < 0.05$) in Model M5, which indicates that individual learning is a partial mediator between exploitative learning and affective commitment. It can be seen from Model 5 that individual learning can explain 6% variance ($[0.51 − 0.48]/0.51$), and the partial mediating effect is shown in Figure 3.12.

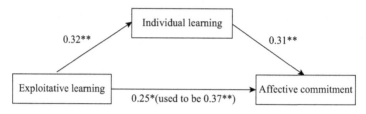

Figure 3.12 Partial mediating effect of individual learning between exploitative learning and affective commitment

3.1.3.4.2.4 The mediating role of individual learning between explorative learning and affective commitment

According to the same procedure, the HLM analysis results in Table 3.18 show that the main effect of explorative learning on affective commitment will be reduced from $\gamma_{01} = 0.59$ ($p < 0.001$) in Model M4 to $\gamma_{01} = 0.43$ in Model M5 ($p < 0.01$), which indicates that individual learning is a partial mediator between explorative learning and affective commitment. It can

Table 3.18 The mediating role of individual learning between explorative learning and affective commitment

Model	Parameter estimate						
	γ_{00}	γ_{01}	γ_{10}	σ^2	τ_{00}	τ_{11}	Effect
M1: null model							
L1: $OC_{ij} = \beta_{0j} + \Gamma_{ij}$	3.36**			0.51	0.057**		
L2: $\beta_{0j} = \Gamma_{00} + U_{0j}$							
M2: the relationship between independent variable and mediator variable							
L1: $I_{ij} = \beta_{0j} + \Gamma_{ij}$	2.42***	**0.32****		0.30	0.033***		
L2: $\beta_{0j} = \gamma_{00} + \gamma_{01}(FF_{ij}) + U_{0j}$							
M3: the relationship between mediator variable and dependent variable							
L1: $OC_{ij} = \beta_{0j} + \beta_{1j}(I_{ij}) + \Gamma_{ij}$							
L2: $\beta_{0j} = \gamma_{00} + U_{0j}$	3.36**		**0.33*****	0.48	0.039**	0.012	0.06
$\beta_{1j} = \gamma_{10} + U_{1j}$							
M4: the relationship between independent variable and dependent variable							
L1: $OC_{ij} = \beta_{0j} + \Gamma_{ij}$	2.04**	**0.37****		0.51	0.035**		0.39
L2: $\beta_{0j} = \gamma_{00} + \gamma_{01}(FF_{ij}) + U_{0j}$							
M5: test model of mediator variable							
L1: $OC_{ij} = \beta_{0j} + \beta_{1j}(I_{ij}) + \Gamma_{ij}$							
L2: $\beta_{0j} = \gamma_{00} + \gamma_{01}(BE_{ij}) + U_{0j}$	2.48**	**0.25***	0.31**	**0.48**	0.029*	0.008	**0.06**
$\beta_{1j} = \gamma_{10} + U_{1j}$							

*** $p < 0.001$.
** $p < 0.01$.
* $p < 0.05$.

Notes: σ^2 is the horizontal residual; τ_{00} is the intercept residual, namely U_{0j}; τ_{11} is the slope residual, namely U_{1j}.

"Effect" refers to the effect of independent variable on dependent variable. Here, effect = (baseline model residual − research model residual)/benchmark model residual.

I refers to individual learning, *FF* refers to explorative learning and *OC* refers to affective commitment.

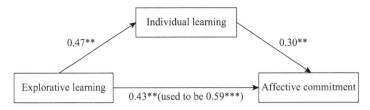

Figure 3.13 Partial mediating role of individual learning between explorative learning and affective commitment

be seen from Model M5 that individual learning can explain 6% variance ([0.51 − 0.48]/0.51), as shown in Figure 3.13.

According to the aforementioned results (Tables 3.15, 3.16, 3.17 and 3.18, Figures 3.10, 3.11, 3.12 and 3.13), individual learning is a full mediator variable between organizational learning and affective commitment; and individual learning has a partial mediating effect among inter-organizational learning, exploitative learning, explorative learning and affective commitment. This validates Hypothesis 6.

3.1.3.4.3 THE MEDIATING EFFECT OF INDIVIDUAL LEARNING BETWEEN THE DIMENSIONS
OF COLLECTIVE-LEVEL LEARNING AND INDIVIDUAL VARIABLES

In a word, the collective-level learning dimensions (collective learning, inter-organizational learning, and explorative learning) must avail the mediating effect of individual learning to have an impact on employee satisfaction. Organizational learning must avail the mediating effect of individual learning to influence affective commitment. Inter-organizational learning, exploitative learning and explorative learning can, on the one hand, have a direct effect on employees' affective commitment and, on the other, have an indirect effect on it through the mediating effect of individual learning. Therefore, the organizational learning has differing effective mechanisms on employee satisfaction and affective commitment.

3.1.3.5 *The moderating role of organizational learning in individual mechanism of action*

3.1.3.5.1 THE MODERATING EFFECT OF ORGANIZATIONAL LEARNING ON THE RELATIONSHIP
BETWEEN EMPLOYEE SATISFACTION AND TURNOVER INTENTION

3.1.3.5.1.1 Results of hierarchical linear model and hierarchical regression analysis For the five collective-level dimensions, the results of the hierarchical linear model analysis are shown in Table 3.19. The results of Model M2 show that there is a significant negative relationship between employee satisfaction and turnover intention ($\gamma_{10} = -0.43$, $p < 0.001$); the results of Model M3 show that organizational level learning has a significant negative effect on the negative relationship coefficient between them ($\gamma_{12} = -1.47$, $p < 0.01$), while the negative relationship coefficient between the two is significant ($\gamma_{12} = 0.69$, $p < 0.01$), indicating that organizational level learning and exploitative learning play a moderating role in the relationship between employee satisfaction and turnover intention.

Table 3.19 The moderating effect of collective-level learning dimension on employee satisfaction and turnover intension

Model	Parameter estimate														
	γ_{00}	γ_{01}	γ_{02}	γ_{03}	γ_{04}	γ_{05}	γ_{10}	γ_{11}	γ_{12}	γ_{13}	γ_{14}	γ_{15}	σ^2	τ_{00}	τ_{11}
M1: null model															
L1: $TI_{ij} = \beta_{0j} + \Gamma_{ij}$	2.92***												0.64	0.083***	
L2: $\beta_{0j} = \gamma_{00} + U_{0j}$															
M2: random coefficient model															
L1: $TI_{ij} = \beta_{0j} + \beta_{1j}(SA_{ij}) + \Gamma_{ij}$	2.93***						−0.43*						0.52	0.066***	0.104***
L2: $\beta_{0j} = \gamma_{00} + U_{0j}$															
$\beta_{1j} = \gamma_{10} + U_{0j}$															
M3: slope as dependent variable model															
L1: $TI_{ij} = \beta_{0j} + \beta_{1j}(SA_{ij}) + \Gamma_{ij}$	3.45***	−0.11	−0.21	−0.28	0.33	0.17	1.91	−0.57	−1.47**	0.49	−0.04	0.69**	0.52	0.058***	0.031*
L2: $\beta_{0j} = \gamma_{00} + \gamma_{01}(G_{ij}) + \gamma_{01}(O_{ij}) + \gamma_{03}$ $(BE_{ij}) + \gamma_{04}(EF_{ij}) + \gamma_{05}(FB_{ij}) + U_{0j}$															
$\beta_{1j} = \gamma_{10} + \gamma_{11}(G_{ij}) + \gamma_{12}(O_{ij}) + \gamma_{13}$ $(BE_{ij}) + \gamma_{14}(EF_{ij}) + \gamma_{15}(FB_{ij}) + U_{0j}$															

*** $p < 0.001$.
** $p < 0.01$.
* $p < 0.05$.

Notes: σ^2 is the horizontal residual, τ_{00} is the intercept residual, namely U_{0j}; τ_{11} is slope residual, namely U_{1j}; *G* refers to collective learning, *O* refers to organization-level learning, *FB* refers to inter-organizational learning, *BE* refers to exploitative learning and *FF* refers to explorative learning.

Table 3.20 Hierarchical regression analysis of the moderating effect of individual learning on the relationship between employee satisfaction and turnover intention

		Coefficient	R^2	ΔR^2
Step 1	Independent variable			
	Employee satisfaction	−0.38***	0.14	0.14***
Step 2	Employee satisfaction	−0.38***	0.14	0.00
	Individual learning	0.00		
Step 3	Employee satisfaction	−0.31	0.14	0.00
	Individual learning	0.06		
	Employee satisfaction × individual learning	−0.11		

*** $p < 0.001$

The results of the hierarchical regression analysis of individual learning dimension in Table 3.20 show that there is no significant interaction effect between individual learning and employee satisfaction on turnover intention ($\beta = -0.11$), which does not confirm the moderating effect of individual learning on the relationship between employee satisfaction and turnover intention.

In order to expound this moderating effect, we test the regression coefficient of employee satisfaction vs. turnover intention under both high and low variables (among which, we take the "variable level" in Table 3.21 1 SD above or low than mean as the criterion). To specify, organizational level learning has a significant negative effect on the negative relationship coefficient between them (which can also be seen from the coefficient in Table 3.21). To put it simply, the relationship between employee satisfaction and turnover intention is stronger in companies with a higher organizational-level learning level (i.e., companies with large adjustment in organizational features) than those with a low organizational-level learning level. The moderating effect is shown in Figure 3.14. In contrast, exploitative learning has a significant positive effect on the negative relationship coefficient between them, as shown in Table 3.21; that is, the relationship between employee satisfaction and turnover intention is stronger in the companies with a low level of exploitative learning than those with a high level of exploitative learning. The moderating effect is shown in Figure 3.15.

In a word, organizational-level learning strengthens the relationship between employee satisfaction and turnover intention, while exploitative learning weakens the relationship. This verifies both Hypotheses 9 and 10.

Table 3.21 Regression analysis results of employee satisfaction vs. turnover intention under specific conditions

Variable	*Level*	*Coefficient*	*T*	*P*
Organizational-level learning	Low	−0.33***	−7.44	0.000
	High	−0.42***	−8.37	0.000
Exploitative learning	Low	−0.42***	−9.65	0.000
	High	−0.33***	−6.48	0.000

*** $p < 0.001$

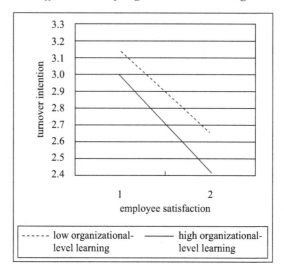

Figure 3.14 Moderating effect of organizational-level learning on the relationship between employee satisfaction and turnover intention (strengthened)

Figure 3.15 Moderating effect of exploitative learning on the relationship between employee satisfaction and turnover intention (weakened)

3.1.3.5.2 THE MODERATING EFFECT OF ORGANIZATIONAL LEARNING ON THE RELATIONSHIP BETWEEN AFFECTIVE COMMITMENT AND TURNOVER INTENTION

3.1.3.5.2.1 Results of hierarchical linear model and hierarchical regression analysis   The results of hierarchical linear model analysis of five collective level dimensions are shown in M2, Table 3.22.

Table 3.22 Moderating effect of collective level learning dimension on the relationship between affective commitment and turnover intention

Model	Parameter estimate														
	γ_{00}	γ_{01}	γ_{02}	γ_{03}	γ_{04}	γ_{05}	γ_{10}	γ_{11}	γ_{12}	γ_{13}	γ_{14}	γ_{15}	σ^2	τ_{00}	τ_{11}
M1: null model															
L1: $TI_{ij} = \beta_{0j} + \zeta_{ij}$	2.92***												0.64	0.083***	
L2: $\beta_{0j} = \gamma_{00} + U_{0j}$															
M2: random coefficient model															
L1: $TI_{ij} = \beta_{0j} + \beta_{1j}(OC_{ij}) + \zeta_{ij}$	2.94***						−0.52***						0.52	0.066***	0.104***
L2: $\beta_{0j} = \gamma_{00} + U_{0j}$															
$\beta_{ij} = \gamma_{10} + U_{0j}$															
M3: slope as dependent variable model															
L1: $TI_{ij} = \beta_{0j} + \beta_{1j}(OC_{ij}) + \zeta_{ij}$	3.14**	−0.12	−021	−0.4	0.36	0.42	0.69	−0.22	−0.70*	−0.09	0.24	0.49**	0.49	0.038***	0.012*
L2: $\beta_{0j} = \gamma_{00}(G_{ij}) + \gamma_{01}(O_{ij})$ $+ \gamma_{03}(BE_{ij}) + \gamma_{04}(EF_{ij}) + \gamma_{05}$ $(FB_{ij}) + U_{0j}$															
$\beta_{ij} = \gamma_{10} + \gamma_{11}(G_{ij}) + \gamma_{12}(O_{ij})$ $+ \gamma_{13}(BE_{ij}) + \gamma_{14}(EF_{ij}) + \gamma_{15}$ $(FB_{ij}) + U_{0j}$															

*** $p < 0.001$.
** $p < 0.01$.
* $p < 0.05$.

Notes: σ^2 is the horizontal residual, τ_{00} is the intercept residual, namely U_{0j}; τ_{11} is slope residual, namely U_{1j}. G refers to collective learning, O refers to organization-level learning, and BE refers to inter-organizational learning, FB refers to exploitative learning and FF refers to explorative learning, OC refers to affective commitment and TI refers to turnover intension.

These results show that there is a significant negative relationship between affective commitment and turnover intention ($\gamma_{10} = -0.52$, $p < 0.01$); the M3 result indicates that organizational-level learning has a significant negative effect on the negative relationship coefficient between them ($\gamma_{12} = -0.70$, $p < 0.05$), while exploitative learning has a significant positive effect ($\gamma_{15} = 0.49$, $p < 0.05$). This indicates that organizational-level learning and exploitative learning have a moderating effect on the relationship between organizational effective commitment and turnover intention.

The results of hierarchical regression analysis of the individual learning dimension in Table 3.23 showed that there was no significant interaction between individual learning and affective commitment on turnover intention ($\beta = 0.05$, $p = 0.835$), failing to verify individual learning's moderating effect on the relationship between affective commitment and turnover intention.

Specifically, organizational-level learning has a significant negative effect on the negative relationship coefficient between the two (as shown in Table 3.24); that is, in companies with a high level of organizational-level learning (companies with large adjustment in organizational characteristics), the relationship between affective commitment and turnover intention is stronger than that of companies with a low level of organizational-level learning. The moderating effect is shown in Figure 3.16. In contrast, exploitative learning has a significant positive effect on the negative relationship coefficient between the two (as shown in Table 3.24); that is, in companies with a low level of exploitative learning, the relationship between affective commitment and turnover intention is stronger than that in companies with a high level of exploitative learning. The moderating effect is shown in Figure 3.17.

Table 3.23 Hierarchical regression analysis of individual learning's moderating effect on the relationship between affective commitment and turnover intention

Step 1	Independent variable	Coefficient	R^2	ΔR^2
	Affective commitment	−0.47***	0.22	0.22***
Step 2	Affective commitment		0.22	0.00
	Individual learning	0.00		
Step 3	Affective commitment	−0.50**	0.22	0.00
	Individual learning	−0.03		
	Affective commitment × individual learning	0.05		

*** $p < 0.001$.
** $p < 0.01$

Table 3.24 Regression analysis results of employee satisfaction vs. turnover intention under specific conditions

Variable	Level	Coefficient	T	P
Organizational-level learning	Low	−0.43***	−9.78	0.000
	High	−0.48***	−9.67	0.000
Exploitative learning	Low	−0.52***	−12.17	0.000
	High	−0.41***	−8.02	0.000

*** $p < 0.001$

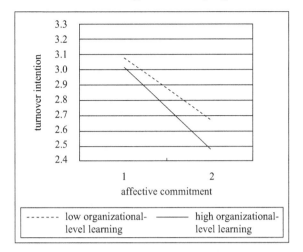

Figure 3.16 Moderating effect of exploitative learning on the relationship between affective commitment and turnover intention (strengthened)

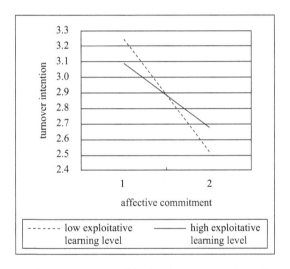

Figure 3.17 Moderating effect of exploitative learning on the relationship between affective commitment and turnover intention (weakened)

In conclusion, organizational-level learning can strengthen the relationship between affective commitment and turnover intention, while exploitative learning can weaken the relationship between them. This validates both Hypotheses 11 and 12.

Synthesizing the aforementioned two aspects, we can conclude that organizational-level learning can strengthen the negative relationship among employee satisfaction, affective commitment and turnover intention at the individual level, while exploitative learning can weaken the negative relationship among the three. The above results confirm the view of Crossan et al. (1999): the effectiveness of organizational learning is not necessarily positive. The results of this study align with the case studies of Crossan and Berdrow (2003).

When taking task performance as the dependent variable, it can be seen from Table 3.9 that there is no significant correlation among employee satisfaction, affective commitment and task performance (the correlation coefficients are $r = -0.04$ and $r = 0.07$ respectively, which are not significant), so Hypotheses 13 and 15 are not verified; therefore, there is no moderating effect of organizational learning on the relationship, and thus Hypotheses 14 and 16 are not verified.

3.1.4 Summary

3.1.4.1 The influence of organizational learning on employees' work attitude and task performance

The following conclusions can be drawn.

1. The effect of the dimensions of collective level learning (collective learning, organizational level learning, inter-organizational learning and explorative learning) on job satisfaction must be realized via individual learning.
2. The organizational-level learning's effect on affective commitment must be mediated by individual learning. This shows that the adjustment of organizational characteristics must also involve individual participation in order to affect individual affective commitment. However, the mediating effect of individual learning among inter-organizational learning, exploitative learning, explorative learning and affective commitment shows that they affect individual affective commitment from two directions: direct and indirect via individual learning. These partial mediating effects also indicate that there may exist other mediators that affect employees' affective commitment through other mediating variables. This remains to be verified through further research.
3. The mediating effect of individual learning between collective-level learning dimension and employee satisfaction and affective commitment is different, and this difference is merits further discussion.
4. From the direct and indirect relationship between organizational learning and employee satisfaction and affective commitment, we can conclude that in order to improve these two kinds of working attitudes of employees, collective-level organizational learning is a breakthrough point, and we should take individual learning as the key link. Collective-level learning dimensions requires the active participation of individual employees in order to have an positive impact.
5. Only individual learning has a significant negative impact on turnover intention. However, the moderating effect of organizational learning to be mentioned later indicates that organizational learning has an indirect effect on turnover intention.
6. Organizational learning has no significant effect on individual task performance, indicating that organizational learning is the improvement of an organization's learning capability, and it has no direct effect on the immediate

task performance of employees. This is also one of the reasons that account for the difficulty in implement organizational learning in practice. Despite its attractiveness to many firms, learning organization is prone to failure in firms since they cannot reap short-term benefits.

3.1.4.2 The moderating effect of organizational learning

The results show that a high level of organizational-level learning and a low level of explorative learning will make employees more emotional, and their dissatisfaction and lack of affection for the unit will likely make them want to resign. To put it in another way, the relationship between employee satisfaction and affective commitment on one hand and turnover intention on the other is magnified in firms with major organizational adjustment and poor execution of policies and strategies. As far as organizational-level learning is concerned, a substantial adjustment of a firm's characteristics, such as strategy, structure and procedure, may break the original balance and reallocate interests and power. This is bound to increase the difficulty for employees to adapt, make the employees with a low degree of satisfaction and affective commitment more anxious and, as a result, increase their tendency to leave the firm. This also implies that organizational learning has potential effects on employees' psychology and also suggests that managers should pay attention to associating organizational learning with employees' satisfaction, affective commitment and other psychological states in the management and implementation of organizational learning, so as to enhance the positive effect of management and intervention measures; If a firm wants to initiate significant adjustment in organizational strategy and organizational structure, it must choose a proper time when employees' satisfaction and affective commitment are relatively high. From the perspective of using learning, a firm with poor performance in implementing a corporate strategy and system—that is, a firm that fails to make strategy and planning affecting every employee—will undermine the prestige of the firm and managers in the eyes of employees, making it easier for employees to leave the firm because of dissatisfaction and lack of affection.

3.1.4.3 The overall analysis of the effect of organizational learning on individuals

The mediating effect of individual learning shows that no matter how well the firm learns, its employees' satisfaction will not be very high without their own active learning. However, in terms of affective commitment, in a firm doing well in organization learning (collective-level learning), individual learning can directly and indirectly improve employees' affective commitment. Therefore, the influence of organizational learning on affective commitment is greater than that on employee satisfaction. In firms with a high level of organizational learning, employees' affective commitment will be stronger. But further study is needed to explain the reason for this difference. The partial mediating effect of individual learning between collective-level organizational learning and affective commitment suggests that there may be other mediating variables to be studied further.

In a word, if a firm has a high level of organizational learning, the two kinds of working attitudes of employees will be higher, but at this time, we should pay attention to the individual learning, a key intermediary link. In terms of turnover intention, only individual learning has significant negative correlation with employee turnover intention, but the moderating effect of organizational learning dimension at the collective level indicates that organizational learning has an indirect effect on turnover intention.

In terms of the moderating effect, why do employees with high employee satisfaction and affective commitment have lower turnover intention in firms with a high organizational-level learning and low exploitative learning? This is because when firms constantly adjust their organizational structure, policies and strategies along with the external environment and their own development needs, this relative macro adjustment boosts employees' hope of the firm and confidence in the future, which will potentially incentivize employees who are satisfied and identify with the firm to stay in the firm. However, if the firm can downplay the implementation and execution of established policies and strategies, it will give employees greater work autonomy and maneuvering, and it will make those employees who are satisfied and identify with the firm more willing to stay in the firm. On the contrary, if the firm blindly implements the established strategies and policies, it will create constraint for the employees, suppress the individual working ability and enthusiasm and make them more inclined to leave than to stay. This also shows that although exploitative learning is an important part of organizational learning, overemphasis on the exploitation of existing knowledge will produce bad results. Therefore, managers must strike a balance between the exploitation of existing knowledge and the exploration of new knowledge.

We can see that organizational learning will interact with the psychological state of employees at that time, and then affect the behavior of employees. Consequently, the complexity of organizational learning lies in the "holistic harmony" in management and implementation, which means to make the internal organization learning and all aspects of the firm cooperate and achieve balance. The implementation and intervention of organizational learning (as well as the construction of learning organization) can have a prime effect only when the employees have a positive working attitude.

3.2   The effect of organizational learning on organization

The study of organizational behavior has always emphasized research on individuals. What impact, then, does organizational learning across the individual and collective levels have on the variables at the collective level? This will be the focus of the section.

3.2.1   Research hypothesis

3.2.1.1   Organizational learning and organizational innovation

Learning and innovation are often inseparable. Organizational learning is a frequently discussed term by many foreign scholars conducting organizational innovation research. Slater and Narver (1995) believe that organizational innovation has an impact on organizational learning. At the same time, there have emerged related empirical studies. For example, Hurley and Hult (1998) found that organizational learning has a significant impact on innovation. The confirmatory factor analysis of 187 R&D vice presidents by Calantone et al. (2002) showed that the path coefficient between learning orientation and corporate innovation ability defined by Calantone is 0.49 ($p < 0.01$). Hult et al. (2002) found that organizational learning has a direct impact on organizational innovation. Lian Yahui (2002) investigated 142 employees in a high-tech company in Taiwan. The regression coefficient between organizational learning facilitating factors and knowledge performance is 0.50. Yang et al.'s (2004) structural equation modeling (SEM) of the survey data of 863 people (one person in each firm) indicates that the regression coefficient between the dimension of "establishing systems to capture and share learning" and knowledge performance is 0.35. Therefore, the following hypothesis is set forth:

Hypothesis 17:

Organizational learning has a significant positive effect on organizational innovation.

3.2.1.2 Organizational learning and financial performance

The relationship between organizational learning and financial performance is a controversial research field. Day (1994) holds that learning has a direct impact on performance outcomes. Watkins and Marsick (1993) and Ellinger et al. (2002) demonstrate that financial performance is significantly related to learning organizational behavior perception. The results of Zheng Jinchang and Zhou Yunwei (2001) show that the total score of the learning organization questionnaire is significantly related to the three objective organizational performances of firms in the past four years. Yang et al. (2004) show that the regression coefficient between the dimension "providing strategic leadership for learning" and financial performance is 0.42. Lian Yahui (2002) showed that the regression coefficient between organizational learning facilitating factors and financial performance was 0.39. The research results of Calantone et al. (2002) show that the path coefficient from learning orientation in their definition to firm performance is 0.24. The research results of Chen and Zheng (2005) show that there are significant positive relations between the seven aspects of firm learning ability and firm performance (comprehensive performance).

However, contrary to the above views, Goh and Rhan's (2002) empirical study on the relationship between organizational learning capability and organizational performance found that the five learning abilities they studied had no significant correlation with financial performance. Research by Yeung et al. (1999) shows that there are different degrees of correlation between learning disabilities and business performance of firms. However, we believe that the results do not show that there is a strong direct relationship between the three.

We posit the following theoretical hypothesis:

Hypothesis 18:

Organizational learning has a significant positive effect on financial performance.

3.2.1.3 The role and effect of organizational innovation

Are organizational innovation and financial performance parallel when organizational learning influences the process of organizational innovation and financial performance at the organizational level? Organizational financial performance is the core goal of an organization, and organizational learning and organizational innovation are the methods to attain this goal. In the relationship between organizational learning and organizational innovation, the former is the premise of the latter. Only by improving organizational learning capability can firms have the basis of innovation. Therefore, this study hypothesizes that relationship between organizational learning and financial performance is mediated by organizational innovation.

Hypothesis 19:

Organizational innovation is the full mediator variable of organizational learning's effect on financial performance.

Therefore, the research framework of this study can be summarized as shown in Figures 3.18 and 3.19. First, study the direct effects of organizational learning on these two variables (see Figure 3.18, including Hypotheses 17 and 18); then, study the mediating effect of organizational innovation on organizational learning's impact on organizational financial performance (see Figure 3.19, including Hypothesis 19).

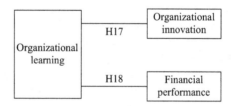

Figure 3.18 Research framework 1: direct effect of organizational learning on collective-level (H17,H18)

Figure 3.19 Research framework 2: the mediating role of organizational innovation between organizational learning and financial performance (H19)

3.2.2 *Methodology and procedures*

3.2.2.1 *Measures*

We used the six-item questionnaire of Calantone et al. (2002) for the organizational innovation. The main content of the questionnaire includes companies trying new ideas and process innovation, etc. For questionnaire evaluation, we used the Likert five-point scale, from 1 (completely inconsistent) to 5 (completely consistent). The questionnaire includes 1 negative item and 5 positive items. Organizational innovation ability is a structure of the collective level. According to the compositional model of Chan (1998), this study adopted the reference-shift consensus model; that is, all the subjects of the items are companies, such as "company trying new ideas" and so on.

This research adopts the four-item questionnaire of Calantone et al. (2002) for financial performance, which includes the evaluation of return on investment, return on assets, return on sales and overall profit. The questionnaire uses the six-point scale for evaluation, with six grades from low to high. According to Kozlowski and Klein's (2000) classification and Chan's (1998) point of view, the compositional model used in this study is the reference shift consensus, and the subject of questionnaire items is "unit," such as "unit's return on investment."

3.2.2.2 *Subjects and statistical analysis methods*

This study used the data of 908 people from 43 companies mentioned in this study, as shown in Table 3.1. The exploratory factor analysis, general regression analysis (OLS), hierarchical regression analysis (HRA) and statistical software SPSS 10.0 were applied.

3.2.3 *Research results*

3.2.3.1 *Test of other research questionnaires*

In this study, the principal component analysis method was used to conduct exploratory factor analysis on the survey data of the organizational innovation questionnaire and the corporate financial performance questionnaire. The results showed that the factor load and internal consensus coefficient of the two scales met the basic requirements of metrics. The specific factor loading of each item is shown in Tables 3.25 and 3.26. The results show that the data support the structure of the questionnaire.

Table 3.25 Factor analysis results of organizational innovation questionnaire

Item	V40	V41	V39	V42	V44	V43	Eigen value	Explained variance	Coefficient α
Load	0.81	0.80	0.80	0.76	0.67	0.40	3.10	51.72%	0.83

Table 3.26 Factor analysis results of financial performance

Item	V40	V41	V39	V42	V44	V43	Eigen value	Explained variance	Coefficient α
Load	0.88	0.87	0.84	0.82	2.92	72.87%	0.87	0.88	0.87

3.2.3.2 *The test of using the average of individual data as the collective-level variable*

In this study, organizational innovation and financial performance are the collective-level constructs, which require aggregating individual perception data into a collective-level construct and test intra-group homogeneity and intergroup differences (Kozlowski & Klein, 2000; Zohar, 2000).

The results of r_{wg} and ICC (1), evidence of intra-group homogeneity, are shown in Tables 3.27 and 3.28. The results show that, regardless of the uniform distribution or negative skew distribution, the r_{wg} reaches above 0.72, greater than the empirical 0.70 (Klein et al., 2000). According to James (1982), ICC (1) should be between 0 and 0.5, and ICC (1) in this study was 0.37 and 0.14. This shows that the two collective constructs in this study have sufficient internal homogeneity. The results of ICC (2), the reliability index of individual data mean of these two collective-level variables, are shown in Table 3.28, which are both higher than the empirical standard of 0.70 (Klein et al., 2000). This shows that it is reliable to use the average as the measurement index of these two collective-level variables.

The intergroup difference was tested by analysis of ANOVA, and the results in Table 3.29 show that the intergroup differences of these two collective-level variables are extremely significant, indicating that there are significant differences among different companies.

Table 3.27 Mean and median of r_{wg} of the two collective-level variables

		Organizational innovation	Financial performance
Mean	Uniform distribution	0.88	0.72
	Negative skew distribution	0.90	0.79
Median	Uniform distribution	0.89	0.80
	Negative skew distribution	0.91	0.84

Table 3.28 ICC (1) and ICC (2) of two collective level variables (average $N = 21$)

	Organizational innovation	Financial performance
ICC (1)	0.37	0.14
ICC (2)	0.92	0.77

Table 3.29 Results of analysis of variance of differences between groups of two collective
level variables

	Intra-group mean square	*Intergroup mean square*	*DF*	*F*
Organizational innovation	4.078	0.310	42/807	13.14***
Firm financial performance	3.460	0.784	42/567	4.41***

*** $p < 0.001$

In a word, sufficient intra-group homogeneity and intergroup differences provide evidence for aggregating individual data into a collective-level construct.
Therefore, we can use the average of a company's individual data as observations
of the two collective-level contructs.

3.2.3.3 Descriptive statistics for research variables

Since the hierarchical linear model (HLM) cannot test the influence of individual-
level variables on collective-level variables (Hofmann et al., 2000), the average
of individual-level variables was calculated in each company. The means, standard deviations and correlations for research variables are shown in Table 3.30.

3.2.3.4 The relationship between organizational learning and
organizational innovation and financial performance

3.2.3.4.1 THE DIRECT EFFECT OF ORGANIZATIONAL LEARNING ON ORGANIZATIONAL
INNOVATION AND CORPORATE FINANCIAL PERFORMANCE

This study conducted regression analysis on organizational learning, including
average individual learning, with organizational innovation and financial performance, respectively. The results are shown in Table 3.31.

The results show that organizational-level learning ($\beta = 0.62$, $p < 0.001$) and
exploitative learning ($\beta = 0.40$, $p < 0.01$) have a significant positive effect on
organizational innovation, though not every dimension has a significant impact
on organizational innovation, which explains 81% of the variance of organizational innovation. This validates both Hypothesis 1 and Slater and Narver's
(1995) viewpoints, and it is consistent with the research results of Hurley and
Hult (1998), Lian Yahui (2002), Calantone et al. (2002) and Hult et al. (2002).
Inter-organizational learning has a significant positive effect on corporate financial performance ($\beta = 0.67$, $p < 0.05$), which indicates that organizational learning can directly affect financial performance and explain 41% of the variance of
corporate financial performance. This verifies Hypothesis 2 and the viewpoint of
Day (1994), and it is consistent with the research results of Zheng Jinchang and
Zhou Yunwei (2001), Ellinger et al. (2002), Lian Yahui (2002), Calantone et al.
(2002) and Yang et al. (2004).

Table 3.30 Means, standard deviations and correlations for research variables

Variable	M	SD	1	2	3	4	5	6	7
1C	3.75	0.25	–						
2O	3.65	0.32	0.56**	–					
3BE	3.37	0.34	0.48**	0.70**	–				
4FB	3.56	0.44	0.43**	0.76**	0.64**	–			
5FF	2.95	0.34	0.31*	0.60**	0.84**	0.58**	–		
6OI	3.43	0.42	35*	0.84**	0.66**	0.81**	0.55**	–	
7FP	3.63	0.55	0.23	0.37*	0.60**	0.42**	0.52**	0.51**	–

** $p < 0.01$.
* $p < 0.05$.

Notes: The variables of individual level are averaged according to companies, so the sample is 43.
C refers to collective learning, *O* refers to organizational level learning, *BE* refers to inter-organizational learning, *FB* refers to exploitative learning, *FF* refers to explorative learning, *OI* refers to organizational innovation and *FP* refers to financial performance.

Table 3.31 Regression analysis results of organizational learning on organizational innovation and financial performance

	Organizational innovation			Financial performance		
	Standardization coefficient	R^2	*F*	*Standardization coefficient*	R^2	*F*
Inter-organizational learning	0.22	0.81***	26.17	0.67*	0.41**	4.20
Exploitative learning	0.40**			0.16		
Explorative learning	−0.13			0.12		
Organizational-level learning	0.62***			−0.07		
Collective learning	−0.18			0.18		
Average individual learning	−0.07			−0.43		

*** $p < 0.001$.
** $p < 0.01$.
* $p < 0.05$

3.2.3.4.2 THE MEDIATING EFFECT OF ORGANIZATIONAL INNOVATION IN THE IMPACT
     OF ORGANIZATIONAL LEARNING ON FINANCIAL PERFORMANCE

According to Baron and Kenny, to verify the mediating role takes three steps
(as shown in Table 3.32). The results show that in regression 3, the result of the
second step shows that when the mediator variable (organizational innovation)
is added, only organizational innovation still has a significant positive effect on
financial performance, while organizational learning dimensions have no significant effect on financial performance. This indicates that organizational innovation is a full mediator variable between organizational learning and financial
performance, which can be shown in Figure 3.20. This result is different from the
two opinions in the literature. That is to say, organizational learning has no direct
impact on financial performance, but it indirectly affects financial performance
through organizational innovation.

These results also show the following two direct effects. First, organizational-level learning and exploitation have a significant effect on organizational innovation, which is consistent with the research results of Calantone et al. (2002) and
Hult et al. (2002); second, inter-organizational learning has a significant positive
effect on financial performance, which supports the view of Day (1994), Ellinger
et al. (2002), Calantone et al. (2002) and Yang et al. (2004).

Table 3.32 Results of multiple regression analysis on the mediating role of organizational
          innovation

Variable	Regression 1	Regression 2	Regression 3	
	Organizational innovation	*Financial performance*	*Financial performance*	
			Step 1	*Step 2*
Organizational learning				
Average individual learning	−0.07		−0.43	−0.39
Collective learning	−0.18		0.18	0.28
Organizational-level learning	0.62***		−0.07	−0.43
Inter-organizational learning	0.22		0.67*	0.55
Exploitative learning	0.40*		0.16	−0.07
Explorative learning	−0.13		0.12	0.20
Organizational innovation				
Organizational innovation		0.45***		0.58*
R^2	0.81	0.26	0.41	0.48
ΔR^2	0.81***	0.26*	0.41*	0.37*
F	26.17	14.02	4.20	4.52

*** $p < 0.001$.
* $p < 0.05$.

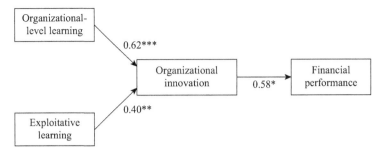

Figure 3.20 Full mediating effect of organizational innovation between organizational learning and financial performance

At the organizational level, organizational learning has an indirect effect on financial performance through organizational innovation; that is, the result does not indicate organizational learning has a direct impact on financial performance, nor does it indicate that organizational learning has no impact on financial performance. This reconciles the debate between two opposite viewpoints in the literature, which is also a characteristic of the research results; at the same time, the conclusion is also a feature of the research results. In addition, the results also show that organizational learning has a strong direct impact on organizational innovation. The full mediating effect of organizational innovation reveals the underlying relationship between organizational learning and financial performance. On the one hand, organizational learning must have an impact on financial performance; but on the other hand, it also shows that organizational learning does not have an direct impact on financial performance, which means that it must improve the organization's innovation ability before it can indirectly improve its financial performance. On the one hand, the results give managers the confidence that organizational learning has an effect on financial performance, and they can take many measures (including creating learning organizations) to improve the learning of organizations. On the other hand, they also need to be well prepared. The effectiveness of organizational learning cannot be achieved overnight; rather, it should be viewed and tested from a long-term perspective. This result also reveals why long-term business management models such as organizational learning intervention (including the creation of learning organizations) are often short-lived in the management practice of many countries, mainly because many high-level decision-makers do not see the results of such intervention in the near future, and they may not have the patience to test and examine the long-term effects of these management interventions.

3.3 The integrating model of organizational learning on individual and organization

Building on the previous research results, this study proposes an integrated theoretical model of trans-level mechanism of organizational learning shown in Figure 3.21. Organizational learning spans both individual and collective levels.

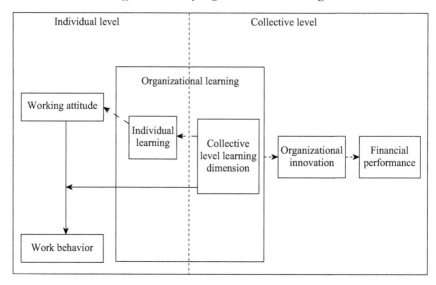

Figure 3.21 Integrated model of organizational learning effectiveness on individual and organization

The moderating role of organizational learning dimensions at the collective level and the mediating role of individual learning and organizational innovation holds great value for understanding and exploring the effectiveness mechanism of organizational learning.

Organizational learning is a phenomenon that crosses individual and collective level. The individual level includes the individual leaning dimension, and collective learning includes the other five dimensions.

On the individual level, while organizational learning influences individual working attitudes (employee satisfaction and affective commitment), the five collective-level dimensions influence working attitudes through individual learning (the individual plays the mediating role). That is to say, individual learning is the bridge between collective-level learning dimensions and individual variables in organizational learning. Simultaneously, when individual work attitude affects individual work behavior, collective-level learning dimension has a moderating effect.

On the collective level, organizational learning has effects on organizational financial performance through the full mediating effect of organizational innovation. That is, to have an effect on organizational financial performance, the internal and long-term organizational learning ability must improve organizational innovational capability.

Therefore, this effect model of organizational learning offers important inspirations for exploring the influential mechanism of organizational learning, organizational learning management and human resource management practices of companies.

Notes

1 Shared construct is a shared feature of collective members. Shared construct exists only when individuals in the group share a similar perception. Shared construct posits that the construct has similar functions, content, meaning and organizational construct at different levels. It is formed by the linear combination of emergence. Therefore, when researchers explore shared construct, it is necessary to clarify the intra-group consensus or credibility of individual characteristics.
2 The direct consensus model depends on the intra-group consensus, because only when there is consensus can the structure of the collective level exist. In this case, the intra-group consensus should be calculated to verify the existence of the collective-level structure.
3 The referent-shift consensus model is very similar to the direct consensus model, except that the reference-shift construct changes from individual to collective.

4 The generative mechanism of organizational learning*

In the process of organizational learning, for an organization to learn well and fast requires a lot of factors, including both internal and external factors. In this chapter, we focus on the internal factors. For Chinese enterprises, leadership is the superior and core element of multilevel learning capability and the fundamental element of organizational learning, followed by the organizational culture and human resource management (HRM) of the organization. These three aspects constitute the "troika" of leadership, cultural "soft" environment and practical "hard" environment of organizational learning and the main factors that facilitate organizational learning within the organization. Based on constructing the theoretical model of the generative mechanism of organizational learning, we study in this chapter how these three aspects influence organizational learning through empirical research.

4.1 Theoretical model of the generative mechanism of organizational learning

Against the backdrop of economic globalization, what kind of leadership can promote a company's organizational learning? How do leaders promote organizational learning? These are the core issues that determine whether companies can achieve long-term development. Unfortunately, there are limited empirical studies on the mechanism of leadership's role in organizational learning in the literature (Berson et al., 2006; Vera & Manor, 2004). In practice, Chinese companies' leaders take more traditional measures such as imparting knowledge to and exchanging experience with employees when promoting organizational learning (China Entrepreneur Survey System, 2006). To put it simply, they do not know exactly "what to do" and "how to do" to better promote organizational learning of the company.

For the question of "what to do," it has been confirmed by some research results (Amitay et al., 2005; Jansen et al., 2007; Lam, 2002) that transformational leadership is an important leadership behavior that promotes organizational learning. However, this study holds a contingency view on the relationship between the two. On one hand, though it is true that some aspects of transformational leadership can promote organizational learning, some transformational leadership behaviors can hinder organizational learning; on the other hand, transactional

* This part was partially supported by grants from The National Natural Science Foundation of China (Project No. 71871025).

leadership can also promote some aspects of organizational learning, albeit with hindrance aspects as well, which cannot be denied.

In terms of "how to do," this study contends that leaders of Chinese companies can depart from both the "soft" and "hard" aspects to effectively facilitate organizational learning. On one hand, leaders can build an enabling learning atmosphere as the soft environment for the company to learn. On the other hand, they can enhance human resources management to reinforce the "hard" measures. Only when the leaders pay attention to both "soft" and hard" measures can they really promote the organizational learning of companies.

4.1.1 Transformational leadership and transactional leadership

Bass (1997) summarized transformational leadership and transactional leadership as "the full range leadership," which is a comprehensive summary of leadership. "Transformational leadership is charismatic, inspirational, intellectually stimulating, and individually considerate" (Avolio et al., 1999). Transformational leadership helps get others to go beyond their own self-interests for the good of the group, while transactional leadership motivates individuals primarily through contingent-reward exchanges and active management-by-exception (Avolio et al., 1999). Operating within an existing system, transactional leaders seek to strengthen an organization's culture, strategy, and structure. Bass (1985, 1997) views them as distinct dimensions, which allows a leader to be transactional, transformational, both, or neither. Research results on transformational leadership show that transformational leadership has a significant impact on individual work attitude and work performance (Lowe et al., 1996; Li & Shi, 2003, 2005), group atmosphere and group performance (Wu & Wu, 2006), and organizational innovation (Jung et al., 2003; Keller, 2006).

4.1.2 The relationship between transformational leadership and transactional leadership and organizational learning

The literature shows that there has been some theoretical analysis and empirical research on the relationship between leadership and organizational learning. In terms of theoretical analysis, Vera and Manor (2004), with their systematic theoretical model, proposed that both transformational and transactional leaders stimulate exploration and exploitation, yet transformational leaders usually inspire learning that challenges the status quo, and transactional leaders facilitate learning that reinforces existing practices. Berson et al. (2006) conducted a systematic theoretical analysis on the nexus between leadership and organizational learning and believed that leaders play a role in promoting organizational learning through culture development and human resource management practices. Senge believes that organizational learning needs a coaching leadership.

In terms of empirical research, recent empirical studies have explored the relationship between different leadership styles and organizational learning. Amitay et al.'s (2005) findings attest to the central role of organizational leaders in determining the effectiveness of organizational learning. The research results of Nemanich et al. (2009) show that transformational leadership influences the whole explorative learning and exploitative learning through partial mediation of learning culture. All the aforementioned studies have explored the relationship between transformational leadership and organizational learning, but none of them studied the role of transactional leadership in organizational learning. The studies of Rui Mingjie and Lv Yufang (2005) show that leadership is an important variable in promoting organizational learning. Yu Haibo et al. (2008b) found that transformational leadership plays a positive role in promoting organizational learning, but it also hinders organizational learning in some aspects. They have also found that paternalistic leadership style of benevolent leadership can promote organizational learning, while authoritarian leadership has a significant negative effect.

However, the empirical research on the relationship between transformational leadership, transactional leadership and organizational learning needs to be strengthened. Jansen et al. (2007) found that transformational leadership has a significant positive impact on explorative learning, but not on exploitative learning; transactional leadership exerts significant positive influence on exploitative learning, but has a significant hindrance effect on explorative learning. Bass (1990, 1997) also held the belief that transactional leadership can facilitate organizational learning. This view is different from the general view that organizational learning needs transformational leadership more than transactional leadership.

In conclusion, these studies have explored the relationship between transformational leadership and organizational learning, and all showed that transformational leadership can influence organizational learning through some mediator variables. But how transformational leadership and transactional leadership jointly influence organizational learning requires further study.

4.1.3   The mediating effect of human resource management practice and organizational culture

4.1.3.1   The mediating effect of human resource management practice

In terms of the relationship between leadership and human resource management practice, a consensus has been reached in the literature that the leaders determine the human resource management practices. First of all, different organizations pay varying degrees of attention to human resource management. For example, the organizations under transformational leadership pay more attention to human resource management than the companies under transactional leadership. Secondly, leadership styles can profoundly impact the human resource management practice. Mumford (2000) argued that to manage creativity and innovation, effective human resource practices must consider the individual, the group, the organization and the strategic environment confronting the organization. The results of Waldman et al. (1987) show that transformational leadership can influence the effect of organizational performance evaluation. Therefore, it can be said that leadership influences human resource management practice, but more empirical research is needed.

Some empirical studies on the relationship between human resource management practices and organizational learning have concluded that human resource management practices can promote organizational learning. The research results of López et al. (2006) support that selective hiring, strategic training and employee participation in decision-making have significant positive effects on organizational learning, and their findings do not support the notion that compensation and reward systems focusing on performance will positively influence organizational learning. Another research of López et al. (2005) shows that human resource management practices have a significant positive effect on organizational learning, and the relationship between human resource practices and organizational performance is mediated by organizational learning. Bhatnagar and Sharma (2005) proved that the role of human resource management is positively related to organizational learning capability. At the same time, the relationship between human resource management practices and organizational learning is covered in some empirical studies. The results of Jerez-Gómez et al. (2005b) show that contingent compensation has a significant positive effect on organizational learning. Gómez et al. (2004) found that investment in training is conducive to the acquisition, generation and dissemination of new knowledge, and the improvement of individual commitment to organizational learning. Through empirical research, Chen Guoquan (2007) concluded four aspects of learning-oriented human resource management, which are recruitment, training, performance management and employee development. The analysis of He Huitao and Peng Jisheng (2008) shows that human resource management practices have an impact on organizational learning. The empirical study of Yu Haibo et al. (2008a) found that strategic training, employee participation, performance management and compensation management have a significant effect on different aspects of organizational learning. In short, the research on the relationship between human resource management practice and organizational learning is not systematic, and this highlights the need for further studies.

In terms of the relationship among the three variables, it was found that transformational leadership improves organizational performance through capital-enhanced human resource management. This serves as a great inspiration for the further study of the role of human resource management in the relationship between leadership and organizational learning: human resource management practice has a mediating effect, but more empirical research is needed to support this notion.

4.1.3.2 The mediating effect of organizational culture

Literature on organizational learning shows that learning climate plays a significant role in the relationship between leadership and organizational learning. Bass and Avolio (1993) believes that transformational leadership will create a transformational climate, and transactional leadership will create a transactional climate. Studies have shown that learning climate is a necessary condition for organizational learning (Tannenbaum, 1997; Goh, 1998; Watkins & Marsick, 1993; Yang et al., 2004). An atmosphere of tolerance for diversity of opinions and skills (Ford, 1996), or safe atmospheres in which different opinions are not punished (Edmondson, 1999) are conducive to learning. Therefore, many relevant research results and some theoretical viewpoints suggest that learning climate has a mediating effect between leadership and organizational learning (Berson et al., 2006). Leaders can create a climate of freedom, feedback, clear and shared organizational vision and trust (Redmond et al., 1993; Amabile et al.,

1996; Shalley & Gilson, 2004), which is conducive to knowledge generation and sharing. Some studies also show that transformational leadership influences the organization's patent awards through the partial mediating effect of empowerment and innovation culture (Jung et al., 2003); since leaders support an atmosphere of fault tolerance, employees learn in conducting after-action review (Ron et al., 2006). However, the mediating effect of organizational culture between transformational leadership/transactional leadership and organizational learning requires the support of further empirical research.

4.1.4 *The construct of the generative mechanisms of organizational learning*

The management practice front and theory front need to explore the mediating effect of transformational leadership and transactional leadership (and the paternalistic leadership with Chinese characteristics) on organizational leadership (as shown in Figure 4.1), and in-depth and systematic empirical studies are required. More specifically, efforts are needed in the following issues.

First, difference in the mediating effect of transformational leadership and transactional leadership (and paternalistic leadership with Chinese characteristics) on organizational leadership remains to be explored further. Theoretically, it is generally believed that organizational leadership needs transformational leadership more than any other type of leadership (Vera & Manor, 2004). As a result, there are some empirical studies on the relationship between transformational leadership and organizational learning, but the relationship between transactional leadership and organizational learning is insufficiently covered. Therefore, it is essential to explore the effective mechanism of transformational leadership and transactional leadership (as well as paternalistic leadership) on organizational learning.

Second, the effect of human resource management practices and organizational culture (including learning climate) in the relationships between transformational leadership/transactional leadership (as well as paternalistic leadership) and organizational learning needs to be further studied. Though some studies conclude that transformational leadership and transactional leadership will affect human resource practice and learning atmosphere, which will affect organizational learning, there is few studies on the role of human resource management practices and

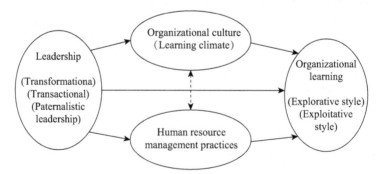

Figure 4.1 Effectiveness mechanism of leadership on organizational learning: the mediating role of organizational culture and human resource management practice

organizational culture (including learning climate) in the relationship between leadership and organizational learning. The theoretical analysis of Berson et al. (2006) suggests that leaders promote organizational learning through some mediator variables. Therefore, this highlights the importance of studying the effect of human resource management practices and organizational culture (including learning climate) in the relationship between transformational leadership and transactional leadership (and paternalistic leadership), and organizational learning.

4.2 Leadership—the foundation of generative mechanisms of organizational learning

In today's innovation-oriented China, companies are becoming increasingly aware of the importance of enhancing organizational learning capability, and corporate leaders also attach increasing importance to organizational learning. However, although they recognize the importance of organizational learning, they do not actually know exactly what to do and how to do it in order to better promote organizational learning. So far, there is a lack of systematic studies on the relationship between leadership and organizational learning (Vera et al., 2004; Berson et al., 2006). Vera and Manor (2004) and Berson et al. (2006) theoretically analyzed the relationship between leadership and organizational learning. Amitay et al. (2005), Rui and Lv (2005), Jansen et al. (2007) and Yu Haibo et al. (2008c) studied the effect of transformational leadership and paternalistic leadership on organizational learning. However, there is no empirical study on the specific mechanism of how leadership affects organizational learning. The *Leadership Quarterly*, a famous international journal, allotted a special issue in 2008 to systematically study the relationship between leadership and organizational learning. This shows that from the theoretical point of view, the effect of leadership on organizational learning mechanism is an important issue.

Studies on leadership were carried out from different perspectives (House & Aditya, 1997), in which transformational leadership and transactional leadership are known as "the full range leadership" (Bass, 1997). As for the Chinese culture, many scholars in the Taiwan Region and Hong Kong SAR believe that paternalistic leadership is a leadership style different from that in the West. In this study, we will discuss the relationship between transformational, transactional, paternalistic leadership and organizational learning, so as to provide more scientific inspiration for Chinese corporate leaders to lead in organizational learning.

4.2.1 The influence of transformational leadership on organizational learning

4.2.1.1 Literature review and research hypotheses

4.2.1.1.1 RESEARCH OVERVIEW OF THE RELATIONSHIP BETWEEN TRANSFORMATIONAL LEADERSHIP AND ORGANIZATIONAL LEARNING

The relationship between transformational leadership and organizational learning has been studied in the literature. Amitay et al. (2005) found that leadership is the defining factor of organizational learning efficiency, but their research focuses on the relationship between departmental leadership style and organizational learning. Vera and Manor (2004) believe that transformational leadership often leads to organizational learning that challenges the status quo, while transactional leadership is more likely to lead to organizational learning that reinforces the status quo. Senge (1990) also discussed that organizational learning needs the coaching leadership. Unfortunately, there are only theoretical analyses, and more empirical research is needed to support them.

4.2.1.1.2 THE RESEARCH HYPOTHESES ARE SET FORTH

This study adopts the five-factor view of transformational leadership of Rafferty and Griffin (2004) and splits the transformational leadership behaviors into five dimensions: vision, inspirational communication, intellectual stimulation, supportive leadership and personal recognition; for the study of organizational learning, we use the six-factor questionnaire with 29 items developed by our study. The following hypotheses are set forth.

Hypothesis 1:

Visionary leadership behavior promotes organizational learning, and there is a significant positive relation between the two.

Hypothesis 2:

There is a significant positive relation between inspirational communication leadership behavior and organizational learning.

Hypothesis 3:

There is a significant positive relation between the intellectually stimulating leadership behavior and organizational learning.

Hypothesis 4:

There is a significant positive relation between supportive leadership behavior and organizational learning.

Hypothesis 5:

There is a significant positive correlation between personally recognized leadership behavior and organizational learning.

4.2.1.2 Methodology

4.2.1.2.1 SUBJECTS

We distributed 300 questionnaires to 10 companies in Beijing, Shanghai, Shenyang and Qingdao and received 276 valid responses. The basic information of the subjects is as follows: 33.0% are employees in state-owned enterprises, 23.2% in private companies and 43.8% in foreign-funded companies. In terms of development stages of the companies, 8.3% are in the start-up stage, 38.0% in the growth stage, 22.8% in the mature stage and 30.8% in the re-innovation stage. In terms of position, general staff account for 74.6%, front-line managers account for 15.6% and middle- and high-level management account for 9.8%.

The transformational leadership scale is based on Rafferty and Griffin's (2004) transformational leadership questionnaire, which covers five dimensions, each including three items. The organizational learning scale adopts the organizational learning scale developed by this study, which includes 29 items. The five-point Likert scoring method was used in both scales. The subjects were asked to evaluate with their own companies. The internal consistency reliability α coefficient of each dimension of the organizational learning scale is as follows: individual learning is 0.79, collective learning is 0.84, organizational level learning is 0.80, inter-organizational learning is 0.85, explorative learning is 0.64 and exploitative learning is 0.83. The internal consistency reliability α coefficient of each dimension of the transformational leadership scale is as follows: vision is 0.74, incentive communication is 0.69, intellectual stimulation is 0.79, supportive leadership is 0.77 and personal recognition is 0.87. It shows that the reliability of each scale meets the basic requirements of metrology.

This study adopts SPSS 10.0 and AMOS 4.0 to carry out the statistical analysis and structural equation modeling.

4.2.1.3 Research results

We use the statistical analysis software AMOS 4.0 to analyze the survey data. Through structural equation modeling, it was found that the quality of the three items of transformational leadership and two items of explorative learning were not ideal in the structure of the four latent variables. Therefore, the five items were removed, and then the structural equation modeling was carried out. The statistical analysis results of the fit index of the model are shown in Table 4.1. The results show that x^2/df and RMSEA both achieve good fitness, and the other four indicators all reach above 0.95, which indicates that the validation model fits well (Bollen, 1989). This shows that the fit indexes of the two-dimensional model formed by transformational leadership and organizational learning meet the requirements of metrology. The factor loading and error of the structural equation model are shown in Table 4.2. The results also show that the factor

Table 4.1 Comparison of fit indexes for the model of the relationship between transformational leadership and organizational learning

	x^2	df	x^2/df	NFI	IFI	TLI	CFI	RMSEA
Model zero	36,786.18	780	47.16					
Validation model	1881.43	666	2.83	0.95	0.97	0.96	0.97	0.08

Table 4.2 Load and error of latent variables of transformational leadership and organizational learning on manifest variables

Manifest variables	Vision	Inspirational communication	Intellectual stimulation	Supportive leadership	Personal recognition
X_1	0.87 (0.20)	0.59 (0.64)	0.69 (0.76)	0.80 (0.64)	0.83 (0.27)
X_2	0.82 (0.23)	0.71 (0.54)	0.94 (0.18)	0.78 (0.65)	0.66 (0.22)
X_3	0.50 (0.99)				0.79 (0.36)
X_1	0.63 (0.55)	0.66 (0.31)	0.55 (0.47)	0.67 (0.75)	0.72 (0.39)
X_2	0.67 (0.45)	0.71 (0.38)	0.43 (0.37)	0.62 (0.41)	0.63 (0.54)
X_3	0.57 (0.54)	0.73 (0.32)	0.60 (0.49)	0.65 (0.45)	0.69 (0.38)
X_4	0.64 (0.56)	0.68 (0.35)	0.67 (0.78)	0.69 (0.49)	0.69 (0.50)
X_5	0.68 (0.32)		0.68 (0.50)	0.69 (0.70)	0.75 (0.30)
X_6	0.50 (0.67)			0.40 (0.45)	0.51 (0.84)

Note: The subscript numbers of letters of manifest variables represent the number of manifest variables, respectively. Numbers in brackets indicate error.

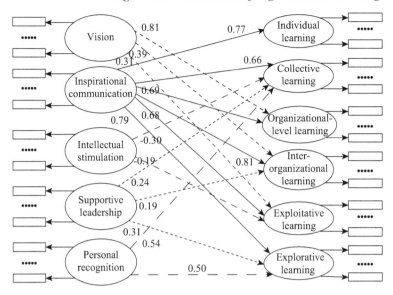

Figure 4.2 Relationship between transformational leadership and organizational learning

loading of each item is large while the error loading is small, which proves that the structure of this model is better.

The construct model is shown in Figure 4.2. First, the visionary leadership behavior plays a significant role in promoting organizational learning, inter-organizational learning, and exploitative learning. Furthermore, the coefficient of the promoting effect visionary leadership behavior on organizational learning is relatively large, which is partially consistent with Hypothesis 1. Second, the leadership behaviors of inspirational communication have a significant positive effect on the six organizational learning dimensions, which verifies Hypothesis 2. Third, the intellectually stimulating leadership behaviors have a significant inhibiting effect on collective learning and exploitative learning, which does not support Hypothesis 3. Fourth, the leadership behaviors of supportive lerdership play a significant role in promoting collective learning, inter-organizational learning and explorative learning, which partially supports Hypothesis 4. Fifth, personally recoginzed leadership behaviors have a significant promoting effect on collective learning and explorative learning, which supports Hypothesis 5. These results are basically consistent with the results of Amitay et al. (2005), but it should be noted that intellectual stimulation has a significant inhibiting effect on collective learning and exploitative learning, and this has not been found in previous studies.

4.2.1.4 Analysis and discussion

In general, transformational leadership plays a significant role in promoting organizational learning. It should be noted, however, that the intellectually stimulating leadership behaviors of leaders in Chinese companies exert a significant inhibiting effects on organizational learning.

The main reason that visionary leadership behaviors significantly facilitate organizational learning, inter-organizational learning and exploitative learning is that when the leader of an organization has a clear strategic orientation, that person can inspire the organization to form a shared vision and promote the employees' recognition of the organizational vision. This in turn will greatly facilitate the formulation and implementation of organizational strategy and promote the refinement of the organizational culture and the organizational system. Further, since the leader has done a good job in forming the organizational vision, the employees and whole departments can understand and identify with the strategy and objective of the entire organization so that, when communicating and cooperating with other organizations, they will have clear objectives and stronger motivation. This, as a result, can promote inter-organizational learning.

The inspirational communication leadership behaviors play significant roles in promoting the six dimensions of organizational learning, which suffices to prove that when leaders embrace an open attitude towards the department and employees in the organization, such leadership behaviors will produce tremendous radiating power that facilitates every aspect of organizational learning. The effects of leaders' active communication are elaborated. First, it will constantly stimulate individual employees to strive for better and improve their work; second, it will play an exemplary and incentive role in creating a culture of openness and trust and strengthening cooperation among members of the organization; third, leaders' active communication style can facilitate the formulation and implementation of organizational strategy and the improvement of organizational culture; fourth, it can also encourage individual employees and departments to communicate and actively cooperate with other organizations with an open mind; fifth, it will promote the creation and diffusion of new knowledge in the organization, exploration and exploitation of organizational knowledge.

The intellectually stimulating leadership behaviors have significant inhibiting effects on collective learning and exploitative learning, but this result has not been found by a priori studies. This result suggests that Chinese company leaders should avoid radical or risky behaviors in the process of leading organizational learning, so as to prevent the adverse effect on organizational learning. The reason is that, in the Chinese culture, the leaders' obsession with new working methods and ideas often puts individual employees under great pressure, which will make the employees pay excessive attention to the generation of their own new ideas and new working methods, thus hindering the communication and cooperation among members. Further, this is bound to affect the exploitation of new knowledge and hence hinder organizational learning. The underlying cultural reasons need to be further studied.

Supportive leadership behaviors can promote collective learning, inter-organizational learning and explorative learning because if leaders care about the feelings and interests of their subordinates, a sound working climate of mutual understanding in the company can be created easily. Since leaders are so considerate to their subordinates, as members of such a fair organization, the subordinates will more likely take leaders as role models to understand and support each other. Moreover, this kind of working climate will also affect the flow cooperation between the company and other organizations, and the employees and departments, can work together with mutual understanding and reach more of a consensus. Of course, the enabling working climate brought about by supportive leadership is more conducive to the generation of new ideas in the organization. It will form a good work atmosphere that inspires members of the organization and plays a great role in promoting the exploration of organizational knowledge.

Personally approved leadership plays a significant role in promoting collective learning and explorative learning in that leaders recognize the achievements of their subordinates and inspire them. In this way, leaders can set a good example for members in the organization to recognize each other's strengths and engage in more effective communication. This climate of mutual recognition will enable members to engage in better cooperation. Leaders' recognition of other people serve as a role model to affect the work climate of the unit, greatly motivate every member of the organization to generate internal work motivation and generate more new ideas at work. It is conducive to the dissemination of new knowledge within the organization, and it can promote the exploration of knowledge.

Chinese corporate leaders can be inspired by the results of this study in three aspects. First, when leading organizational learning, leaders should grasp the vision of the company, highly identify with the vision of the company, engage in active communication with the members of the organization and pay attention to the personal feelings and needs of members of the organization; second, they should avoid radical work stimulation, so as to avoid inhibiting the organizational learning of the company; third, leaders should value inspirational communication and show their care about subordinates' feelings and personal growth. In conclusion, transformational leaders emphasize experimentation, risk taking, punctuated change, and multiple alternatives, which will greatly promote organizational learning. However, at the current stage, in the process of leading organizational learning in China, leaders should strike a balance between risk-taking and transformation, and avoid going to the extreme.

4.2.2 *The influence of paternalistic leadership on organizational learning*

4.2.2.1 *Question presentation*

Paternalistic leadership is a leadership style with Chinese cultural characteristics prevalent in Chinese enterprises (Zheng Boxun, 2004). Scholars, such as Silin (1976) and Westwood (1997), have studied the paternalistic leadership in Chinese culture. At present, the widely accepted view is that of Zheng Boxun et al. (2000) based on extensive and in-depth research. The research on paternalistic leadership is mainly conducted in two aspects. Firstly, the views of Zheng Boxun et al. (2003) and Zheng Boxun (2004) dominate the research on the construct and measurement of paternalistic leadership. Their triarchic theory holds that paternalistic leadership includes authoritarian leadership, moral leadership and benevolent leadership. Second, the research on the effectiveness of paternalistic leadership is very popular. Many studies have found that paternalistic leadership has unique explanatory power on many aspects of companies, teams and individual employees, and the three factors reflect different explanatory power.

Paternalistic leadership is the concrete representation of transformation leadership, a hot topic in western leadership studies. When comparing the effectiveness of transformational leadership and paternalistic leadership, researchers found that the former does not have stronger explanatory power than latter (Zheng Boxun et al., 2003; Zheng Boxun, 2004). As the literature indicated that transformational leadership can promote organizational learning, and that paternalistic leadership with Chinese cultural characteristics is similar to transformational leadership in many aspects, we posit that paternalistic leadership is correlated to organizational learning. At the same time, the benevolent dimension of paternalistic leadership plays a significant role in promoting organizational learning, while authoritarian leadership has an inhibiting effect on organizational learning, though this study adopts the binary theory of paternalistic leadership. In short, the empirical studies on the influence of paternalistic leadership on organizational learning are still limited.

Therefore, this study adopts the triarchic theory of paternalistic leadership proposed by Zheng Boxun et al. (2003), and the organizational learning study adopts the six-dimension view of Yu Haibo et al. (2006). Based on the analysis presented, we hypothesize that:

Hypothesis 6:

Benevolent leadership has a significant positive effect on all dimensions of organizational learning.

Hypothesis 7:

Moral leadership has a significant positive effect on all dimensions of organizational learning.

Hypothesis 8:

Authoritarian leadership has a significant negative effect on all dimensions of organizational learning.

The studies on the interaction effect among the three aspects of paternalistic leadership are sparsely documented in the literature. Zheng Boxun et al. (2003) found that there was an interaction effect between benevolent leadership and moral leadership in the work attitude of subordinates: subordinates under high benevolent leadership and high moral leadership have the most positive work attitude. They also found that under high authoritarian leadership, there is a significant positive predictive effect between benevolent leadership and subordinates' work attitude, but under low authoritarian leadership, the relationship between them was not significant. The results also show that under low authoritarian leadership, moral leadership has a significant positive predictive effect on the work attitude of subordinates, but under high authoritarian leadership, the effect of moral leadership will be inhibited. Zhou Hao and Lirong Long (2007) also found that moral leadership and authoritarian leadership have a significant interaction effect in distribution justice and procedural justice, while benevolent leadership and authoritarian leadership have a significant interaction effect in leadership justice. These results suggest that there is a similar interaction effect between paternalistic leadership and organizational learning. Therefore, the following hypotheses are set forth.

Hypothesis 9:

Benevolent leadership and moral leadership have a significant interaction effect on all dimensions of organizational learning.

Hypothesis 10:

Benevolent leadership and authoritarian leadership have a significant interaction effect on all dimensions of organizational learning.

Hypothesis 11:

Moral leadership and authoritarian leadership have a significant interaction effect on all dimensions of organizational learning.

4.2.2.2 Methodology

4.2.2.2.1 SUBJECTS

We investigated 30 companies in Beijing, Hebei and Tianjin; we distributed 900 questionnaires and obtained 711 valid questionnaires. Specifically, in the sample, 23.4% are state-owned enterprises, 34.8% private enterprises, 19.8% foreign-funded enterprises and 22.0% firms of other types; 75.8% are front-line workers, 14.5% front-line managers and 9.8% middle-level and senior managers; 72.0% are working for less than 3 years, 16.5% between 3 and 7 years and 11.4% more than 7 years. Among the surveyed, 48.9% have a college degree or below, 39.9% a bachelor's degree and 11.2% a postgraduate degree; 49.5% male and 50.5% female; 68.2% of the surveyed enterprises have between 1 and 500 employees, 17.2% between 501 and 2000 employees and 14.6% more than 2000 employees; 12.4% of employees are working at enterprises in the start-up stage, 44.5% in the growth stage, 26.3% in the mature stage and 16.7% in the re-innovation stage.

4.2.2.2.2 MEASURES

The paternalistic leadership questionnaire of Zheng Boxun et al. (2000) was adopted as the paternalistic leadership questionnaire, which consisted of 33 items, including 11 items on benevolent leadership, 9 items on moral leadership, and 13 items on authoritarian leadership. The organizational learning questionnaire is the 29-item and six-factor questionnaire developed in this study. The Likert five-point scoring method was used in both scales, and the subjects were asked to evaluate the consistent with the companies where they work.

4.2.2.2.3 STATISTICAL METHOD

SPSS 10.0 was used for statistical analysis.

4.2.2.3 Research results

4.2.2.3.1 RESULTS OF DESCRIPTIVE STATISTICS

The descriptive statistics for research variables are shown in Table 4.3. The results show that the internal consistency coefficient of paternalistic leadership and each organizational learning dimension is between 0.69 and 0.89, which meets the basic requirements of psychometrics.

4.2.2.3.2 CONFIRMATORY FACTOR ANALYSIS RESULTS OF EACH MEASURE

The results of confirmatory factor analysis show that x^2/df and RMSEA (critical value is 0.08) of the three-factor model of paternalistic leadership were 5.44 and 0.079 respectively, which meet the model fit standard; the indexes of NFI, IFI, TLI and CFI were all 0.96, indicating that the three-factor model fit well (Bollen, 1989). The indexes of the six-factor model of organizational learning, x^2/df, RMSEA, NFI, IFI, TLI and CFI are 3.21, 0.056, 0.98, 0.99, 0.98 and 0.99 respectively, which all meet the basic requirements, indicating that the six-factor model fits well. Therefore, it can be concluded that the three-factor paternalistic leadership structure model and six-factor organizational learning structure model have a relatively high structural validity.

4.2.2.3.3 THE EFFECT OF PATERNALISTIC LEADERSHIP ON ORGANIZATIONAL LEARNING

4.2.2.3.3.1 The direct effect of paternalistic leadership on organizational learning   In terms of main effect, the results of hierarchical regression analysis (Table 4.4) show that benevolent leadership has a significant effect on all six dimensions of organizational learning, supporting Hypothesis 6. Moral leadership has a significant effect on all six dimensions except explorative learning. These results partially support Hypothesis 7. Authoritarian leadership has a significant effect on collective learning, organizational learning, inter-organizational learning and exploitative learning but no significant effect on the other two dimensions, contradicting Hypothesis 8.

4.2.2.3.3.2 The interaction effect of paternalistic leadership on organizational learning   The hierarchical regression analysis results show that the explanatory variance only increased significantly for explorative learning ($\Delta R^2 = 0.009$, $p < 0.05$) and exploitative learning ($\Delta R^2 = 0.014$, $p < 0.05$). These results partially support Hypotheses 10 and 11, but not Hypothesis 9.

Specifically, there is a significant interaction effect between benevolent leadership and authoritarian leadership on explorative learning ($\beta = 0.11$, $p < 0.05$). The interaction effect diagram is shown in Figure 4.3. The results of regression coefficient (Table 4.5) shows that under high authority leadership and low authority leadership, the regression coefficient of benevolent leadership and explorative learning is 0.73 and 0.59 ($Z = 1.92$, $p < 0.05$, one-tailed test). The results also show that under high authority leadership, the regression coefficient between

Table 4.3 Descriptive statistics, correlations and internal consistency reliabilities for research variables

Variable	M	SD	1	2	3	4	5	6	7	8	9
1. Benevolent leadership	2.98	0.81	(0.89)								
2. Moral leadership	3.17	0.78	0.59**	(0.83)							
3. Authoritarian leadership	3.16	0.68	0.00	-0.09*	(0.86)						
4. Individual learning	3.40	0.73	0.46**	0.49**	0.05	(0.75)					
5. Collective learning	3.56	0.77	0.43**	0.42**	-0.01	0.61**	(0.70)				
6. Organizational-level learning	3.48	0.71	0.42**	0.38**	0.12**	0.56**	0.56**	(0.69)			
7. Inter-organizational learning	3.30	0.73	0.56**	0.39**	0.04	0.52**	0.55**	0.60**	(0.73)		
8. Explorative learning	3.07	0.83	0.58**	0.35**	-0.03	0.41**	0.45**	0.53**	0.65**	(0.72)	
9. Exploitative learning	3.44	0.85	0.47**	0.42**	0.04	0.56**	0.49**	0.57**	0.63**	0.53**	(0.73)

** $p < 0.01$.
* $p < 0.05$.

Note: The data in brackets are coefficient α of internal consistency reliability of each variable.

Table 4.4 Hierarchical regression analysis of the influence of paternalistic leadership on organizational learning

Variables	Individual learning			Collective learning			Organizational-level learning			Inter-organizational learning			Explorative learning			Exploitative learning		
	M1	M2	M3	M1	M2	M3	M1	M2	M3	M1	M2	M3	M1	M2	M3	M1	M2	M3
Step 1: basic variable																		
Nature of enterprises	0.04	−0.01	−0.01	0.11**	0.07	0.07	0.07	0.04	0.05	0.06	0.03	0.03	0.09	0.06	0.06	0.12**	0.08*	0.09*
Scale of enterprises	0.04	0.00	0.01	0.09	0.04	0.05	0.00	−0.04	−0.05	0.01	−0.05	−0.05	0.04	−0.02	−0.02	0.02	−0.02	−0.03
Development stages	0.00	0.03	0.03	0.08	0.11**	0.10*	−0.01	0.02	0.02	0.01	0.03	0.03	−0.07	−0.07	−0.06	0.01	0.04	0.04
Step 2: paternalistic leadership																		
Benevolent		0.29**	0.29**		0.28**	0.28**		0.29**	0.28**		0.52**	0.49**		0.62**	0.59**		0.32**	0.28**
Moral		0.33**	0.33**		0.32**	0.32**		0.24**	0.24**		0.15**	0.17**		0.04	0.06		0.26**	0.28**
Authoritarian		0.07	0.08		0.10*	0.11*		0.17**	0.17**		0.13**	0.13**		0.04	0.04		0.12**	0.12**
Step 3: interaction effect																		
Benevolence × morality			0.09			0.00			−0.07			−0.03			−0.02			−0.02
Benevolence × authority			0.01			−0.02			0.01			0.11*			0.11*			0.15**
Morality × authority			0.00			−0.06			−0.06			−0.08			−0.05			−0.11*
R^2	0.003	0.269	0.275	0.024	0.266	0.271	0.006	0.185**	0.189	0.004	0.345	0.354	0.013	0.416	0.425	0.014	0.233	0.247
ΔR^2	0.003	0.266**	0.006	0.024**	0.242**	0.005	0.006	0.179**	0.004	0.004	0.341**	0.009	0.013	0.403**	0.009*	0.014**	0.219**	0.014*

** $p < 0.01$.
* $p < 0.05$.
Note: The independent variables are all centralized.

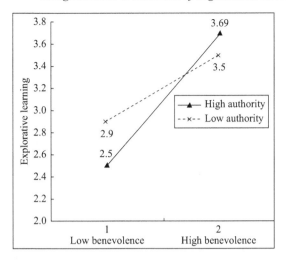

Figure 4.3 Interaction effect between benevolent leadership and authoritarian leadership on explorative learning

Table 4.5 Regression analysis results of interaction effect

Dependent variable	Moderating variable level	Independent variable	Coefficient
Explorative learning	High-authority leadership	Benevolent leadership	0.73**
	Low-authority leadership	Benevolent leadership	0.59**
Exploitative learning	High-authority leadership	Benevolent leadership	0.57**
	Low-authority leadership	Benevolent leadership	0.37**
	High-authority leadership	Moral leadership	0.33*
	Low-authority leadership	Moral leadership	0.63**

** $p < 0.01$.
* $p < 0.05$.

benevolent leadership and explorative learning is greater. This shows that high benevolence and high authority leadership is the most effective in promoting explorative learning, followed by high benevolence and low authority leadership, then low benevolence and low authority leadership; and the least effective is low benevolence and high authority leadership.

In terms of exploitative learning, there is a significant interaction between benevolent leadership and authoritarian leadership ($\beta = 0.15$, $p < 0.01$), moral leadership and authoritarian leadership ($\beta = -0.11$, $p < 0.05$), as shown in Figures 4.4 and 4.5. The result of regression coefficient (Table 4.5) shows that under high authority leadership and low authority leadership, there are significant differences between the regression coefficient of benevolent leadership (0.57) and exploitative learning (0.37) ($Z = 1.98$, $p < 0.05$, single-tailed test), and the regression coefficient between moral leadership and exploitative learning is 0.33 and 0.63 ($Z = 3.04$, $p < 0.01$, single-tailed test). This shows that high benevolence and high authority leadership is the most effective in promoting exploitative learning,

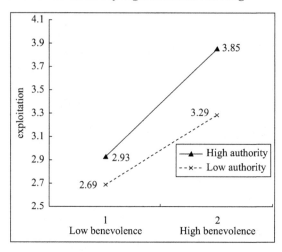

Figure 4.4 Interaction effect between benevolent leadership and authoritarian leadership on exploitative learning

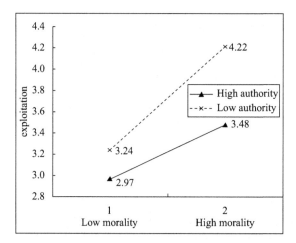

Figure 4.5 Interaction effect between moral leadership and authoritarian leadership on exploitative learning

followed by high benevolence and low authority leadership, then low benevolence and high authority leadership, and the least effective is low benevolence and low authority leadership. Likewise, high morality and high authority leadership is the most conducive to exploitative learning, followed by high morality and low authority leadership, low morality and low authority leadership, and the least conducive is low morality conduct and high authority leadership. These results support Hypotheses 10 and 11.

The results also show that the interaction effect between benevolent leadership and moral leadership in all dimensions of organizational learning is not significant; therefore Hypothesis 9 is not verified.

4.2.2.4 Discussions

On the whole, benevolent leadership has a significant positive impact above medium level on the six dimensions of organizational learning; moral leadership has a significant impact on five of the dimensions; but authoritarian leadership has a significant positive impact on only four dimensions. Therefore, benevolent leadership has the greatest impact on organizational learning, while authoritarian leadership has the slightest impact on organizational learning. This shows that leaders' care for subordinates and selflessness can create an open, positive and good organizational atmosphere, thus promoting organizational learning in all aspects. However, authoritarian leadership shows a relatively small positive impact in this study, while earlier studies (Yu Haibo et al., 2008a) have drawn a conclusion with significant negative impact. Two main reasons account for this difference. One reason is that this study is conducted under the background of the triarchic theory of paternalistic leadership (i.e., three dimensions), while previous studies were based on the binary theory. Thus, we can conclude that if the level of moral leadership of Chinese leaders is not high, then authoritarian leadership will have a negative effect on organizational learning; but if the level of moral leadership is relatively high, then authoritarian leadership still plays a certain role in promoting organizational learning, but only mildly. The second reason is that, on the basis of the leader's moral leadership, the leader's tight control and absolute obedience style can also promote the adjustment of the organizational level, the application of knowledge, and smooth communication between organizations. It will also have some facilitating effect on the communication and cooperation between employees.

As for the crucial explorative learning, only benevolent leadership can have a significant positive effect on it (0.62, $p < 0.01$), which proves that benevolent leadership plays a significant facilitating role in knowledge exploration and that this leadership style with Chinese characteristics is not obsolete in China's advanced corporate management.

The effect of benevolent leadership and authoritarian leadership on explorative learning and exploitative learning figures more prominently in the interaction effect, but the effect varies. Comparing Figures 4.3 and 4.4, we can see that high benevolence and high authority leadership are prime for both explorative learning and exploitation; however, the difference between the two is that low benevolence and high authority is the most detrimental to explorative learning, while for exploitative learning, the low benevolence and low authority leadership is the most detrimental. This proves that benevolent leadership is needed more for explorative learning, and authoritarian leadership can also promote exploitative learning to a certain extent.

However, the interaction effect between moral leadership and authoritarian leadership on exploitative learning is different from the previous two. Figure 4.5 shows that if the level of authoritarian leadership is high, the role of moral leadership in exploitative learning will be inhibited; only when the level of authoritarian leadership is low can moral leadership play a better role in promoting exploitative learning. This shows that for moral leadership to have a promoting effect on exploitative learning, high authority leadership should be avoided because it will greatly offset the role of moral leadership in promoting exploitative learning.

The studies described previously on main effect and interaction effect indicate that in facilitating organizational learning, first, benevolent leadership is needed in the first place because it is the basic condition for leaders to facilitate organizational learning; second, if the level of benevolent leadership is not high, then the level of moral leadership should be elevated or the authoritarian leadership should be maintained at a certain level so as to facilitate organizational learning.

The results of this study present important theoretical and practical value. In terms of theoretical value, first, it carried out research on the relationship between paternalistic leadership and organizational learning ahead of others; second, it has identified some specific relationships between paternalistic leadership and organizational learning, which confirms that paternalistic leadership with Chinese cultural characteristics tremendously impacts modern organizational learning. In terms of practical value, first, if China's organizational leaders desire to improve their organizational learning capability, they need to strengthen their benevolent leadership behavior; second, moral leadership is also an indispensable condition for promoting organizational learning; third, for promoting organizational learning, the most ideal leadership style is a leadership style with high benevolence, high morality and a certain level of authority, and we must avoid the leadership style of low benevolence, low morality and high authority (the most important).

4.2.2.5 Conclusion

Benevolent leadership has a significant positive effect on all six dimensions of organizational learning; moral leadership has a significant positive impact on the other five dimensions of organizational learning apart from explorative learning; authoritarian leadership has a significant, and to a certain extent, positive effect on collective learning, organizational learning, inter-organizational learning and exploitative learning.

Benevolent leadership and authoritarian leadership have a significant interaction effect on both explorative learning and exploitative learning, while moral leadership and authoritarian leadership have a significant interaction effect on exploitative learning. In other words, leadership of high benevolence, high morality and a certain level of authority are the best leadership in promoting organizational learning.

4.2.3 The effect of paternalistic leadership on the balance between explorative learning and exploitative learning

Today, with the deepening of social and corporate reform, the exploration of new knowledge and the exploitation of existing knowledge have always been an eternal paradox in firm innovation and development. This paradox reflected in the field of organizational learning is the balance between explorative learning and exploitative learning (March, 1991). March (1991) believed that maintaining an appropriate balance between exploration and exploitation is a primary factor in system survival and prosperity. The leader is the supreme element in maintaining this balance. Unfortunately, the empirical research on the relationship between explorative learning and exploitative learning is insufficient (Gupta et al., 2006). Therefore, how leaders can lead to achieve equilibrium between these two is one theoretical and practical problem to be solved urgently.

4.2.3.1 Theoretical review and presentation of research questions

4.2.3.1.1 STUDY ON EXPLORATIVE LEARNING AND EXPLOITATIVE LEARNING

The concepts of explorative learning and exploitative learning were first proposed by March (1991), but there are disparate interpretations in the literature. There has been debate about whether both include learning, in particular, two types of different learning. March's (1991) view is that both of them include learning. Exploitation includes things captured by the expansion and refinement of the existing knowledge and technology, while exploration includes the organization's search and discovery of new knowledge and technology. This study follows March's view and uses Crossan et al.'s (1999) definition to regard explorative learning and exploitative learning as two processes of information or knowledge flow. This study holds that exploitative learning refers to the process of information or knowledge flow from the organizational level to the collective and individual levels; it is a process of information or knowledge exploitation, namely transforming organizational knowledge into individual knowledge and gradually changing individual cognition and behavior. Explorative learning refers to the process of information or knowledge flow from the individual level to the collective and organizational levels; it is a process of information or knowledge exploration, which integrates and transforms new individuals' knowledge or behaviors into organizational knowledge, so as to gradually change organizational characteristics (such as organizational culture and organizational strategy).

The balance between explorative learning and exploitative learning is at the center of organizational learning research. March has held the belief that adaptive systems that engage in exploration to the exclusion of exploitation are likely to find that they suffer the costs of experimentation without gaining many of its benefits. As argued by Levinthal and March (1993), "The basic problem confronting an organization is to engage in sufficient exploitation to ensure its current viability and, at the same time, to devote enough energy to exploration to ensure its future viability." There are some empirical studies. For example, Katilac and Ahujac (2002) found a significant positive interaction effect between explorative learning and exploitative learning. He and Wong (2004) also found that relative imbalance between explorative learning and exploitative learning is negatively related to sales growth rate. Among the few Chinese empirical studies on the balance between explorative learning and exploitative learning, Yu Haibo et al. (2008a) found an interaction effect in influencing organizational performance. Sun Yongfeng et al. (2007) discussed incremental innovation and emergent innovation. However, the empirical research on the role of leaders in balancing explorative learning and exploitative learning is limited.

4.2.3.1.2 STUDY OF PATERNALISTIC LEADERSHIP'S EFFECT ON THE BALANCE
　　　BETWEEN EXPLORATIVE LEARNING AND EXPLOITATIVE LEARNING

Some theoretical viewpoints and empirical findings in the literature have discussed the relationship between leadership and organizational learning (Vera & Manor, 2004; Rui & Lv, 2005; Berson et al., 2006; Nemanich et al., 2009). However, there are insufficient findings on the relationship between paternalistic leadership and organizational learning with Chinese characteristics. Yu Haibo et al. (2008a) found that different aspects of paternalistic leadership have positive and negative effect on organizational learning. In short, there is no empirical finding in paternalistic leadership's effect on the balance between explorative learning and exploitative learning.

4.2.3.1.3 PRESENTATION OF QUESTION

In terms of the conceptualization of the balance between explorative learning and exploitative learning, this study adopts the perspective of strategic fit and divides the balance between into two aspects (He & Wong, 2004). One is fit as moderating, which requires that we study the interaction effect of paternalistic leadership on explorative learning and exploitative learning. The other is matching fit, for which we need to study the effect of paternalistic leadership on the difference between the two, which is called comparative balance in this study. In this section, we examine the interaction effect of the three paternalistic leadership dimensions on the balance between explorative learning and exploitative learning.

4.2.3.2　Research methods

The specific sample, measures and statistical method are described in Section 4.2.2.2.1 of this chapter.

4.2.3.3　Research results

4.2.3.3.1 DESCRIPTIVE STATISTICAL RESULTS

The descriptive statistical results of each variable are shown in Table 4.6. The results show that the internal consistency coefficients of each dimension of explorative learning, exploitative learning and paternalistic leadership are between 0.72 and 0.89, which meets the basic requirements of psychometrics.

4.2.3.3.2 CONFIRMATORY FACTOR ANALYSIS RESULTS OF EACH MEASURE

The results of confirmatory factor analysis showed that the six indicators of x^2/df, RMSEA, NFI, IFI, TLI and CFI of one-factor model of paternalistic leadership are 11.45, 0.121, 0.90, 0.91, 0.90 and 0.91 respectively, while the six indicators of three-factor model are 5.44, 0.079, 0.96, 0.96, 0.96 and 0.96. The results show that the three-factor model fit well (Bollen, 1989), and the three-factor paternalistic leadership construct model has high structural validity.

Table 4.6 Descriptive statistics, correlations and internal consistency reliabilities for research variables

Variable	M	SD	1	2	3	4	5	6	7
1. Benevolent leadership	2.98	0.81	(0.89)						
2. Moral leadership	3.17	0.78	0.59**	(0.83)					
3. Authoritarian leadership	3.16	0.68	0.00	−0.09*	(0.86)				
4. Explorative learning	3.07	0.83	0.58**	0.35**	−0.03	(0.72)			
5. Exploitative learning	3.44	0.85	0.47**	0.42**	0.04	0.53**	(0.73)		
6. Explorative × exploitative	10.94	4.71	0.59**	0.43**	0.02	0.88**	0.84**	—	
7. Exploitative-explorative	0.37	0.82	−0.09*	0.08*	0.07	−0.46**	0.51**	−0.02	—

** $p < 0.01$.
* $p < 0.05$.
Note: The data in the diagonals is the internal consistency reliability coefficient α of 4 variables.

As documented in the literature, some scholars believe that explorative learning and exploitative learning are two endpoints of a continuum, and thus a theoretical model of one factor can be obtained. In this study, we challenge this view and regard them as two kinds of learning, and a two-factor model can be obtained. The results showed that x^2/df, RMSEA, NFI, IFI, TLI and CFI of the one-factor model are 5.97, 0.084, 0.96, 0.96, 0.96 and 0.96 respectively, while those of the two-factor model are 3.21, 0.056, 0.98, 0.99, 0.98 and 0.99 respectively. This shows that the one-factor model fit is not ideal, but the two-factor model indicators comply with the requirements. Therefore, from the data fit, explorative learning and exploitative learning are two aspects rather than two endpoints of a continuum.

4.2.3.3.3 THE INFLUENCE OF PATERNALISTIC LEADERSHIP IN THE BALANCE BETWEEN EXPLORATIVE LEARNING AND EXPLOITATIVE LEARNING

The result of hierarchical regression analysis (as shown in Table 4.7) shows that both benevolent leadership and moral leadership have a significant main effect on the interactive balance and comparative balance of explorative learning and exploitative learning, while authoritarian leadership has only a significant main

Table 4.7 Hierarchical regression analysis of paternalistic leadership's influence on organizational learning

Variable	Exploitative learning x × explorative learning			Exploitative learning x - explorative learning		
	Ml	*M2*	*M3*	*Ml*	*M2*	*M3*
Step 1: basic variable						
Nature of company	0.12**	0.08*	0.09*	0.03	0.02	0.02
Scale of company	0.03	−0.03	−0.03	−0.02	0.00	0.00
Development stages	−0.03	−0.01	−0.01	0.09	0.11*	0.10*
Step 2: paternalistic leadership						
Benevolent		0.54*	−0.14		−0.33**	−0.53
Moral		0.18*	0.38		0.21*	0.41
Authoritative		0.11*	−0.10		0.08	0.14
Step 3: interaction effect						
Benevolent × moral bene			0.15			0.04
Benevolent × authoritative			0.67**			0.19
Moral × authoritative			−0.28			−0.22
R^2	0.016	0.406	0.415	0.007	0.089	0.091
ΔR^2	0.016	0.390*	0.009*	0.007	0.082**	0.002

** $p < 0.01$.
* $p < 0.05$.
Note: All independent variables are centralized.

effect on interactive balance, but not on comparative balance; benevolent leadership has a significant negative effect on comparative balance.

In terms of the interaction effect, a look at the regression coefficient will reveal that benevolent leadership and authoritarian leadership have a significant interaction effect on the interactive balance between explorative learning and exploitative learning ($\Delta R^2 = 0.009$, $p < 0.05$). The difference test of regression coefficient showed that there was no significant difference between benevolent leadership 0.73 ($p < 0.01$) and explorative learning 0.67 ($p < 0.01$) under high authority leadership and low authority leadership (Z = 0.93, $p > 0.05$, single-tailed test). Therefore, benevolent leadership and authoritarian leadership have no significant interaction effect on the interactive balance between explorative learning and exploitative learning.

4.2.3.4 *Discussion*

4.2.3.4.1 THE INFLUENCE OF PATERNALISTIC LEADERSHIP ON THE BALANCE BETWEEN EXPLORATIVE LEARNING AND EXPLOITATIVE LEARNING

In terms of the total amount of learning (interactive balance), challenging the obsolete view of paternalistic leadership, the result shows that the three aspects of paternalistic leadership can improve the total amount of interaction between a company's explorative learning and exploitative learning. In terms of improving the total amount of learning, paternalistic leadership is predicted to play a significant role.

The result of the relative comparison between the explorative learning and exploitative learning shows that benevolent leadership can narrow the relative disparity between the two, moral leadership will increase the disparity, while authoritarian leadership has no significant effect. In terms of benevolent leadership, leaders' care for subordinates will weaken the understanding that explorative learning and exploitative learning are contradictory, thus releasing the potential of companies in explorative learning and narrowing the internal relative disparity between explorative learning and exploitative learning. As for moral leadership, leaders lead by example, fairness and justice, which will encourage the staff to take leaders as role models and have internal identification with the company, which will promote the whole company to implement the plan and strategy of leaders and greatly promote exploitative learning. However, this kind of identification will weaken the explorative learning and thus increase the relative disparity between explorative learning and exploitative learning. This is a reminder for Chinese corporate management personnel that when an organization needs to weaken the competitive relation between explorative learning and exploitative learning, they should implement more benevolent leadership; however, if it emphasizes exploitative learning and weakens explorative learning during a specific period, they should implement more moral leadership.

However, in terms of interaction effect, the results did not show any significant effect of the three dimensions of paternalistic leadership on the balance between explorative learning and exploitative learning. Reasons are to be given through further study.

In a word, the three dimensions of paternalistic leadership, namely benevolent leadership, moral leadership and authoritarian leadership, have significant promoting effects on the total amount of exploitative learning and explorative learning. In terms of the relative disparity between explorative learning and exploitative learning, moral leadership will increase the disparity, while benevolent leadership will reduce the disparity. Synthesizing the study results, we can obtain a model of paternalistic leadership influencing explorative learning and exploitative learning (Figure 4.6) to provide better guidance for future research and corporate practice in China.

This result has important theoretical and practical implications. Theoretically, first, it fills the gap of empirical research on paternalistic leadership's influence on the balance between explorative learning and exploitative learning against China's cultural background. Second, it obtained specific results of paternalistic leadership's influence on the balance between explorative learning and exploitative learning and confirmed the great potential of paternalistic leadership with Chinese cultural characteristics on the balance between the two for Chinese companies. Practically, the results provide valuable inspiration for leaders to better lead the balance of organizational learning. First, Chinese corporate leaders can implement paternalistic leadership to improve the total amount of explorative learning and exploitative learning; second, it shows that moral leadership will enlarge the relative disparity between explorative learning and exploitative learning; third, benevolent leadership will narrow the relative disparity between the two.

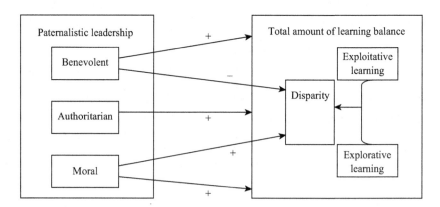

Figure 4.6 Effect of paternalistic leadership on the balance between explorative learning and exploitative learning

4.2.4 The influence of transactional leadership on organizational learning

4.2.4.1 Literature review and research hypotheses

The relationship between transactional leadership and organizational learning is scarcely covered in the literature. Vera and Manor (2004) believe that transactional leadership can also stimulate organizational learning, and the difference is that transformational leadership usually leads to organizational learning that challenges the status quo, while transactional leadership is more likely to lead to organizational learning that reinforces the status quo. The empirical study of Jansen et al. (2007) found that transactional leadership has a significant positive effect on the exploitative learning but has a significant inhibiting effect on explorative learning. Bass (1990, 1997) also argued that transactional leadership can also promote organizational learning. In a word, both theoretical analysis and empirical research show that transactional leadership and organizational learning are significantly related, but this needs to be further tested.

According to Bass (1997) conceptualizations, transactional leadership can be divided into contingent reward and management-by-exception. Contingent reward of transactional leadership refers to the active and positive exchange between leaders and subordinates; leaders recognize that employees have completed the expected tasks, and employees are rewarded. Management-by-exception could be split into two sub-factors: active vs. passive. Active management-by-exception focuses on monitoring task execution for any problems that might arise and correcting those problems to maintain current performance levels. The passive management-by-exception leaders often intervene in the manner of criticism and blame when the problems have occurred or have not reached the prescribed standards.

In terms of the relationship between contingent reward of transactional leadership and organizational learning, the leader's contingent reward will encourage individual employees, teams and even the whole organization, where individual employees are eager to learn more and improve their work, teams strive to continue learning and improve their collective business level, thus promoting the organization to better adjust according to the circumstances so as to improve organizational performance through existing strategies and objectives. Therefore, the contingent reward will promote the learning of the organization. Through the above analysis, we hypothesize that:

Hypothesis 12:

The contingent reward promotes organizational learning, and contingent reward leadership is significantly positively related to organizational learning.

As for the relationship between management-by-exception of transactional leadership and organizational learning, both the monitoring before the problem occurs and the criticism and punishment after the problem occurred can stimulate reflection and learning of individual employees, discussions and improvement of the team, and summary and improvement of past performance within the entire organization. Therefore, management-by-exception will promote organizational learning, despite some passive traits. Based on the preceding analysis, the following hypothesis is set forth:

Hypothesis 13:

Management-by-exception promotes organizational learning, and there is a significant positive correlation between management-by-exception and organizational learning.

4.2.4.2 Methodology

4.2.4.2.1 SUBJECTS

The subjects were employees, including management personnel in enterprises of different nature and scales in Beijing. We distributed 600 questionnaires. Of that number, 500 questionnaires were recovered, including 70 invalid questionnaires, which were eliminated, and 430 valid questionnaires. The effective rate was 86%. Specifically, state-owned enterprises accounted for 31.4%, private enterprises 32.1%, foreign-funded enterprises 14.0%, other enterprises 22.3%, missing 0.2%; front-line employees 64.2%, front-line managers 19.8%, medium-level and senior managers 15.8%, 0.2% not specified. Among these responders, 54.0% have worked for less than 3 years, 26.7% for 3 ~ 7 years, 18.6% for more than 7 years, with 7% not specified; 42.8% had a college degree, 42.6% with a bachelor's degree or above, and 13.7% with a postgraduate degree; male 45.8%, female 52.3%, missing 1.9%; In terms of scale: 74.4% enterprises have between 1 and 500 employees, 15.8% between 500 and 2000 employees, and 8.9% with more than 2000 employees, missing 0.9%; in terms of development stage, 14.2% of employees are in companies in the start-up stage, 51.2% in the growth stage, 23.5% in the mature stage and 11.1% in the re-innovation stage.

4.2.4.2.2 MEASURES

The transactional leadership scale adopts Bass's (1997) leadership style questionnaire, which includes two dimensions: contingent reward and management-by-exception. Each dimension consists of three items. The organizational learning scale, which includes six factors and 29 items, is used in this study. The five-point Likert scoring method was used in both scales. The subjects were asked to evaluate the compliance with their own enterprises.

The coefficient α of internal consistency reliability of transactional leadership is 0.62, the coefficient α of internal consistency reliability of contingent reward is 0.74 and that of management-by-exception is 0.60. The coefficient α of each dimension of organizational learning is as follows: individual learning is 0.84, collective learning is 0.82, organizational-level learning is 0.66, inter-organizational learning is 0.81, explorative learning is 0.79 and exploitative learning is 0.81. It shows that the reliability of each scale meets the basic requirements of metrology.

4.2.4.2.3 STATISTICAL METHOD

SPSS 10.0 was used for statistical analysis.

4.2.4.3 Research result

The descriptive statistics for research variables are shown in Table 4.8, showing that the correlations between various variables have all reached a significant level.

Table 4.8 Descriptive statistics and correlations for research variables

Variable	M	SD	1	2	3	4	5	6	7	8	9
1. Transactional leadership	1.14	0.23									
2. Contingent reward	3.37	0.95	0.83**								
3. Management-by-exception	3.49	0.78	0.74**	0.24**							
4. Organizational leaning	3.55	0.70	0.55**	0.57**	0.27**						
5. Individual learning	3.57	0.75	0.53**	0.54**	0.27**	0.86**					
6. Collective learning	3.74	0.81	0.41**	0.41**	0.22**	0.81**	0.68**				
7. Organizational-level learning	3.73	0.86	0.38**	0.39**	0.20**	0.80**	0.61**	0.56**			
8. Inter-organizational learning	3.47	0.81	0.50**	0.54**	0.22**	0.91**	0.76**	0.69**	0.66**		
9. Explorative learning	3.22	0.91	0.48**	0.53**	0.20**	0.84**	0.67**	0.58**	0.58**	0.76**	
10. Exploitative learning	3.60	0.86	0.45**	0.43**	0.25**	0.84**	0.67**	0.60**	0.63**	0.71**	0.61**

** $p < 0.01$.
Note: The significance of all related coefficients have reached the level of ** $p < 0.01$.

Table 4.9 Hierarchical regression analysis of the effect of transactional leadership on organizational learning and its various dimensions (1) ($N = 430$)

Dependent variable	Organizational learning		Individual learning		Collective learning		Organizational-level learning	
Model	M1	M2	M1	M2	M1	M2	M1	M2
Level 1: control variables								
Nature of company	0.00	−0.03	0.02	0.05	0.04	0.06	−0.02	0.00
Company scale	0.00	−0.06	−0.07	−0.12**	−0.06	−0.10*	−0.06	−0.10*
Company development stage	−0.02	−0.02	−0.02	−0.03	0.08	0.08	−0.05	−0.05
Step 2: independent variables								
Contingent reward		0.54**		0.52**		0.39**		0.37**
Management-by-exception		0.14**		0.15**		0.13**		0.11*
R^2	0.000	0.341	0.007	0.331	0.007	0.192	0.009	0.177
ΔR^2	0.000	0.0341**	0.007	0.324**	0.007	0.186**	0.009	0.168**

** $p < 0.01$.
* $p < 0.05$.

Table 4.10 Hierarchical regression analysis of the effect of transactional leadership on organizational learning and its various dimensions (2) ($N = 430$)

Dependent variable	Inter-organizational learning		Explorative learning		Exploitative learning	
Model	M1	M2	M1	M2	M1	M2
Step 1: control variables						
Nature of company	0.06	0.08	−0.06	−0.04	−0.04	−0.01
Company scale	0.06	−0.01	0.07	0.01	0.10	0.05
Company development stage	0.01	0.00	0.00	0.00	−0.10	−0.10*
Step 2: independent variables						
Contingent reward		0.52**		0.51**		0.39**
Management-by-exception		0.10*		0.06		0.16*
R^2	0.007	0.301	0.007	0.281	0.011	0.215
ΔR^2	0.007	0.294**	0.007	0.274**	0.011	0.203**

** $p < 0.01$.
* $p < 0.05$.

The results of hierarchical regression analysis (Tables 4.9 and 4.10) show that, in general, the two dimensions of transactional leadership have a significant role in promoting organizational learning. Among all dimensions, contingent reward and management-by-exception have a significant effect in promoting all other dimensions of organizational learning except for explorative learning; contingent reward has a significant effect on explorative learning, but management-by-exception does not (regression coefficient is 0.06, $p > 0.05$). At the same time, the results show that contingent reward has greater effect than management-by-exception on organizational learning.

4.2.4.4 Discussion

On the whole, transactional leadership plays a significant role in promoting organizational learning, which supports the views of Bass (1997) and Vera and Manor (2004). Furthermore, contingent reward of transactional leadership has a greater effect than management-by-exception on organizational learning, especially explorative learning.

The contingent reward leadership has a significant effect on organizational learning as well as all its dimensions. This indicates that although the performance orientation of learning and result-based orientation belongs to two different management philosophies, if leaders can give rewards flexibly according to work and management results, the organizational learning capability of companies can be improved so as to realize the unity of performance and learning.

The management-by-exception leadership has a significant promoting effect on organizational learning and some of its dimensions. This can be explained by two main reasons. First, as long as leaders, whether actively or passively, conduct timely summaries and feedback on problems in management, pass on the company's idea and values and implement the company's regulations and rules, there can be opportunities for organizational learning. Second, the management-by-exception leadership does not have a significant effect on explorative learning, indicating that it cannot facilitate innovative learning of the company or systematically stimulate knowledge innovation.

In terms of effect, the contingent reward leadership has a greater effect in promoting organizational learning than management-by-exception. This converges with the results of Jansen et al. (2007) for three main reasons. First, from the nature of leadership behaviors, active rewards are more effective in promoting organizational learning than negative monitoring or even criticism. Active and flexible reward serves as positive guidance and encouragement for learning, while monitoring and even criticism is a negative behavior. Second, in the internal mechanism, the positive emotions and cognitive process triggered by contingent reward can mobilize the intrinsic learning enthusiasm of each member in organizational learning, while the negative emotions and passive changes caused by management-by-exception only lead to passive external changes. Third, in the internal philosophy orientation, contingent reward follows the learning-oriented management philosophy to a certain extent and attaches importance to continuously guiding and stimulating the learning motivation of all subjects in the process of management and learning, so as to achieve improvement and adjustment in all aspects. In contrast, management-by-exception is oriented to short-term results, which is performance orientation. In this process, leaders force the subjects of the organization to change the original working mode or results through a monitoring mechanism or even a criticism mechanism afterwards. It is a leadership behavior oriented to a short-term result, which has a less significant effect on organizational learning.

The results of this study offer practical implications in three aspects. First, corporate leaders can promote organizational learning through flexible contingent reward and even result feedback. Second, leaders should try to restrain from simple monitoring or criticism of leadership behavior to promote organizational learning, because this type of management-by-exception leadership has a much weaker effect in facilitating organizational leadership. Thirdly, management-by-exception leadership fails to promote the explorative learning of an organization, and what's needed more by explorative learning is the flexible contingent reward leadership.

4.2.5 The construct of learning leadership and the evolution of its effect on organizational learning

4.2.5.1 Introduction

Learning leadership should be viewed from the perspective of the effective leadership, because only leadership process and behaviors that facilitate organizational learning can be categorized as learning leadership. For Chinese enterprises, the effective learning leadership is one based on leadership in Chinese culture and integrated with the characteristics of western culture. Therefore, this study will follow the research paradigm of Yukl (1999), expert in the research on effective leadership, to construct a structural model of learning leadership in China at the current stage based on the effective leadership behavior for organizational learning under paternalistic leadership, transformational leadership, transactional leadership and servant leadership; on this basis, this study also explores the role of learning leadership in organizational learning, with focus on the models of learning leadership needed in a company's different stages of development.

4.2.5.2 Theoretical basis and research questions

4.2.5.2.1 STUDY ON TRANSFORMATIONAL LEADERSHIP, TRANSACTIONAL LEADERSHIP AND PATERNALISTIC LEADERSHIP AND THEIR RELATIONSHIP WITH ORGANIZATIONAL LEARNING

The relationship between transformational leadership, transactional leadership and paternalistic leadership with organizational learning has been extensively studied (e.g., Vera & Manor, 2004; Nemanich & Vera, 2007; Jansen et al., 2007; Yu Haibo et al., 2008a; Chen & Zhao, 2010; see details in Section 4.1 of this chapter). Their studies show that transformational leadership can influence organizational learning through some mediator variables, and transactional leadership can significantly promote some aspects of organizational learning. Therefore, we can conclude that both transformational leadership and transactional leadership are important to organizational learning.

The analysis of the relationship between transformational, transactional and paternalistic leadership and organizational learning can be found in Tables 4.3, 4.4 and 4.9.

4.2.5.2.2 SERVANT LEADERSHIP AND ITS RELATIONSHIP WITH ORGANIZATIONAL LEARNING

The study of servant leadership represents a new trend in the research on leadership in the West, and it is extremely important in the process of building a service-oriented society in China. The concept of servant leadership was coined by Greenleaf (1977) as leaders who can put the needs, wishes and interests of others above their own, and the natural feeling that one wants to serve, to serve first. The purpose of servant leadership is to make followers more intelligent, more liberated, better at self-management and more willing to be service providers. In the literature, there are many studies on how servant leadership influences individuals and teams, but more research is needed on the relationship between servant leadership and organizational learning. In view of the purpose of servant leadership, it defines and explores the relationship between leaders and subordinates from a new perspective, and it defines leadership in the mode of mutual services, which is particularly important for organizational learning that needs internal impetus, just as Senge (1990) believed that in order to create a learning organization, we need a coaching leadership that provide greater service for subordinates and enterprises. Therefore, servant leadership is of vital importance for organizational learning.

4.2.5.2.3 THE PRESENTATION OF LEARNING LEADERSHIP AND QUESTIONS TO BE STUDIED

Although learning leadership has been discussed in practice, scholars' definitions of learning leadership are disparate. Senge (1990) believes that learning leadership requires leaders to show coaching leadership style. This study believes that learning leadership is a process of interaction effect between leaders and subordinates, in which leaders constantly motivate subordinates to strive for self-improvement and lead the whole company to continuously improve organizational learning capability.

In exploring the construct of learning leadership, this study uses the research model of competency in strategic human resource management of Ulrich and Brockbank (2005) to define learning leadership. According to the earlier synthetic analysis of the literature, from the perspective of effect, learning leadership may be the integration of four leadership styles to comprehensively play an effective role in promoting organizational learning. It can be concluded that, first, the learning leadership of Chinese companies cannot exist outside the context of Chinese traditional culture and should instead show some paternalistic leadership style with Chinese cultural characteristics. Second, in today's China with deepening reform, learning leadership needs to involve the transformational leadership, and in the maintenance and coordination of daily management, it also needs a certain transactional leadership style. Finally, as China's services attract more attention in world economic development and as China increasingly advocates for a service-oriented society, if firms genuinely want to tap into the potential of learning and growth from within, a servant leadership style is needed. Therefore, the following hypothesis is set forth:

Hypothesis 14:

The structural model of learning leadership is the integration of the four leadership styles covered in this chapter.

In terms of the effect of learning leadership, although this study defines learning leadership from the perspective of leadership style that can promote organizational learning, different aspects of learning leadership have different effects on different aspects of organizational learning. Likewise, according to the contingent theory, in different development stages of a corporate organization, the organization will have to solve different main business management problems, and the environment and requirements for the organization will also vary and the requirements for the learning leadership model will differ. Therefore, this study proposes the following hypotheses:

Hypothesis 15:

Learning leadership has different significant effect on the specific dimensions of organizational learning.

Hypothesis 16:

In different development stages of the company, the model of learning leadership on organizational learning is different.

4.2.5.3 Research process and methods

4.2.5.3.1 MEASURES

This study adopts the paternalistic leadership questionnaire of Zheng Boxun et al. (2000), which includes 3 factors and 33 items. The transformational leadership questionnaire is based on the questionnaire of Bass (1998) with 4 factors and 12 items. The transactional leadership questionnaire is also by Bass (1998), which included 2 factors and 6 items. The servant leadership questionnaire is designed by Liden et al. (2008), including 7 factors and 28 items.

4.2.5.3.2 SUBJECTS

A total of 600 questionnaires were distributed to MBA classes and on-the-job postgraduate classes in several universities in Beijing, and 430 valid questionnaires were obtained. The subjects were from different companies, and the effective rate of the questionnaire was 72%. The specific distribution of the sample is as follows: 31.4% are state-owned enterprises, 32.1% private enterprises, 14.0%

foreign-funded enterprises and 22.3% other enterprises, while 0.2% did not fill the item; 36.5% are enterprises with fewer than 100 employees, 37.9% between 100 and 499 employees, 10.2% between 500 and 999 employees, 5.6% between 1000 and 1999 employees and 8.8% with more than 2000 employees, while 1.0% did not fill the item; 64.2% are front-line employees, 19.8% front-line managers, 15.8% medium-level management and 0.2% did not fill the item. In terms of the development stage of the enterprises, 14.2% are in the start-up stage, 51.2% in the growth stage, 23.5% in the mature stage and 11.2% in the re-innovation stage.

4.2.5.3.3 RELIABILITY AND VALIDITY OF VARIABLES

The data was analyzed by SPSS 10.0 and AMOS 4.0. The results (Table 4.11) of confirmatory factor analysis meet the model fit standard which indicating that the models fit well (Bollen, 1989). And this showed all questionnaires have relatively high structural validity which meet the basic test requirements.

4.2.5.4 Research result and analysis

4.2.5.4.1 DESCRIPTIVE STATISTICAL RESULTS

The descriptive statistics for research variables are shown in Table 4.12, showing that the correlation coefficients among the variables all reach a significant level.

4.2.5.4.2 THE CONSTRUCT OF LEARNING LEADERSHIP STRUCTURE MODEL

4.2.5.4.2.1 Selection of learning leadership behaviors based on four leadership styles   In order to identify the composite items of learning leadership, we conducted a multiple regression analysis by taking the questionnaire items of paternalistic, transformational, transactional and servant leadership as independent variables and organizational learning as the dependent variable. The result shows that there are 24 items that have significant effects on organizational learning, 11 items from paternalistic leadership, 3 items each from transformational leadership and transactional leadership, respectively, and 7 items from servant leadership. The 24 items are used as the items of learning leadership.

Table 4.11 Confirmatory factor analysis and reliability analysis results of each measure

Measures	x^2/df	NFI	IFI	TLI	CFI	RMSEA	Internal consistency reliability
Paternalistic leadership	4.96	0.94	0.95	0.94	0.95	0.08	0.88
Transformational leadership	3.59	0.92	0.94	0.93	0.94	0.08	0.90
Transactional leadership	4.40	0.99	0.99	0.98	0.99	0.08	0.69
Servant leadership	1.97	0.98	0.99	0.99	0.99	0.05	0.96
Organizational learning	2.87	0.97	0.98	0.98	0.98	0.07	0.95

Table 4.12 Descriptive statistics and correlations for research variables (*N* = 430)

Variable	M	SD	1	2	3	4	5	6	7	8	9	10
1. Paternalistic leadership	3.31	0.55										
2. Transformational leadership	3.62	0.80	0.56									
3. Transactional leadership	3.43	0.69	0.55	0.61								
4. Servant leadership	3.42	0.82	0.67	0.82	0.62							
5. Organizational learning	3.55	0.70	0.56	0.64	0.55	0.72						
6. Individual learning	3.57	0.75	0.51	0.61	0.53	0.67	0.86					
7. Collective learning	3.74	0.81	0.38	0.48	0.41	0.57	0.81	0.68				
8. Organizational-level learning	3.73	0.86	0.45	0.48	0.38	0.57	0.80	0.61	0.56			
9. Inter-organizational Learning	3.47	0.81	0.54	0.59	0.50	0.68	0.91	0.76	0.69	0.66		
10. Explorative learning	3.22	0.91	0.52	0.53	0.48	0.63	0.84	0.67	0.58	0.58	0.76	
11. Exploitative learning	3.60	0.86	0.44	0.54	0.45	0.59	0.84	0.67	0.60	0.63	0.71	0.61

Note: All correlation coefficients reach a significant level of $p < 0.01$.

4.2.5.4.2.2 The construct of learning leadership model   We selected 24 leadership behaviors that have a significant effect on organizational learning as the measurement items of learning leadership. First, qualitative analysis was conducted. To avoid the overlapping of measurement items, we invited three experts to do semantic analysis of the 24 items and identify the items with similar semantics. Then, quantitative analysis and exploratory factor analysis and item analysis were carried out. Finally, combining the results of qualitative semantic analysis and quantitative analysis, 10 low-quality items were deleted and 14 items were finalized as the questionnaire items to be used. The result of the exploratory factor analysis on the remaining 14 items shows that the structural model of learning leadership includes three dimensions (Table 4.13).

Table 4.13 Results of exploratory factor analysis of learning leadership structure

Item/factor loading	*Service care*	*Authoritarian supervision*	*Encouraging guidance*
(servant) My leader puts my best interests ahead of his/her own.	0.77		
(transactional) Whenever I feel like it, I can negotiate with my leader about what I can get from what I accomplish.	0.73		
(servant) My leader seems to care more about my success than his/her own.	0.68		
(paternalistic) The leader will take good care of subordinates who have been with him for a long time.	0.65		
(paternalistic) The leader will meet my requirements according to my personal needs.	0.60		
(paternalistic) When the task cannot be completed, the leader will scold us.		0.78	
(paternalistic) The leaders stresses that our performance must surpass that of other units.		0.78	
(paternalistic) The leaders follow the principles and we will be severely punished for breaking the rules.		0.76	
(paternalistic) The leaders adopt strict management methods.		0.72	
(paternalistic) At the meeting, the final decision is made according to the leader's will.		0.60	
(servant) My leader can tell if something is going wrong.			0.75
(transformational) My leader is an inspiration to us.			0.75
(transformational) My leader enables me to think about old problems in a new way.			0.70
(paternalistic) For the ability that I lack in my work, the leadership will give appropriate education and guidance			0.60
α coefficient	0.77	0.74	0.75
Explained variance (56.17%)	19.72%	19.37%	17.08%

Note: the characters in brackets indicate the source of leadership style: paternalistic, servant, transformational and transactional.

Dimension 1 mainly includes the leader's care and concern for subordinates and their interests, so it can be named "servant care." This dimension mainly reflects the characteristics of "putting subordinate first" in servant leadership and "benevolence" in paternalistic leadership. Dimension 2 mainly includes leader's strict management of subordinates, which can be named "authoritarian supervision." This dimension mainly reflects the characteristics of "teaching," "strict" and "authoritarian" in paternalistic leadership. Dimension 3 mainly includes the leader's encouragement, stimulation and guidance to subordinates, so it can be named "encouraging guidance." This dimension mainly reflects the characteristics of "boosting morale" and "intellectual stimulation" in transformational leadership, "analyzing and solving problems" in servant leadership and "understanding and tolerance" in paternalistic leadership. Hypothesis 14 is thus supported.

4.2.5.4.3 THE EFFECT OF LEARNING LEADERSHIP ON ORGANIZATIONAL LEARNING

Table 4.14 shows the fit indexes of the structural equation model of learning leadership on organizational learning and its various dimensions. The results show that the fit indexes of each model meets the requirements of metrology.

4.2.5.4.3.1 The total effect of learning leadership on organizational learning   As shown in Figure 4.7, on the whole, encouraging guidance, followed by servant care, has the greatest effect on organizational learning, and authoritarian supervision has the least effect. This indicates that in organizational learning, what is needed most from leaders is to encourage employees and provide guidance; at the same time, leaders should show consideration about subordinates; authoritarian supervision has some, though slight, effect.

4.2.5.4.3.2 Effect of learning leadership in various concrete aspects of organizational learning   First, for individual learning (Figure 4.8), the effect of learning leadership on organizational learning is basically similar to that of

Table 4.14 Fit indexes of the models

Model/dependent variable	x^2	df	x^2/df	NFI	IFI	TLI	CFI	RMSEA
Organizational learning	370.76	164	2.26	0.99	0.99	0.99	0.99	0.054
Individual learning	433.54	164	2.64	0.98	0.99	0.99	0.99	0.062
Collective learning	295.17	129	2.29	0.99	0.99	0.99	0.99	0.055
Organizational-level learning	276.78	146	1.90	0.99	0.99	0.99	0.99	0.046
Inter-organizational learning	360.09	164	2.20	0.98	0.99	0.99	0.99	0.053
Exploitative learning	305.19	129	2.37	0.99	0.99	0.99	0.99	0.056
Explorative learning	336.80	129	2.61	0.98	0.99	0.99	0.99	0.061

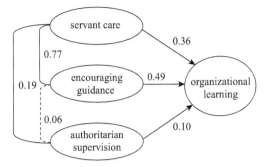

Figure 4.7 Effect of learning leadership on organizational learning

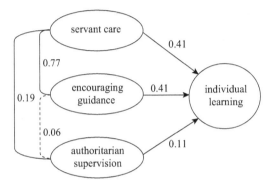

Figure 4.8 Effect of learning leadership on individual learning

overall organizational learning, except that encouraging guidance and servant care have the same effect on individual learning.

Second, for collective learning (Figure 4.9), encouraging guidance is the main facilitator, while servant care plays only a minor role and authoritarian supervision has no significant effect on collective learning.

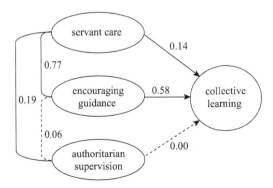

Figure 4.9 Effect of learning leadership on collective learning

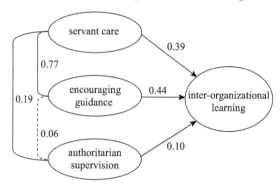

Figure 4.10 Effect of learning leadership on organizational-level earning

Third, for organizational learning (Figure 4.10), encouraging guidance plays the major role, while authoritarian supervision and servant care play a smaller role.

Fourth, for inter-organizational learning (Figure 4.11), the role of learning leadership is similar to that of the overall effect model. Encouraging guidance and servant care have a greater effect, while authoritarian supervision plays a relatively small role.

Fifth, for explorative learning (Figure 4.12), servant care plays a major promoting role, while encouraging guidance plays only a minor role and authoritarian supervision has no significant effect.

Sixth, for exploitative learning (Figure 4.13), encouraging guidance plays a major promoting role, while authoritarian supervision plays a smaller role; servant care has the least effect on exploitative learning.

Through comparing the effect of learning leadership on explorative learning and exploitative learning, we can conclude that the servant care leadership style is more effective in promoting explorative learning, while encouraging guidance is more effective in promoting exploitative learning, and authoritarian supervision promotes only exploitative learning.

Comparing the effect of three dimensions of learning leadership on organizational learning, it can be seen that encouraging guidance has a great effect on

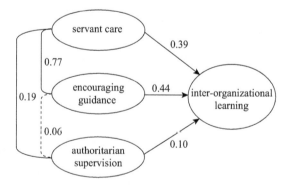

Figure 4.11 Effect of learning leadership on inter-organizational learning

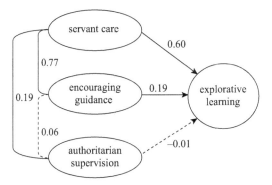

Figure 4.12 Effect of learning leadership on explorative learning

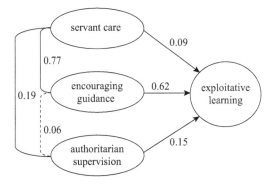

Figure 4.13 Effect of learning leadership on exploitative learning

organizational learning, but its effect on explorative learning is smaller than that of servant care. The specific effects of servant care on organizational learning are, in ascending order of impact: explorative learning, individual learning, inter-organizational learning, collective learning, organizational-level learning and exploitative learning. This manifested the value of servant care for organizational learning. The reason why authoritarian supervision is an important part of learning leadership lies in its influence on company's explorative learning, organizational learning, individual learning and inter-organizational learning. It can be seen that the three aspects of learning leadership play different roles in promoting organizational learning, but are all important parts of a complete learning leadership. These results validate Hypothesis 15.

4.2.5.4.3.3 Changes of the effect of learning leadership on organizational learning with the development stage of the organization   According to the four stages of company development (start-up, growth, maturity and re-innovation), the relationship between learning leadership and organizational learning was analyzed through hierarchical regression analysis. The results (as shown in Table 4.15 and Figure 4.14) are summarized as follows.

Table 4.15 Regression analysis results of the effect of learning leadership on organizational learning in different stages of organization's development

	M1	M2	M3	M4
	Start-up	*Growth*	*Mature*	*Re-innovation*
Basic variable				
Unit nature	0.14	0.00	−0.08	0.00
Enterprise scale	−0.19	0.04	−0.19	−0.02
Learning leadership				
Authoritarian supervision	0.21*	0.01	0.12	0.07
Encourage guidance	0.40**	0.48**	0.25**	0.37**
Servant care	0.40**	0.39**	0.43**	0.43**
R^2	0.553**	0.622**	0.338**	0.353**
ΔR^2	0.592**	0.631**	0.373**	0.428**

** $p < 0.01$.
* $p < 0.05$.

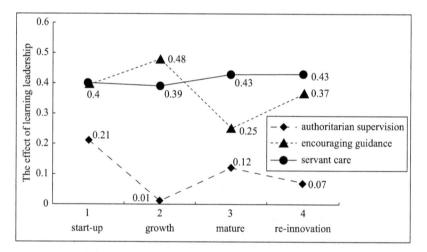

Figure 4.14 Comparison of learning leadership's effect on organizational learning in different development stages of the organization

In terms of the three dimensions of learning leadership, authoritarian supervision plays a significant role in the organizational learning of a company in the start-up stage but does not have a significant effect in the three later stages. The promoting effect of encouraging guidance decreases along with the development of the company before mounting a rebound, and it plays a dominant role in the growth stage of the company. The promoting effect of servant care increases along with the company's development and begins to have a dominant role in the mature stage of a company.

From the perspective of different development stages of an organization, in the start-up stage, organizational learning needs a learning leadership style that integrates the three dimensions. In the growth stage, encouraging guidance needs to play the dominant role with emphasis on servant care; in the mature stage, the servant care learning leadership style should be dominant with emphasis on encouraging guidance; in the re-innovation stage, the servant care should dominate with emphasis on encouraging guidance. These results validate Hypothesis 16.

4.2.5.5 *Discussion*

4.2.5.5.1 THE STRUCTURAL MODEL OF LEARNING LEADERSHIP

The results show that the learning leadership of Chinese firms includes three dimensions: servant care, authoritarian supervision and encouraging guidance. This structural model has the following three characteristics.

The structural model of learning leadership in Chinese firms is an integration of paternalistic leadership, servant leadership and transformational leadership (Figure 4.15). Among them, servant care is similar to the M (benevolent leadership) in Ling Wenquan's CPM (Ling et al., 1987) and benevolence in paternalistic leadership by Zheng Boxun et al. (2003), including the content of "subordinates first" in servant leadership and "contingent reward" in transactional leadership. Authoritarian supervision is composed of three manifestations of paternalistic leadership, namely "instructions," "austere" and "authoritarian." Encouraging guidance consists of "boosting morale" and "intellectual stimulation" in transformational leadership, analyzing and solving problems in servant leadership and "understanding and tolerance" in paternalistic leadership.

The structural model of learning leadership demonstrates the characteristics of the integration of Chinese and western cultures: namely the integration of Chinese traditional Confucianist and legalist culture with western cultural thoughts of "freedom, equality, fraternity" and "self-actualization." Servant care is the requirement of "benevolence" of Chinese traditional Confucianism to the modern

Figure 4.15 Source of learning leadership: the integration of paternalistic, transformational and servant leadership

companies' learning leadership, and it is also the requirement of "equality and fraternity" in western culture. Authoritarian supervision is the requirement of legalism and politicized Confucianism in Chinese traditional culture; the main features of legalism are law and punishment, power centralization and art of control; political Confucianism is manifested mainly in the three cardinal guides specified in the feudal ethical code. Encouraging guidance is the requirement of "freedom" and "self-actualization" in western culture. This kind of thought is manifested mainly in encouraging subordinates and leading them to innovate; at the same time, encouraging guidance also reflects the "benevolence" in Chinese Confucianism, manifested as education and guidance of subordinates.

Third, the structural model of learning leadership embodies the main style of companies' learning leaders towards people and work. The service and care for people represents the quality requirements of "going out of one's way to enlist the services of the talented and the learned"; for work, leaders should be strict and at the same time encourage and guide their subordinates. This kind of leadership style is an all-dimensional requirement for corporate leaders, which means that leaders should not only respect subordinates but also value their interests and achievements and encourage and guide them in work. Therefore, the learning leadership of Chinese firms requires leaders to improve themselves in all aspects. This is the biggest challenge in the establishment of learning organization and learning society.

4.2.5.5.2 THE ROLE OF LEARNING LEADERSHIP IN ORGANIZATIONAL LEARNING

4.2.5.5.2.1 The general and specific effects of learning leadership on organizational learning   In learning leadership, encouraging guidance has the strongest effect, followed by servant care, and authoritarian supervision has the least effect. The result also shows that the paternalistic authoritarian supervision leadership style in traditional Chinese culture does play a role in promoting organizational learning of the firm, but its effect is more prominent in some aspects of organizational learning, such as exploitative learning and so on.

Specifically, encouraging guidance of learning leadership has great value for all the aspects of organizational learning, but its effect on explorative learning is smaller than that of servant care. This converges with the research results emphasizing the transformational leadership's value for organizational learning (Jansen et al., 2007) in the literature. The main reason is that leaders' encouragement, guidance, and help to their subordinates is the application process of leadership or organizational knowledge in employees' work, and it is an essential process of exploitation.

Viewing from the dimension of servant care, its value for organizational learning, in descending order, is explorative learning, individual learning, inter-organizational learning, collective learning, organizational-level learning and exploitative learning. This gives inspiration to corporate management in three ways. First, leaders should have a clear positioning: serve and support subordinates. Second, leaders should put subordinates first, show care to them and take the success and interest of subordinates seriously. This is what's needed the most for the long-term organizational learning of firms. Last, in the process of leading, corporate leaders should show personalized consideration and respect to subordinates so as to boost their working morale and passion for learning.

The value of authoritarian supervision for learning leadership lies its promotion for exploitative learning, organizational learning, individual learning and interorganizational learning. This finding is similar to the research results in the literature. This shows that the paternalistic authoritarian supervision leadership style in traditional Chinese culture still has value for current organizational learning.

4.2.5.5.2.2 Comparison between learning leadership's effect on explorative learning and exploitative learning   The result of this study shows that the servant care leadership style promotes explorative learning more, and encouraging guidance promotes exploitative learning more, while the authoritarian supervision promotes only exploitative learning. It can be concluded that to realize in-depth knowledge exploration and learning of companies, leaders need to manifest the servant care leadership style rather than authoritarian supervision; in contrast, to realize knowledge exploitation, leaders need to show more encouraging guidance leadership style, and the authoritarian supervision leadership style can also play a certain promoting role.

4.2.5.5.3 THE EVOLUTION OF EFFECTS OF LEARNING LEADERSHIP ON ORGANIZATIONAL
LEARNING IN ORGANIZATIONAL DEVELOPMENT STAGES

The results show that the evolution path of the learning leadership role is as follows. The three-in-one learning leadership is needed in the start-up stage, with the combination of servant care and encouraging guidance in the later stages; in the growth stage, the leadership mode dominated by encouraging guidance and supplemented by servant care is needed; in the mature stage and re-innovation stage, companies need the leadership model dominated by servant care and supplemented by encouraging guidance. In different stages of corporate development, the learning leadership modes are: omnipotent, encouraging, servant and servant (Figure 4.16). This converges with the conclusion drawn by Wu Chunbo et al. (2009) that "with the development of China's private companies, paternalistic leadership and transformational leadership are needed."

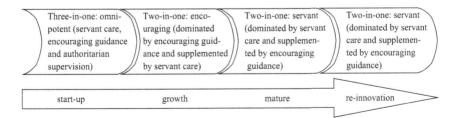

Figure 4.16 Contingent evolution model of learning leadership in different stages of corporate development

The reasons are as follows. In the start-up stage, where companies shift from disorderly development to orderly development, leaders need to boost the morale of employees and care about them; leaders should provide punctuated guidance and at the same time be strict with their work. Therefore, a leadership model integrating the three aspects of learning leadership is needed. In the growth stage, the main task for companies is to promote businesses. What's needed the most is leaders' encouragement to employees in improving their work; at the same time, leaders should serve and care about the employees and bring value addition. In the mature period, the main purpose of the company is to maintain a stable development status, which requires leaders to uphold the people-oriented concept and pay attention to the interests and achievements of subordinates. Therefore, learning leadership style dominated by servant care is needed. In the stage of re-innovation, the main task of a company is to achieve a qualitative leap on the basis of its original development, which requires that learning leaders serve and care about their subordinates, boost their morale and constantly improve their work, so as to achieve the new development goals of the company.

4.2.5.5.4 DIRECTION OF FUTURE RESEARCH

This study makes theoretical contributions in two aspects. One is its contribution to leadership theory. First, this study constructs the structural model of learning leadership in Chinese companies and obtains a measurement that can be used as a reference for future research. Second, from the perspective of cultural sources, the structural model of learning leadership obtained in this study shows the characteristics of cultural integration between China and the West. The other is contribution leadership effect contingent theory. First, viewing from the evolution of effect, the effect of learning leadership on organizational learning will show different models at different stages of a company's development. Second, from the perspective of different emphasis, different ways of organizational learning need learning leadership with different emphasis, and companies in the later stage of development need a servant care learning leadership style. The encouraging guidance in learning leadership is more effective in promoting exploitative learning.

In the future, from the perspective of research ideas, the top-down model can be adopted to construct the structure of learning leadership in order to verify the structural model of learning leadership obtained in this study. From the perspective of research methods, we can further explore the specific mechanism of learning leadership and its effect on organizational learning through case studies and a tracking method to enrich the research results. From the perspective of research problems, we can introduce more mediating variables and moderating variables to explore the internal mechanism of learning leadership so as to enhance organizational learning capability.

4.2.5.6 *Conclusion*

The structural model of learning leadership in Chinese firms includes servant care, encouraging guidance and authoritarian supervision. This is a result of cultural integration between China and the West.

From the static point of view, encouraging guidance has the greatest effect on organizational learning, followed by servant care. Authoritarian supervision also has a significant effect on organizational learning; servant care mainly promotes explorative learning, while encouraging guidance mainly promotes exploitative learning.

In terms of different development stages of a company, all three aspects of learning leadership play significant promoting roles in the start-up stage; in the growth stage, the two-in-one learning leadership model dominated by encouraging guidance and supplemented by servant care is needed; in the mature and re-innovation stages, the company needs a learning leadership style dominated by servant care and supplemented by encouraging guidance.

4.3 Organizational culture—soft factor of the generative mechanism of organizational learning

In literature, some theoretical analysis and empirical studies in the literature concluded that organizational culture has an important impact on organizational learning. In terms of theoretical point of view, Goh (1998) argues that the culture of daring to try offers strong support for learning at all levels of the organization; Berson et al. (2006) believe that learning culture includes three aspects: participation, openness and psychological security. In empirical research, Schein (1992) defined learning culture from 13 aspects. Watkins and Marsick (1993) and Yang et al. (2004) emphasized the importance of seven characteristics of learning organization to organizational learning through a series of studies; Yu Wenzhao et al. (2002) proposed ten dimensions of an organizational culture of continuous learning. The research mentioned here focuses on the culture per se that promotes organizational learning. Through empirical studies, Edmondson (1999) has proved that safety culture has a significant impact on group learning; Chen Guoquan (2007) found that three aspects supporting organizational learning culture have a significant positive impact on organizational learning; Li Yang (2004) shows that organizational culture has a significant impact on organizational learning. Due to the broad connotations of organizational culture and the fact that researchers explore organizational culture from different perspectives, great differences remain, despite many similarities. Therefore, systematic empirical research is required to dig deeper into their relationship.

In this section, we will discuss the influence of organizational culture on organizational learning. As indicated in the literature, organizational learning requires many proper conditions and cultural facilitators, which can be called the internal facilitating factors of organizational learning from the culture perspective.

4.3.1 The influence of internal facilitating factors on organizational learning

4.3.1.1 Literature review and questions presentation

As for the internal facilitating factors of organizational learning, they are defined as the managerial actions and conditions in the organization that stimulates organizational learning. DiBella and Nevis (1998) have identified what they call the normative perspective of a learning organization and argue that learning takes place only under certain conditions or circumstances. In terms of culture, the internal facilitating factors of organizational learning refer to the climate and systems that can promote the learning of individuals, groups and organizational levels in the organization; it is a part of corporate culture, and its existence, if any, and its varying degrees will directly affect organizational learning.

Abroad, there are mainly four researches on the internal facilitating factors of organizational learning from the perspective of organizational learning culture. First, Pedler et al. (1991) summarized and put forward five levels and 11 characteristics of learning companies to showcase the spirits and behaviors of learning organizations. The second is the 7C learning organization characteristic model developed by Watkins and Marsick (1993). The third is Tannenbaum's (1997) coverage of eight factors that promote organizational learning. However, the understanding of learning in his research is more focused on formal training and development. The fourth consists of the ten promoting factors of organizational learning put forward by DiBella and Nevis (1998). They have carried out case studies in many organizations. These four models have been supported by some researches, but the internal facilitating factors of organizational learning as conditions for organizational learning have strong cultural characteristics, and many aspects are not suitable for the management practice of Chinese companies.

In China, there are also some scholars who have explored the internal facilitating factors of organizational learning. For example, Zhang et al. (2004) studied the six enterprises in Chinese mainland by using Watkins and Marsick's (1993) scale. The result shows that this scale meets the basic requirement of psychometrics. Yu Wenzhao et al. (2002) studied the organizational culture of continuous learning and found ten dimensions. A survey of the China Entrepreneur Survey System (2006) shows that the characteristics of companies, the quality and training of employees and the company's understanding of environment and development goals all have a certain impact on organizational learning. Xie Hongming et al. (2006) and Sun Weizhong et al. (2005) conducted theoretical analysis in some influencing factors on organizational learning. Therefore, this study will construct the structure of internal facilitating factors of organizational learning in Chinese companies from the perspective of culture.

The internal facilitating factor and organizational learning approach are two core elements to measure organizational learning (DiBella & Nevis, 1998). However, we have not seen any study on the relationship between the internal facilitating factors and organizational learning orientation in China.

4.3.1.2 The Construction of Internal Facilitating Factors in Organizational Learning

4.3.1.2.1 RESEARCH PROCESS

4.3.1.2.1.1 Item collection and compiling of initial questionnaire In this stage, we mainly took the following four steps to collect items on the internal facilitating factors of organizational learning to compile the initial questionnaire.

Step 1 is the literature review. We summarized the items related to internal facilitating factors of organizational learning in the literature and obtained 23 items in total.

Step 2 is case summary. We collected 9 cases of corporate organizational learning at home and abroad and after an in-depth understanding of the cases, we divide the 23 items into 12 categories for statistics, as shown in Table 4.16. This step validates some of the items in the literature.

Step 3 is the interview. A total of 10 middle-level managers from three enterprises were interviewed, and the interview recordings were sorted out. The following conclusions were made based on the recordings: (1) company learning needs an institutional guarantee; (2) communication within a company is critical for individual learning to spread to the group and organization; (3) the climate of openness and trust in a company is essential; (4) the learning behavior in a company requires that leaders and managers at all levels behave as role models; (5) companies often do not provide relevant learning opportunities, time or resources; (6) the effect of training in reality is often unsatisfactory; (7) companies often fail to notice the informal learning of employees. We validated some items and collected more items on internal facilitating factors of organizational learning.

Step 4 is the open-ended questionnaire. A total of 41 valid open-ended questionnaires were retrieved from the three companies. The questions are as follows. (1) What aspects do you think will promote the generation of learning climate in your company? (2) What factors do you think hinder the development of your organization? (3) What factors do you think affect the dissemination and application of employees' new ideas? (4) What factors do you think will stimulate and promote reform and innovation? According to the frequency statistics of the items collected by the open-ended questionnaire, 52 items with a frequency of greater than 3 were selected.

Finally, based on the results of these four steps and after several rounds of discussions, the research group finalized 35 items; we then invited four experts (PhDs in industrial and organizational psychology) and three practitioners (middle-level managers of three companies) to modify the items. Based on the opinions of experts and practitioners and after discussion in the research group, we finalized 32 items as the initial questionnaire of this study.

4.3.1.2.1.2 Subjects   The questionnaire (using the Likert five-point scale from "1—completely inconsistent" to "5—completely consistent" to evaluate the status quo of companies) was distributed to 500 people from 14 companies, and 268 valid questionnaires were retrieved. The basic information of the subjects is as follows: 61.1% of the surveyed employees are from state-owned enterprises, 39.9% from private enterprises, 44.4% from joint-stock system, 4.5% in foreign-funded enterprises and 3.4% in others. In terms of the development stage of enterprises, 19.8% are in the start-up stage, 71.3% in the growth stage, 7.5% in the mature stage and 1.5% in the re-innovation stage; 72.4% of the surveyed are general staff, 5.6% are front-line management staff, 16.4% are middle-level

Table 4.16 Results of organizing organizational learning cases

Company	1	2	3	4	5	6	7	8	9	10	11	12
Haier	✓	✓	✓	✓	✓	✓	✓	✓	✓	✓	✓	
Lenovo	✓	✓	✓	✓	✓	✓	✓	✓	✓		✓	
Baosteel	✓				✓	✓						
Shanghai UMC				✓	✓	✓	✓					
AHJW	✓				✓	✓						
Shanghai FOSUN Group	✓					✓					✓	
Microsoft	✓	✓	✓	✓	✓	✓	✓	✓	✓			✓
General Motors	✓	✓	✓	✓	✓	✓	✓	✓	✓	✓	✓	✓
UK Rover	✓	✓		✓	✓	✓	✓	✓	✓			

Note: 1. Open climate; 2. Structure; 3. Performance; 4. Reward; 5. Training and education; 6. Information sharing; 7. Continuous improvement of opportunities; 8. Explorative experiment; 9. Leadership; 10. Systematic thinking; 11. Teamwork; 12. Advocating diversity.

managers and 3.7% are senior managers. In terms of literacy, 2.6% have a degree of middle school and below, 25.0% junior college, 50.0% undergraduates and 22.4% postgraduates.

We carried out item analysis and exploratory factor analysis on the results of 268 questionnaires. The results showed that 9 items were of low quality, and hence were deleted. The remaining 23 items were analyzed by factor analysis. The variance maximization orthogonal rotation in principal component analysis was used. The results are shown in Table 4.17. It can be seen that there are four internal facilitating factors of organizational learning in Chinese enterprises, which can explain 52.1% of the total variance, and the internal consistency coefficients of these four factors meet the requirements of psychometrics. The names and content of these four internal drivers are as follows.

The first factor can be named "continuous development." It refers to organizations and individuals that constantly seek development and improvement. The main contents are that units encourage every individual to acquire new knowledge and skills, employees seek truth from facts and self-reflection and so on.

The second factor can be named "organizational support." It refers to an organization's support for learning through rules and regulations, budget, assessment and reward. The main contents are that the unit takes learning attitude and learning capability as key standards for formulating the reward system, and the unit supports education and training of various kinds.

The third factor can be called "open cooperation." It refers to the work and interpersonal communication among employees in the organization with an open and cooperative attitude. Employees trust each other, share information and support and tolerate each other. The main contents include mutual trust and mutual recognition as work partners, discussions and sharing of ideas.

The fourth factor can be named "respect for individuality," which means that the organization respects each employee's individuality and innovativeness and encourages them to formulate development plans that suit themselves according to the development needs of the organization; the main contents account for the fact that we all have self-development plans and implementation methods.

These four factors are different from previous research results in the literature. The respect for individuality is reflected in the previous results, but it is not clearly put forward. The other three factors are reflected, to varying degrees, in the previous research results of scholars (Pedler et al. 1991; Watkins & Marsick, 1993; Tannenbaum, 1997; DiBella & Nevis, 1998). This model is concise and clear, and it can basically include components of the earlier models. Among them, continuous development, open cooperation and respect for individuality are the software of the organization, while organizational support is about the organizational mechanism and the corporate standard system. This is consistent with the "learning atmosphere" and "learning structure" generalized by Örtenblad (2002). Therefore, these four factors generalize the internal factors of promoting organizational learning from two aspects.

Table 4.17 Results of exploratory factor analysis on internal facilitating factors of organizational learning (*N* = 268)

Factor	Continuous development	Organizational support	Open cooperation	Respect for individuality
My organization encourages everyone to acquire new knowledge and skills	0.686			
My organization often reflects on and summarizes the past	0.650			
My organization attaches importance to stimulating the learning motivation of employees	0.637			
My organization encourages the behavior of improving work efficiency through participating in education and training	0.611			
Employees can combine personal ideals with organizational goals	0.566			
Employees seek truth from facts and perform self-reflection	0.538			
Employees try and participate in determining the types and forms of reward systems		0.709		
The staff and workers of the organization can get the funds for education and training according to the principle		0.659		
My organization supports various levels of education and training		0.613		
Learning attitude and learning ability should be regarded as the important standards for the establishment of reward system		0.599		
The roles and positions of the staff and workers are flexible		0.597		
Accounting, budgeting and reporting systems all encourage learning		0.564		
Employees trust each other and treat each other as work partners			0.687	

Employees' ideas are discussed together and shared openly			0.632	
Employees can accept and tolerate different opinions when communicating with each other			0.584	
My organizational evaluation system is mainly for learning and development			0.551	
My organization encourages bold questioning and self-criticism in front of the collective			0.539	
My organization consciously combines people with different abilities and different views			0.501	
We don't think that all parts of a department have to follow the same rules				0.659
The task members of an enterprise include customers, suppliers and employees of the cooperative enterprise				0.651
When implementing major changes, we often set up several typical units				0.633
My organization takes seriously the initiative of all employees				0.543
We all have self-development plans and implementation methods				0.512
Explained variance (52.1% of total variance)	14.1%	13.9%	12.4%	11.7%
Internal consistency coefficient	0.79	0.80	0.77	0.75

4.3.1.3 Relationship between the internal facilitating factors of organizational learning and the orientation of organizational learning

In order to explore the relationship between the internal facilitating factors of organizational learning and the orientation of organizational learning, an 18-item organizational learning orientation questionnaire was used to assess the degree between the two opposite aspects in pairs, and the Likert five-point scale ("1—completely consistent with the left" to "5—completely consistent with the right") was adopted. The results of the organizational learning orientation questionnaire show that the α coefficient of the internal consistency of the five factors are 0.60, 0.62, 0.61, 0.63 and 0.60, respectively.

The correlation matrix between the internal facilitating factors of organizational learning and organizational learning orientation is shown in Table 4.18, from which we can see that the four facilitating factors of organizational learning have a moderate degree of significant positive correlation with learning speed (incremental–transformational), which indicates that the higher the level of facilitating factors, the more companies tend to practice transformational learning. The four factors have significant positive correlation with learning engagement (individual–group). The results show that the higher the level of internal facilitating factors of organizational learning, the more inclined the company is to carry out group learning. The three factors are significantly negatively related to the form of knowledge dissemination (formal–informal). It shows that if a company encourages and supports learning, attaches importance to continuous development and has an open cultural atmosphere, then the company will pay more attention to the formal knowledge dissemination during learning. The three factors have a significant positive correlation with the source of knowledge (internal–external), indicating that if the company encourages learning, values development, and creates an open climate, then it will spend greater effort in obtaining relevant knowledge from the external environment. However, there is no significant correlation between the internal facilitating factors of organizational learning and the learning orientation of learning effect, which indicates that the former cannot help to predict whether organizational learning brings about cognitive change or behavioral change. The results presented here demonstrate that the internal facilitating factors of organizational learning can promote the organization to acquire new knowledge from the external environment, then conduct formal knowledge dissemination within the organization by setting up corresponding systems and norms and then carry out transformational group learning based on the acquisition and dissemination of new knowledge.

4.3.1.4 Discussion

4.3.1.4.1 THE STRUCTURE OF INTERNAL FACILITATING FACTORS OF ORGANIZATIONAL LEARNING

The results show that the promoting of organizational learning must meet the following four conditions. First, organizational learning requires that individuals, groups and the entire organization have a spirit of continuous improvement and development. Second, organizational learning should be supported and guaranteed by specific rules and regulations. Third, organizational learning needs an open and cooperative organizational atmosphere. Fourth, organizational learning requires

Table 4.18 Correlation between internal facilitating factors of organizational learning and organizational learning orientation

Factor	Learning speed (incremental–transformational)	Learning engagement (individual–group)	Form of knowledge dissemination (formal–informal)	Source of knowledge (internal–external)	Learning effect (cognition–behavior)
Continuous development	0.34**	0.23**	−0.22*	0.17**	−0.10
Organizational support	0.38**	0.19**	−0.23*	0.14*	−0.09
Open cooperation	0.35**	0.30**	−0.14*	0.14*	−0.02
Respect for personality	0.32**	0.19**	−0.08	0.09	−0.12

** $p > 0.01$.
* $p > 0.05$.

respect for individuality and a specific work style of each individual and department in the organization, and it requires the diversification of task members and
even rules and regulations.

All in all, in order to effectively promote organizational learning, the organization must have an enabling atmosphere of continuous development, open
cooperation and respect for individuality, and the organization must have such
a "learning structure" of rules and regulations that support learning. The two are
complementary because "learning structure" is the direct guarantee of organizational learning that can promote the building of the "learning climate"; in turn, the
learning climate promotes the smooth implementation of the "learning structure"
to improve the efficiency and effectiveness of that "learning structure." "Learning climate" is the facilitating factor for better learning. Therefore, organizational
support is a basic guarantee. Continuous development, open cooperation and
respect for individuality are the facilitating factors to further improve organizational learning. The results in this study offer significant inspiration for corporate
management practices and establishment of learning organization. On the one
hand, the organization can improve its organizational learning capability through
organizational support of learning and the creation of learning climates in the
management practice. On the other hand, the organization should first establish a
basic supporting learning mechanism, and then continuously create the organizational learning climate of the entire company, because the building of this climate
evidently takes more long-term efforts.

4.3.1.4.2 THE RELATIONSHIP BETWEEN INTERNAL FACILITATING FACTORS
AND ORGANIZATIONAL LEARNING ORIENTATION

The study result shows that the internal facilitating factors of organizational learning prompt companies to acquire new knowledge from the external environment
and carry out formal knowledge dissemination and transformational group learning. Therefore, if Chinese companies want to improve their organizational learning
capability or create learning organizations, they can make efforts in the internal
facilitating factors of organizational learning, so as to continuously correct the practice of attaching undue importance to acquiring new knowledge from within; these
factors can also encourage companies to acquire new knowledge from the external
environment. The improvement of internal facilitating factors can also continuously change the status quo of overdependence on the slow informal knowledge
dissemination and promote the establishment of a formal knowledge dissemination
mechanism and system within the company. At the same time, they will enhance
the quality of collective learning, so as to promote the company to continuously
improve the status quo of focusing on incremental organizational learning, realize
transformational learning and strengthen the core competitiveness of companies.

The results of the research on the relationship between the two have important
implications for corporate management practice and the establishment of learning
organization. First, if corporate leaders desire to fundamentally change or improve
the concept and value orientation of organizational learning, then improving the
internal facilitating factors of organizational learning is a good starting point.

Second, leaders can diagnose and intervene in the status quo of organizational learning from both the internal facilitating factors and the basic orientation of organizational learning, so as to promote the organizational learning of the company.

To sum up, the results show that the internal facilitating factors of organizational learning in Chinese companies are composed of four factors: continuous development, organizational support, open cooperation and respect for individuality. The internal facilitating factors of organizational learning can stimulate companies to acquire new knowledge from the outside, conduct formal knowledge dissemination and transformational group learning. For Chinese corporate management practice, the combination of internal facilitating factors of organizational learning and organizational learning orientation (Yu Haibo et al., 2004), which is what DiBella and Nevis (1998) emphasized as the early diagnosis measure of organizational learning, provides measures and ideas for companies to intervene in organizational learning and create learning organizations, and it can also be used as evaluation measures after intervention.

4.3.2 The full mediation of organizational culture between leadership and organizational learning

4.3.2.1 Research hypothesis

4.3.2.1.1 THE RELATIONSHIP BETWEEN TRANSFORMATIONAL AND TRANSACTIONAL LEADERSHIP AND ORGANIZATIONAL LEARNING

According to the discussion in "the relationship between transformational, transactional leadership and organizational learning," the following hypotheses are set forth:

Hypothesis 18:

Transformational leadership promotes organizational learning, and there is a significant positive correlation between them.

Hypothesis 19:

Transactional leadership promotes organizational learning, and there is a significant positive correlation between them.

4.3.2.1.2 THE MEDIATION OF ORGANIZATIONAL CULTURE

According to the mediating effect of organizational culture covered in Section 4.1, the following hypotheses are set forth:

Hypothesis 20:

Organizational culture plays a mediating role when transformational leadership influences organizational learning.

Hypothesis 21:

Organizational culture plays a mediating role when transactional leadership influences organizational learning.

4.3.2.2 Research method

4.3.2.2.1 SUBJECTS

We distributed 236 questionnaires to 13 companies in Beijing, Shandong Province and Jiangsu Province. After 12 invalid questionnaires were excluded, we recovered 224 questionnaires with an effective rate of 94.9%. Specifically, state-owned companies accounted for 21.9%, private companies 40.2%, foreign-funded companies 10.2% and other companies 27.7%; 83.0% subjects are first-line employees, 12.5% front-line managers and 4.5% middle and high-level managers; 49.6% of subjects have worked for less than 3 years, 44.2%, 3–7 years and 6.2% more than 7 years; 32.1% have a junior college degree and below; 55.4% a bachelor's degree; and 12.5% above a bachelor's degree; 52.2% are male and 47.8% female. In terms of company scale, 88.4% have 1500 people, 7.6% have between 500 and 2000 employees; 7.1% of the employees are in the start-up stage, 57.6% in the growth stage, 19.7% in the mature stage and 15.6% in the re-innovation stage.

4.3.2.2.2 MEASURES

The transformational leadership and transactional leadership scale are based on the Transformational Leadership Questionnaire and Transactional Leadership Questionnaire of Bass (1998). Cameron and Quinn's (1999) scale that included 20 items was used as the organizational culture scale. The organizational learning scale was based on a 29-item questionnaire developed in this study. The Likert five-point scoring method was used in the scale, and the subjects were asked to evaluate the compliance with their own units. The coefficient α of the organizational learning scale is 0.97, the coefficient α of the transformational leadership scale is 0.95, the coefficient α of the transactional leadership scale is 0.65 and the reliability coefficient α of the organizational culture scale is 0.98. It shows that the reliability of each scale meets the basic requirements of metrics.

4.3.2.2.3 RESEARCH METHOD

Statistical analysis and structural equation modeling were conducted by using SPSS 10.0 and AMOS 4.0.

4.3.2.3 Research result

4.3.2.3.1 DESCRIPTIVE STATISTICS OF EACH RESEARCH VARIABLE

The average, standard deviation and correlation matrix results of each study variable are shown in Table 4.19. The results show that transformational leadership and transactional leadership are significantly correlated with organizational culture and organizational learning.

Table 4.19 Means, standard deviations and correlations for research variables

Variable	M	SD	1	2	3	4	5	6
1. Nature of company	2.44	1.12	–					
2. Company scale	1.53	0.81	−0.13*					
3. Company's development stage	2.44	0.84	−0.35**	0.05				
4. Transformational leadership	3.30	0.94	−0.22**	0.03	0.28**			
5. Transactional leadership	3.19	0.62	−0.07	0.22**	0.05	0.72**		
6. Organizational culture	3.37	1.05	−0.35**	0.03	0.48**	0.85**	0.63**	
7. Organizational learning	3.42	0.83	−0.33**	0.07	0.44**	0.86**	0.68**	0.83**

** $p < 0.01$.
* $p < 0.05$.

4.3.2.3.2 THE MEDIATING EFFECT OF ORGANIZATIONAL CULTURE BETWEEN LEADERSHIP AND ORGANIZATIONAL LEARNING

The result of hierarchical regression analysis for transformational leadership (Table 4.20) is as follows. First, transformational leadership plays a significant role in promoting organizational learning (M2), which verifies Hypothesis 18. Second, when both transformational leadership and organizational culture were put into the regression equation (M3), the role of transformational leadership changed from very significant (0.79, $p < 0.01$) to insignificant (−0.04, $p > 0.05$), while organizational culture had a significant effect on organizational learning (0.83, $p < 0.01$). This shows that organizational culture plays a full mediating role between transformational leadership and organizational learning, which supports Hypothesis 20. For the transactional leadership, the results show that there was significant correlation between transactional leadership and organizational learning(M5), which verifies Hypothesis 19. However, when both transactional leadership and organizational culture were put into the regression equation (M6), the role of transactional leadership changed from significant (0.68, $p < 0.01$) to insignificant (0.01, $p > 0.05$), while organizational culture had a significant effect on organizational learning (0.78, $p < 0.01$). This also shows that organizational culture plays a full mediating role between transactional leadership and organizational learning, which supports Hypothesis 21.

4.3.2.4 Analysis and discussion

4.3.2.4.1 DIFFERENCE IN THE ROLE OF TRANSFORMATIONAL LEADERSHIP AND TRANSACTIONAL LEADERSHIP

The result shows that the transformational leadership has a greater effect on organizational learning than the transactional leadership, mainly because transformational leadership can better stimulate the internal impetus of organizational learning, while transactional leadership stimulates the external impetus. Transformational leadership stimulates the internal learning potential of every

Table 4.20 Relationship between transformational leadership, transactional leadership and organizational learning: the mediating effect of organizational culture ($N = 224$)

Dependent variable	Organizational learning						Organizational culture			
Model	M1	M2	M3	M4	M5	M6	M7	M8	M9	M10
Step 1: control variables										
Nature of company	-0.20**	-0.08	-0.10	-0.20**	-0.17**	-0.10**	-0.20**	-0.08	-0.20	-0.17
Company scale	0.03	0.03	-0.02	0.03	-0.12**	-0.02	0.03	0.03	0.03	-0.12
Company development stage	0.37**	0.19**	0.23**	0.37**	0.35**	0.23**	0.37**	0.19	0.37	0.35
Step 2: independent variables										
Transformational leadership		0.79**	-0.04					0.79**		
Transactional leadership					0.68**	0.01				0.68*
Step 3: mediating variable										
Organizational culture			0.83**			0.78**				
R^2	0.232**	0.796**	0.816**	0.232	0.666**	0.816**	0.232**	0.796**	0.232**	0.666**
ΔR^2	0.232**	0.563**	0.020**	0.232	0.434**	0.150**	0.232*	0.563**	0.232**	0.434**

** $p < 0.01$.
* $p < 0.05$.

employee through visionary guidance of the company and personalized consideration for employees; it also boosts the morale of the entire company to make everyone learn and improve together. In contrast, the contingent reward and management-by-exception in transactional leadership make positive or negative feedback based on the work results of employees, teams and even the entire organization, which stimulates more passive learning motivation and willingness.

4.3.2.4.2 THE FULL MEDIATING ROLE OF ORGANIZATIONAL CULTURE

The study results indicate that organizational culture plays a full mediating role in the relationships between transformational leadership, transactional leadership and organizational learning. This study contributes theoretical in three ways. First, if a leader wants to manage organizational learning, then organizational culture that suits organizational learning must be built, which is a key pathway between leadership and organizational learning. Second, organizational culture is a necessary soft condition for leaders to promote organizational learning. If an organization wants to fundamentally improve its learning capability, it must rely on its leaders to create an organizational cultural. Third, it provides a great perspective for understanding the relationship between leaders and organizational culture. Leaders promote organizational learning by building organizational culture, but whether or not leaders can be attracted and cultivated by a strong organizational culture to maintain organizational learning capability remains to be tested by further empirical research.

4.3.2.4.3 THE INSPIRATIONS OF THIS STUDY FOR LEADERS TO LEAD ORGANIZATIONAL
         LEARNING IN CHINESE COMPANIES

This study offers three inspirations for Chinese company leaders. First, the building of organizational culture is an important strategy for leaders to manage organizational learning. Second, transformational leaders' building of a learning-oriented organizational culture is a good pathway to improve organizational learning capability and set up a learning organization. Third, transactional leadership can also promote organizational learning by building a relevant organizational culture. This conclusion does not verify the view held by many that such transactional leadership cannot improve organizational learning capability; in addition, it suggests that transactional leaders can also promote organizational learning by creating a cultural atmosphere suitable for the organization.

4.4 Human resource management practice—hard factor of the generative mechanism of organizational learning

4.4.1 The direct influence of human resource management practice on organizational learning

4.4.1.1 Literature review and research hypothesis

Human resource management practice is closely related to organizational learning, as the former is a driver of the latter. Some theoretical and empirical studies have concluded that human resource management can promote organizational learning (López et al., 2005, 2006; Bhatnagar & Sharma, 2005). At the same time, some empirical studies have also proved that there is a significant relationship between specific human resource areas and organizational learning (Jerez-Gómez et al., 2005b; Gómez et al.,, 2004). This study will explore the relationship between the two and posit the following hypothesis:

Hypothesis 22:

Human resource management practice has a significant positive effect on organizational learning.

4.4.1.2 Research object and research process

4.4.1.2.1 SUBJECTS

We distributed 300 questionnaires to several companies in Beijing and recovered 241 valid questionnaires. Of the subjects, 25.3% are from SOEs, 27% from private companies, 25.7% from foreign-funded enterprises and 22% from other types of companies; 69% are front-line workers, 17% managers, 14% middle-level and senior managers. In terms of development stage, 8.3% of companies are in the start-up stage, 45.4% in the growth stage, 30.8% in the mature stage and 14.8% in the re-innovation stage.

4.4.1.2.2 MEASURES

The organizational learning questionnaire adopts the six-factor and 29-item questionnaire. The questionnaire on human resource management practice adopts the seven-factor and 17-item questionnaire in Section 4.4.2. Both questionnaires use the Likert five-point scoring method and asked the subjects to evaluate the compliance with their own companies.

4.4.1.3 Research results

4.4.1.3.1 DESCRIPTIVE STATISTICAL RESULTS

The descriptive statistical results of each variable are shown in Table 4.21. The results show that the internal consistency coefficient α of human resource management practice dimensions and organizational learning is between 0.68 and 0.89, indicating that the validity of each scale meets the basic requirements of psychometrics.

4.4.1.3.2 THE INFLUENCE OF HUMAN RESOURCE MANAGEMENT PRACTICE ON ORGANIZATIONAL LEARNING

In order to study the influence of human resource management practice on organizational learning, we conducted structural equation modeling on the data of the questionnaire. The results showed that the x^2/df (2626.44/1050 = 2.50) and RMSEA (0.078) of the model met the model fit standard, and the four indexes NFI, IFI, TLI and CFI (respectively 0.92, 0.95, 0.95, 0.95) all reached above 0.90, indicating

Table 4.21 Descriptive statistics,correlations and internal consistency reliabilities for research variables

Variable	M	SD	4	5	6	7	8	9
1. Selective hiring	3.47	0.81	(0.68)					
2. Strategic training	3.51	0.89	0.56**	(0.80)				
3. Compensation reward	3.52	1.10	0.30**	0.35**	(0.77)			
4. Employee participation	2.91	0.85	0.26**	0.43**	0.32**	(0.71)		
5. Performance management	3.30	0.93	0.44**	0.53**	0.35**	0.47**	(0.87)	
6. Organizational learning	3.40	0.61	0.44**	0.61**	0.40**	0.56**	0.56**	(0.88)

** $p < 0.01$.
Note: The data in brackets on the diagonal is the internal consistency α coefficient of each variable.

that the model fit well (Bollen, 1989). The specific path coefficients are shown in Table 4.22. The results show that selective hiring has a significant negative effect on inter-organizational learning and explorative learning; strategic training has a strong positive effect on all six dimensions of organizational learning; compensation reward has a significant positive effect on inter-organizational learning and explorative learning; except for collective learning, employee participation has a significant positive effect on individual, organizational, inter-organizational, explorative learning and exploitative learning; performance management plays a significant role in promoting individual learning and exploitative learning. These results partially support Hypothesis 22.

4.4.1.4 Discussion

Overall, human resource management practice has a significant effect on organizational learning. More specifically, it mainly includes the following aspects. Selective hiring has a significant negative effect on inter-organizational learning and explorative learning, which shows that the internal selection system that companies emphasize is detrimental to the communication and cooperation between organizations and to the exploration of new knowledge. This is because the absence of new employees hinders the learning of organization. This signifies that Chinese companies should strategically improve the existing selection and employment system instead of merely focusing on specific operational skills. Otherwise, the communication between companies will be detrimental to exploration of new knowledge.

Strategic training plays a significant role in promoting all six dimensions of organizational learning. This suffices to explain that strategic training underpins organizational learning because it promotes the development of the whole organization through promoting the learning of employees. Organizational learning belongs to the category of human resource development and is the basis of human resource development. This also suggests that in order to promote organizational learning in Chinese companies, a training system can be the first step.

Table 4.22 Path coefficient of human resource management practice on organizational learning

Variable	Individual learning	Collective learning	Organizational-level learning	Inter-organizational learning	Explorative learning	Exploitative learning
Selection	−0.05	0.13	−0.14	−0.26**	−0.14*	−0.11
Training	0.63**	0.68**	0.79**	0.83**	0.48**	0.78**
Compensation reward	0.12	−0.01	0.09	0.14*	0.15*	0.05
Employee participation	0.16*	0.11	0.22**	0.47**	0.78**	0.20**
Performance management	0.29**	0.10	0.02	0.03	0.11	0.18*

** $p < 0.01$,
* $p < 0.05$.

Compensation management plays a significant role in promoting inter-organizational learning and explorative learning, which is contrary to selection and employment. This shows that the increasingly frequent and in-depth compensation reform in Chinese companies has shifted the focus of Chinese companies' pay reform to mixed compensation and performance bonuses. This will promote inter-organizational learning and the development of new knowledge.

Employee participation plays a significant role in promoting all dimensions of organizational learning except collective learning. This is sufficient to illustrate the importance of ensuring employees' full participation in organizational learning through a variety of human resource management systems. Employees' participation in decision-making means that their new knowledge and ideas can be understood by others, shared and fully applied. With certain authorization in the organization, employees have more opportunities to participate in the various affairs of the organization. This is employee-oriented organizational learning.

Performance management plays a significant role in promoting individual learning and exploitative learning. This shows that a complete set of performance management systems has a great effect on stimulating individual self-reflection and improving their work performance. It also shows that the performance management system that disseminates and fully leverages existing knowledge is an institutional and systemic guarantee.

In a word, the aforementioned research results offer two inspirations for corporate management practice. First, organizations must rely on sound and strategic-oriented human resource management to improve organizational learning. Specifically, selective hiring should be more flexible and external-oriented; performance management should attach due importance to openness, transparency and performance feedback; compensation management should value flexible and variable salary modes and performance incentives; a sound and strategy-oriented training system should be established; employee participation should be guaranteed and encouraged. Second, if the organization does not have a sound human resource system, it will hinder organizational learning. This reminds company managers that when promoting organizational learning, they must pay attention to the matching degree between the existing human resource system and organizational learning, and they must analyze whether the existing human resource system is suitable for promoting organizational learning. The results of this study point out the direction of future organizational learning management.

4.4.2 The mediating role of human resource management practice between paternalistic leadership and organizational learning

4.4.2.1 Introduction

The relationship between leadership and organizational learning has not been sufficiently validated (Crossan et al., 2011). There is no empirical study on what mechanism of paternalistic leadership with Chinese cultural characteristics can promote organizational learning. This highlights the urgent need to explore the mechanism of paternalistic leadership on organizational learning, so as to understand the leadership mechanism of organizational learning in theory and to provide scientific reference for Chinese corporate leaders to promote organizational learning in management practice.

4.4.2.2 Literature review and research hypotheses

4.4.2.2.1 THE RELATIONSHIP BETWEEN PATERNALISTIC LEADERSHIP AND ORGANIZATIONAL LEARNING

Hypothesis 23:

Paternalistic leadership has a significant effect on promoting organizational learning.

4.4.2.2.2 THE EFFECT OF HUMAN RESOURCE MANAGEMENT PRACTICE IN THE RELATIONSHIP BETWEEN PATERNALISTIC LEADERSHIP AND ORGANIZATIONAL LEARNING

In the research on the relationship between leadership and human resource management practice, the result of Waldman et al. (1987) showed that transformational leadership would influence the effect of organizational performance evaluation. Transformational leadership can improve organizational performance through human resource management based on capital promoting. Mumford (2000) argued that to manage creativity and innovation, effective human resource practices must consider the individual, the group, the organization and the strategic environment confronting the organization. Therefore, leaders influence the human resource management practice of the organization. Based on the analysis presented, this study posits the following hypothesis:

Hypothesis 24:

Paternalistic leadership has a significant positive effect on human resource management practice.

In the research of the relationship between human resource management and organizational learning, theoretical analysis overwhelms empirical research, but some empirical studies concluded that human resource management can promote organizational learning (Gómez et al., 2004; Bhatnagar & Sharma, 2005; Jerez-Gómez et al., 2005b; López et al., 2006). The following hypothesis is set forth:

Hypothesis 25:

Human resource management practice has a significant positive effect on organizational learning.

Synthesizing the aforementioned analysis and hypothesis, and inspired by Mumford (2000) who holds that leadership can promote organizational performance and organizational innovation through the mediating effect of human resource management practice, this study posits the following hypothesis on the basis of verifying the structure of human resource management practice:

Hypothesis 26:

The relationship between paternalistic leadership and organizational learning is mediated by human resource management practice.

4.4.2.3 Research methods

4.4.2.3.1 SUBJECTS

We distributed 600 questionnaires to several companies and on-the-job graduate student classes in Beijing and recovered 461 valid questionnaires with an effective rate of 76.8%. Specifically, 25.3% of the subjects are from SOEs, 27% from private companies, 25.7% from foreign-funded companies and 22% from other types of companies; 36.9% of the companies have fewer than 100 employees, 35% with 100–499 employees, 10.8% with 500–999 employees, 7.8% with 1000–1999 employees, and 9.5% with 2000 or more employees; 69% are frontline workers, 17% managers, 14% middle-level and senior managers. In terms of the development stage, 8.3% companies are in the start-up stage, 45.4% in the growth stage, 30.8% in the mature stage and 14.8% in the re-innovation stage.

4.4.2.3.2 MEASURES

The paternalistic leadership questionnaire of Zheng Boxun et al. (2000) was adopted as the paternalistic leadership questionnaire. The organizational learning questionnaire contains 29 items. The human resource management practice questionnaire includes five aspects and uses the three subscales of López et al. (2006): selective hiring, strategic training and employee participation in decision-making. The compensation management questionnaire uses three items from López et al. (2006) and one from Wright et al. (2005). The performance management questionnaire uses one item from the Wright et al. (2005) questionnaire and compiled four items according to the performance evaluation standard, performance communication and performance management system in performance management. The Likert five-point scoring method was used in all three questionnaires. The subjects were asked to evaluate the consistency with the actual situation of their own units.

4.4.2.3.3 STATISTICAL METHOD

The statistical analysis was conducted using SPSS 10.0 and AMOS 4.0.

4.4.2.4 Research results

4.4.2.4.1 THE RESULTS OF EXPLORATORY AND CONFIRMATORY FACTOR ANALYSIS ON THE HUMAN RESOURCE MANAGEMENT PRACTICE QUESTIONNAIRE

In order to test the human resource management practice questionnaire, we conducted an explorative factor analysis of the data from the 241 questionnaires. It was found that two items in compensation management had low degree of correlation and low factor loading and communality, so these two items were removed. Then, an explorative factor analysis of the remaining 17 items was carried out, and five factors were extracted. The result shows that the five factors can explain 67.59% of the total variance (as shown in Table 4.23). Except for selective hiring, whose consistency α coefficient is 0.68, the internal consistency coefficient α of each dimension is higher than the 0.70 benchmark of psychometrics.

To verify the structure of human resource management practice questionnaire, confirmatory factor analysis was conducted on the remaining 220 data records. The result showed that x^2/df = 1.94, RMSEA = 0.066 (critical value is 0.08) and NFI, IFI, TLI and CFI were 0.98, 0.99, 0.98 and 0.99 respectively. These results are in line with the model fit standard, indicating that the five-factor model fits well (Bollen, 1989). Therefore, human resource management practice questionnaire has high validity.

4.4.2.4.2 RESULTS OF CONFIRMATORY FACTOR ANALYSIS ON PATERNALISTIC LEADERSHIP AND ORGANIZATIONAL LEARNING

The results of confirmatory factor analysis on paternalistic leadership and organizational learning showed that the three-factor paternalistic leadership model and six-factor organizational learning model had x^2/df = 3.59/2.59, RMSEA = 0.08/0.08 (the critical value is 0.08) and NFI, IFI, TLI, and CFI indexes were 0.92/0.97, 0.94/0.98, 0.93/0.98 and 0.94/0.98, respectively. These results are consistent with the model fit standard, indicating that the model fit well (Bollen, 1989). This shows that paternalistic leadership and organizational learning has high structural validity. The internal consistency coefficient α of benevolent leadership, moral leadership, authoritarian leadership and organizational learning questionnaire was 0.90, 0.85, 0.85 and 0.92 respectively.

4.4.2.4.3 DESCRIPTIVE STATISTICAL RESULTS

The descriptive statistics for research variables are shown in Table 4.24. Other than the correlation coefficient between authoritarian leadership and each variable is not significant, the correlation coefficients among other variables all reached a significant level.

Table 4.23 Exploratory factor analysis results of human resource management practice questionnaire

Item/factor load	Performance management	Strategic training	Employee participation	Selective hiring	Compensation management
The company has an open and transparent performance management system	0.83				
There are clear quantitative standards for the performance appraisal of companies	0.79				
The company carries on the formal performance appraisal to the staff regularly	0.73				
The performance appraisal of employees in companies integrates individual work performance and group performance	0.69				
Managers often have performance interviews with employees	0.67				
The training program attaches importance to general quality and corporate culture		0.75			
The staff training and development policy covers all personnel in the company		0.74			
Employees can be trained throughout the work process		0.72			
Employee participates in decision-making process			0.81		
Companies inform employees of economic and strategic information			0.71		
Implementation of personnel authorization in companies			0.66		
In order to make up for the vacancy, internal promotion is prior to external recruitment.				0.77	
New members of the department or team also participate in recruitment activities				0.69	
In the selective process, companies not only evaluate the candidates' knowledge and experience, but also their ability of work in groups and continuous learning				0.51	
Recruitment and selection is a common thing in the company				0.49	
The salary of the organization is a mixed salary composed of fixed part and variable part					0.89
Companies pay incentive bonus according to employee performance					0.81
Coefficient α	0.87	0.80	0.71	0.68	0.77
Explained variance (67.59%)	18.95%	15.22%	13.00%	10.45%	9.97%

Table 4.24 Descriptive statistics and correlations for research variables

Variable	M	SD	1	2	3	4	5	6	7	8
1. Benevolent leadership	2.91	0.84								
2. Moral leadership	3.11	0.83	0.62**							
3. Authoritarian leadership	3.17	0.70	0.04	0.02						
4. Selective hiring	3.42	0.79	0.22**	0.20**	0.06					
5. Strategic training	3.37	0.89	0.33***	0.28***	0.04	0.54**				
6. Compensation reward	3.33	0.82	0.24**	0.19***	0.02	0.42**	0.48**			
7. Employee participation	3.00	0.85	0.32**	0.17***	−0.05	0.25**	0.38**	0.45**		
8. Performance management	3.27	0.90	0.33***	0.28***	−0.04	0.41**	0.50**	0.46**	0.51**	
9. Organizational learning	3.31	0.64	0.63**	0.53**	0.07	0.29**	0.47**	0.33**	0.33**	0.40**

** $p < 0.01$

4.4.2.4.4 THE MEDIATING EFFECT OF HUMAN RESOURCE MANAGEMENT PRACTICE IN THE INFLUENCE OF PATERNALISTIC LEADERSHIP ON ORGANIZATIONAL LEARNING

To test the full mediating effect of human resource management practice in the relationship between paternalistic leadership and organizational learning, we compared the fit indexes of the full mediation model and the partial mediation model. The results (Table 4.25) show that $\Delta x^2 = 274.45$, $\Delta df = 3$, $\Delta x^2/\Delta df = 91.49$, This shows that the partial mediation model is better than the full mediation model ($p < 0.01$). Moreover, the $\Delta x^2/df$ and RMSEA of the partial mediation models all meet the model fit standard, and NFI, IFI, TLI and CFI are all above 0.90, which indicates that the partial mediation model fits well (Bollen, 1989). Therefore, partial mediation model is a suitable model. The results show that selective hiring and performance management have no significant impact on organizational learning. Therefore, we obtain the modified partial mediation model by removing these two dimensions. The analysis results show that all the indexes of the model meet the requirements (Table 4.25), indicating that the model fits well.

The path coefficient of the modified partial mediation model is shown in Figure 4.17. The result shows that benevolent leadership promotes organizational learning through the mediating effect of strategic training, compensation management and employee participation. On the one hand, moral leadership has a direct effect in organizational learning; on the other hand, it indirectly facilitates

Table 4.25 Fitting indexes of the model

Model	x^2	df	x^2/df	NFI	IFI	TLI	CFI	RMSEA
Zero model	69,591.15	1596	43.60					
Full mediation model	4513.63	1461	3.09	0.94	0.96	0.95	0.96	0.067
Partial mediation model	4239.18	1458	2.91	0.94	0.96	0.96	0.96	0.064
Modified partial mediation model	3577.01	1109	3.23	0.94	0.96	0.96	0.96	0.067

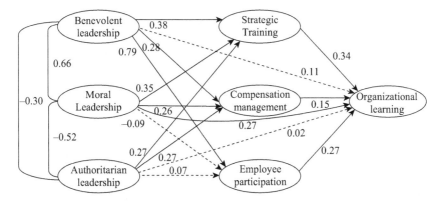

Figure 4.17 Modified partial mediation model

organizational learning through partial mediation of strategic training and compensation management; authoritarian leadership promotes organizational learning through the full mediation of strategic training and compensation management.

In terms of the effect of paternalistic leadership on organizational learning (Table 4.26), moral leadership has the greatest impact on organizational learning, followed by benevolent leadership and authoritarian leadership. This supports Hypothesis 1.

In terms of the mediation, human resource management practice plays the most important role in benevolent leadership, followed by moral leadership and authoritarian leadership. This validates Hypotheses 24, 25 and 26.

The mediation effect of strategic training on paternalistic leadership and organizational learning was the greatest ($0.13 + 0.12 + 0.09 = 0.34$), followed by employee participation in decision-making (0.21), and the mediation of compensation management was the smallest ($0.04 + 0.04 + 0.04 = 0.12$). Strategic training and compensation management play the mediation role in all three aspects of paternalistic leadership and organizational learning, but employee participation in decision-making plays only a mediating role between benevolent leadership and organizational learning.

4.4.2.5 Conclusion and discussion

4.4.2.5.1 THE RELATIONSHIP BETWEEN PATERNALISTIC LEADERSHIP AND ORGANIZATIONAL LEARNING

From the perspective of the effect model, moral leadership has not only an indirect effect on organizational learning through human resource management practice, but also a direct effect. In contrast, benevolent leadership and authoritarian leadership can promote the organizational learning capability and establishment of learning organization only by strengthening the human resource management practice, elevating the training level of the organization, enhancing the organization's compensation management system and giving employees opportunities to participate in management.

4.4.2.5.2 THE MEDIATING MECHANISM OF HUMAN RESOURCE MANAGEMENT PRACTICE IN THE RELATIONSHIP BETWEEN PATERNALISTIC LEADERSHIP AND ORGANIZATIONAL LEARNING

In terms of the three aspects of paternalistic leadership, human resource management practice has the greatest mediating effect on benevolent leadership. This shows that the care, help and attention of paternalistic leaders to subordinates can be better reflected in the human resource management practice, so as to promote the organizational learning of the entire company.

Viewing from the perspective of specific human resource management practices, strategic training is the mediator variable of the three aspects of paternalistic leadership that affect organizational learning, and it has the greatest mediating effect. These results are consistent with those of López et al. (2006) and Gómez et al. (2004), and they also prove the view of Ulrich and Todd (1993) and shows that strategic training can be used as an important lever for leaders to promote organizational learning.

Table 4.26 Effects breakdown of path analysis

Independent variable	Effect type	Strategic training	Compensation management	Employee participation in decision making	Organizational learning
Benevolent leadership	Direct effect	0.38	0.28	0.79	0.38
	Indirect effect	(0.13)	(0.04)	(0.21)	
Moral leadership	Direct effect	0.35	0.26		0.27
	Indirect effect	(0.12)	(0.04)		0.16
Authoritarian leadership	Direct effect	0.27	0.27		
	Indirect effect	(0.09)	(0.04)		0.13

Note: Figures in brackets indicate the indirect effect of paternalistic leadership on organizational learning through human resource management practices.

Employee participation in decision-making is a full mediator variable for benevolent leadership to promote organizational learning, and its mediating effect is relatively large. This result is consistent with the result of López et al. (2006) and also proves the opinion of Pedler et al. (1991). This also highlights that in the relationship between managers and employees, employee participation should be valued; even in some cases, employees should be authorized to make decisions so as to promote the organizational learning of companies.

Compensation management is the mediator variable of three aspects of paternalistic leadership that affect organizational learning. This result is consistent with the result of Gómez et al. (2004) but inconsistent with that of López et al. (2006). This is because benevolent leadership places greater emphasis on communication with employees in compensation management, which can improve the efficiency of compensation communication and promote organizational learning.

Selective hiring and performance management do not have a significant mediation effect between paternalistic leadership and organizational learning. This is inconsistent with the results of López et al. (2006). The reason may be that although the leaders can affect the selective hiring of the organization, for it to have an effect on organizational learning takes time. In terms of performance management, some companies simply equate it with performance appraisal because the pursuit of performance management is not development-oriented or process-oriented, but more result-oriented in a bid to allocate revenues directly according to the performance evaluation results.

4.4.2.5.3 THE THEORETICAL AND PRACTICAL IMPLICATION OF THIS STUDY

In theory, this study provides a new understanding of the relationship between leadership and organizational learning: human resource management practice is one of the channels and levers between the two, and it is the hardware management measure. In practice, it can inspire Chinese company leaders that to lead the organizational learning in the company, they should establish a complete scientific and strategy-based training system, a scientific and democratic staff participation decision-making mechanism and a compensation management system based on strategy and performance. It also inspires them to fully tap the potential of the leadership style with Chinese cultural characteristics to promote organizational learning.

In future research, in terms of content, we will further study the different effect mechanisms of paternalistic leadership on organizational learning through human resource management practice in different types and stages of companies; we can also study the "hardware" (human resource management practice) and "software" (organizational atmosphere or organizational culture) of paternalistic leadership to promote organizational learning mechanism. At the same time, since leadership has a great influence on the strategic level, we can explore the different mediating effects of human resource management strategy and practices between leadership and organizational learning. In terms of research methods, we can validate and expand the specific mechanism of paternalistic leadership with Chinese cultural characteristics in the process of promoting organizational learning and creating learning organization through case tracking.

5 Future trend of organizational learning research

5.1 The multilevel nature of organizational learning methodology

Building on the literature review and our empirical studies, we come to the conclusion that organizational learning is a trans-level phenomenon. This, on one hand, signifies the complexity of organizational learning, and on the other hand, demonstrates its importance in the operation and management of organizations. The trans-level nature of organizational learning presents certain challenges for the studies, which requires that the trans-level research should be carried out with a multilevel perspective.

Ever since Rousseau integrated the multilevel perspective into theoretical research (Hofmann, 2002), organizational discipline has been moving towards a new paradigm that can bridge the gap between macro and micro approaches with a single unified theory, that is, multilevel theory (Kozlowski & Klein, 2000). The purpose of the multilevel theory is to achieve a more integrated understanding of the phenomena at different levels of the organization. It is based on the belief that micro-phenomena permeate the macro-phenomena, which are formed by the interaction of microelements. Multilevel theory not only can evaluate at multiple levels but also can illuminate top-down and bottom-up processes, and only in this way can a more scientific and applicable organizational discipline be established.

The trans-level nature of organizational learning determines that multilevel theory methodology should be adopted, which entails attention in the following three aspects.

First, the research level. As demonstrated in this study, organizational learning is a phenomenon across the individual, collective, organizational and inter-organizational levels. From the perspective of the research level, organizational learning can be mainly divided into individual and collective levels. Therefore, in the design and operation of organizational learning research, the priority is to determine whether the research is merely at the organizational level or includes multiple levels of individual and collective. In the implementation of the research, research objects and data acquisition methods will be determined along with the determination of the research level. If the research is carried out only at the organizational level, perhaps only one leader can deliver a report in an organization; if the research is carried out at different levels, then the selection of research objects and data acquisition require observation and data acquisition of multiple objects in multiple organizations and within each organization. This is the first issue that needs to be figured out in organizational research.

Second, the measurement of variables. When the research level is hammered out, so are the research object and data acquisition methods; attention should then be given to the measurement of variables at the collective level. The structure of the collective level can be divided into three types: global structure, shared structure and configural structure (Kozlowski & Klein, 2000). Chan (1998) summarized five models: the additive model, direct consensus model, reference shift consensus model, dispersion model and process model. Different methods are adopted for measuring variables of different properties. Therefore, different understanding of organizational learning determines different methods of measuring organizational learning and its specific dimensions. This important issue of measurement method merits special attention in the study of organizational learning.

Third is statistics. We carry out research, particularly empirical research, on organizational learning based on the multilevel theory. In the process of data statistics, we also need to carry out trans-level statistical analysis as required by multilevel theory. However, the traditional regression analysis and structural equation model are not suitable for data analysis of the trans-level organizational learning. Therefore, HLM or Mplus software should be applied to conduct trans-level analysis of organizational learning data so as to analyze and answer more accurately the relevant problems and organizational learning patterns. Undoubtedly, with further development of methodology and data statistics, this study will also provide new research perspectives and ideas for the study of complicated organizational learning phenomena to explore deeper into the pattern of trans-level organizational learning.

5.2 Multilevel interaction in the organizational learning process

Different opinions about what organizational learning is in the literature lead to different interpretations of the organizational learning process. This study proposes and validates the organizational learning process from two aspects: comprehensive learning levels and information or knowledge flow. This is mainly determined by the complexity of the organizational learning process per se. Therefore, the following issues should be noted when understanding and defining the organizational learning process.

First, what are the relationships among individual, collective, organizational and inter-organizational levels in organizational learning? Multilevel theory and evolutionary theory are the two important directions for future organizational learning research (Crossan et al., 2011). Some theories such as Kim's (1993) analyzed the relationship between individual learning and collective learning. This study also regards the knowledge or information flow process as a linkage among all levels. With the systems view, Chen (2007) regards individual learning, collective learning and organizational-level learning as a system with information input and output. One type of individual learning is connected with another through information output and so on; it forms collective learning. Likewise, different collective learning forms organizational learning; in a certain organizational learning system, individual learning is connected with another through information output, and in the same vein, the knowledge input and output are connected with the learning of other organizations to form inter-organizational learning. This systems view has important implications for understanding the relationship between different levels of learning, which also needs to be verified and amplified by empirical research.

Second, what is the relationship between the two kinds of learning in organizational learning, namely explorative learning and exploitative learning, from the perspective of information or knowledge flow? What is the complex relationship between their balance and organizational innovation and performance? This has become a hot topic and a core issue in organizational learning research (Crossan et al., 2011; Zhang et al., 2015; Zhang & Yu, 2015; Lee et al., 2016). What is the balance between the two types of organizational learning proposed by Argyris and Schön (1978), Senge (1990) and March (1991)? Although there are debates over whether they are two types or two endpoints in the literature, from the current stage of Chinese companies, explorative learning and exploitative learning compete for scarce resources. How to balance the two in organizational learning is an issue that must be heeded while defining organizational learning. If we look at these two types of learning dynamically, then how to understand the role of top-down and bottom-up processes in the organizational learning process is also a key issue. This study discovers the relationship between their balance and organizational performance through empirical research (Yu et al., 2008b), but it is only a preliminary study. In the future, further study digs deeper into how to balance the two with the evolution of organizational development stages and what the mechanism of the balance is on organizational innovation and organizational performance. We can draw from the dynamic balance framework of Yin and Yang in Chinese traditional culture (explorative learning is Yang, exploitative learning is Yin) to have more in-depth studies of the balance and dynamic effect of explorative learning and exploitative learning.

Third, how does the spiraling cycle of organizational learning evolve? Does it have a relative beginning and ending stage? Evolutionary theory establishes the direction for future organizational learning research (Crossan et al., 2011). In the West, many organizational learning models attempt to understand the process from a singular and linear perspective, which is clearly inaccurate. But it is totally different in the Chinese culture as Chinese scholars understand organizational learning from a cycling perspective. In fact, it is more in sync with the reality of organizational learning in China to regard organizational learning as a spiraling process, because organizational learning is indeed an everlasting process for an organization. It's natural that when an event takes place or when a leader is in office, organizational learning can be regarded as something within a certain period of time, and we can know the relative beginning and end stage of organizational learning. But on the whole, it is more appropriate to regard organizational learning as a process of survival and development of an organization. Then, it is followed by another problem: organizational learning is so all-encompassing that we don't know how to define it accurately. We can consider drawing from the framework of the dynamic balance of Yin and Yang to undertake an in-depth study of the spiraling cycling of evolutionary organizational learning process so that we can gradually explore the theoretical framework of Chinese-style organizational learning.

Fourth, is organizational learning a unity of knowledge, behaviors or interpersonal interactions, or is it purely a knowledge issue? This question is related to the definition of learning and influenced by people's understanding of learning. When reviewing the literature on the definition of organizational learning, this study divides the definition of organizational learning into three categories: knowledge, behavior and interpersonal interactions. However, according to the literature, most studies understand the organizational learning process from the perspective of knowledge, but there is no denying the fact that organizational learning, which contains four levels, does not exist without interpersonal interactions. Therefore, in understanding organizational learning, a key issue in the organizational learning process is more properly integrating knowledge as the object, behavior as the subject and interpersonal interaction.

In a word, how an organization learns is a focus as well as the biggest controversy in the study of organizational learning, and it needs to be further clarified under the guidance of empirical studies. It is an urgent matter that requires further study in both academic and practical fields.

5.3　Multilevel and complex effective mechanism of organizational learning

Prior empirical studies and many literatures have shown that organizational learning has significant impacts on individual attitude and behavior, group behaviors and organizational performance. This prior research has shown that organizational learning can exist as a background of individual behavior and cognition, in which it can play a moderating role; at the organizational level, it affects organizational performance through the full mediation of organizational innovation. All these indicate that important as it is, it takes time before organizational learning manifests its role. This important issue leaves plenty of room for future research, as mainly reflected in the following aspects.

First, through what kind of mediating link does organizational learning exert its influence on organizational performance? The results of empirical research in this book and results in the literature show that organizational learning influences organizational performance through complex organizational innovation. Organizational innovation is already a long-term project, and coupled with the complexity of organizational learning, it will take some time before the effect of organizational learning on organizational performance is manifested. This illuminates us that when organizational learning works on organizational performance, there will be many other channels besides organizational innovation. Then what are these mediating variables? Some studies have shown that organizational learning can promote organizational innovation and performance through knowledge sharing and acquisition (Shu et al., 2015); of course, further study is required to find out whether there is a non-linear relationship between organizational learning and organizational performance.

Second, what mediating links and moderating environment does organizational learning go through to have an impact on individual employee performance? The collective level of organizational learning needs to be mediated by individual learning to act on individual attitudes and behaviors. Individual learning is not easy, so naturally it takes time before its effect is manifested. The moderating effect of collective learning inspires us to posit that organizational learning is the foundation of organizational capability, and the organization should lay a solid foundation so as to be truly competitive. This also inspires the question, how does organizational learning play the role of its background conditions, affect individual behavior and performance and finally affect organizational performance? More mediating links are involved in this process, and in-depth multilevel empirical research is needed to explore these mediating variables and moderating variables.

Third, both the theoretical research and management practice should objectively understand the long-term effect of organizational learning. Organizational learning is a hot topic of academic research, and it is urgently needed in organizational management practice. However, these external factors should not serve as excuses for ignoring the fact that organizational learning is long term in nature. To truly grasp how and through which links organizational learning affects performance, researchers must carry out field studies in the enterprise and track its learning process on a long-term basis so that an objective and actual mechanism of organizational learning can be presented; managers should not rush for quick results and leaders would wish in vain that the short-term (half year or even shorter) promotion could fundamentally impact organizational performance. Chinese corporate leaders should bear this in mind so as to avoid setbacks; otherwise, it will backfire. Evolutionary theory and multilevel theory are two important directions for future organizational learning research (Crossan et al., 2011). In the future, we can grasp the internal mechanism of organizational learning from the perspective of evolution and multilevel correlation.

All in all, our work over the years speaks volumes about the importance of organizational learning, but for the role and impact to manifest requires patience in both academic and practical fields; otherwise, it will be detrimental to the management of organizational learning.

5.4 Multilevel and integrating generative mechanism of organizational learning

Many factors can promote organizational learning, including the fundamental facilitating forces and promoting factors. The fact that this study conducted empirical research on three factors of organizational learning does not mean that these three factors are what organizational learning is all about. They are only what the author deems the most important. It is fair to say that the complexity of organizational learning determines that the facilitating factors are multidimensional and should be understood from the following aspects.

First, the fundamental facilitating force of organizational learning is underpinned by the survival and development of an organization. Following the original understanding of organizational learning, many scholars regard organizational learning as a metaphor for individual learning. This means that organizational learning is like individual learning in that individual learning is the fundamental way out for individual survival, development and even the search for the meaning and value of life; therefore, organizational learning can also be regarded as the fundamental matter of organizational survival, development and even prosperity. Future research can be based on goal orientation theory (Chadwick & Raver, 2015) to explore the mechanism of individual goal orientation emerging into team and organizational goal orientation, thus promoting organizational learning; or to explore a social network's internal facilitating mechanism on organizational learning based on the social network theory (Lee et al., 2016); what's more, it can be based on the identification theory (Lee et al., 2016) to explore the internal mechanism of identity in promoting shared knowledge from the emotional perspective so as to improve organizational learning capability.

Second, the external impetus of organizational learning comes from the turbulent environment and intensifying competition. Many scholars believe that organizational learning comes from the organization's overall response and reactions to the external environment, and the organization's response to adapt to the external environment reflects organizational learning capability. Recent theoretical discussions also hold that the mechanism and process of organizational learning can be examined based on the institutional theory (Chandler & Hwang, 2015), so as to better understand the integration of multiple external factors in its generative mechanism.

Third, leadership, organizational culture and human resource management are the key internal factors that facilitate organizational learning. This is the view that the author has been holding and that this study has validated. For Chinese companies, leaders are the engines of organizational learning and role models for individual employees in the organizations. However, leaders' impetus alone does not lead to quick and efficient organizational learning. Such a sound soft environment as organizational culture is needed (the organizational culture here is more focused on core values), because it, like air, is pervasive in the organization. It is a fundamental facilitating force for individuals, groups and the entire organization. However, sometimes, with a soft environment alone, it is difficult to achieve the expected results. To learn better and faster, organizations need a systematic environment that matches the organizational culture; that is human resource management. The author of this book believes that, fundamentally, organizational learning is implemented by people in the organization, and human resource management practice is a direct force to promote the learning of members of the organization. Therefore, only by integrating leadership, organizational culture and human resource management can organizational learning enjoy a good internal environment.

Fourth, the most important part, yet also most difficult, is that since there are many internal and external factors that promote organizational learning, how to integrate these factors? What role do these factors play in promoting organizational learning? This is the fundamental question about how to promote organizational learning. This aspect is insufficiently covered, so it is urgent to explore and verify it through in-depth empirical research (Lee et al., 2016). In the future, knowledge management theory, organization theory, leadership theory and identification theory can be integrated to construct the promotion model of organizational learning in different stages and levels from the evolutionary and multilevel perspectives, so as to deeply reveal the generative mechanism of organizational learning and provide scientific reference for improving organizational learning capability.

In a word, the aforementioned studies have come to a lot of findings and pointed out the direction to promote organizational learning. But on the whole, research in this area is limited, and it also provides venues for future studies.

5.5 Three-dimensional theory of organizational learning

Organizational learning research in the last four decades has reached many in-depth conclusions, including theories and views that have been gradually recognized by the academic circle. It also exerts great influence in the practical field. However, academic research on the mechanism and principle of organizational learning presents a somewhat downward trend. We are seeing an increasing number of researches that regard organizational learning as a key part. At the same time, in view of the current research on organizational learning in China, a unified organizational learning theory has not yet been fully formed, and organizational learning research of various organizations in China needs to be continuously integrated to achieve this goal. Based on the conclusion of this study and the illumination of many scholars, we can integrate the theories of organizational learning from the following three dimensions to establish the three-dimensional theory of organizational learning.

First, the level of organizational learning: multilevel and trans-level. This is a theoretical point of view obtained from many years of research on organizational learning and accepted by most researchers. Generally speaking, organizational learning includes four levels: inter-organizational, organizational, collective and individual. After a series of explorations, this study concludes that organizational learning is a process that includes the four levels and their interactions; it is a trans-level phenomenon, a process of continuous change generated by the continuous interaction of lower-level subjects, between subjects, and between subjects and higher-level backgrounds based on learning at a higher level. Though many scholars also categorize organizational learning into external learning and internal learning (Argote & Ophir, 2002; Chen, 2016), many research theories show that the aforementioned four levels can explain the internal and external integrating rules of organizational learning more deeply and specifically. Therefore, the future integrated theory of organizational learning needs to consider the important characteristics of organizational learning, namely the four levels and trans-level.

Second, the degree of organizational learning: explorative learning and exploitative learning. Ever since March (1991) proposed that organizational learning includes two types of learning, exploration and exploitation, the two types have been interpreted as ambidextrous by later studies. Ambidextrous learning has also become a hot topic in recent decades. Academic circles have been paying extensive and sustained attention to ambidextrous learning itself, especially the balance of ambidextrous learning (He & Wong, 2004; Jiang & Zhao, 2006; He & Peng, 2008). A series of empirical studies indicate that explorative learning and exploitative learning are very important components of organizational learning, and also a very critical development issue of companies. Therefore, the integrated theory of organizational learning should consider explorative learning and exploitative learning in ambidexterity and the balance between the two.

Third is the time of organizational learning: past and future. The essential definition of organizational learning emphasizes organization's full application of past experience as well as the rapid adaptability to the future environmental changes. Many studies (Chen, 2016; Argote & Epple, 1990; Argote & Miron-Spektor, 2011) have also found the performance and rules of organizational learning from past experience. In view of the development practice of Chinese companies and other kinds of organizations, they should not only sort out the good experience of the past and apply it to the organization, but also set roadmaps for the future. Therefore, the integrated theory of organizational learning also needs to consider the balance between the past and the future.

Therefore, in the future, we can gradually explore and establish a three-dimensional theory with organizational learning level (scope), degree and time through theoretical construct, model testing and case analysis. This can not only provide a panoramic conceptual view of the characteristics of organizational learning, but also provide an important perspective for the construct of theory as well as in-depth and concrete guidance for organizational management practice.

Appendix

Organizational learning questionnaire (29 items, compared with the learning practices of your company)

Items	Compeletely inconsistent	Relatively inconsistent	Not sure	Relatively consistent	Completely consistent
1. My colleagues have clear work goals.	①	②	③	④	⑤
2. My colleagues sum up their work experience in time.	①	②	③	④	⑤
3. The organizational structure of the company changes appropriately order to adapt to the strategic changes.	①	②	③	④	⑤
4. Our company often exchanges work experience with cooperative companies.	①	②	③	④	⑤
5. My colleagues actively seek help from others to solve work problems.	①	②	③	④	⑤
6. Our company publicizes the established strategy to employees in various forms.	①	②	③	④	⑤
7. My colleagues have a lot of new ideas in their work.	①	②	③	④	⑤
8. Our company can convey its policy to every employee.	①	②	③	④	⑤

(*Continued*)

Items	*Compeletely inconsistent*	*Relatively inconsistent*	*Not sure*	*Relatively consistent*	*Completely consistent*
9. Our company planning points out the work direction for the staff.	①	②	③	④	⑤
10. My colleagues often try and test new ideas.	①	②	③	④	⑤
11. The organizational structure of the company constantly adjusts according to business needs.	①	②	③	④	⑤
12. Communication between colleagues is smooth.	①	②	③	④	⑤
13. The company planning constantly adjusts according to the internal and external changes.	①	②	③	④	⑤
14. My colleagues can break old thinking habits and look at problems from a new perspective.	①	②	③	④	⑤
15. Our company can engage in personnel exchanges and training with other companies.	①	②	③	④	⑤
16. Our company carries out trainings on belief and rules.	①	②	③	④	⑤
17. The personal opinions of employees can be taken into account when making decisions.	①	②	③	④	⑤
18. Colleagues often exchange freely work-related information.	①	②	③	④	⑤

(*Continued*)

Items	Compeletely inconsistent	Relatively inconsistent	Not sure	Relatively consistent	Completely consistent
19. Our company often learns from the good practices of other companies.	①	②	③	④	⑤
20. Employees often participate in collective decision-making.	①	②	③	④	⑤
21. Our company searches for and retains the experience and lessons of other companies.	①	②	③	④	⑤
22. The company will adjust strategy to adapt to the change of external environment.	①	②	③	④	⑤
23. Colleagues often solve the disagreement in their work through discussions and consultations.	①	②	③	④	⑤
24. Our company often cooperates with other companies for common development.	①	②	③	④	⑤
25. Colleagues often cooperate and help each other in their work.	①	②	③	④	⑤
26. The company's business process is constantly adjusted.	①	②	③	④	⑤
27. The company planning often adopts the department's work suggestions.	①	②	③	④	⑤
28. Both general staff and managers have an impact on corporate strategy.	①	②	③	④	⑤

(*Continued*)

Items	Compeletely inconsistent	Relatively inconsistent	Not sure	Relatively consistent	Completely consistent
29. Our company discusses future development with customers.	①	②	③	④	⑤

Individual learning: 1, 2, 5, 7, 10, 14
Collective learning: 12, 18, 23, 25
Organizational level learning: 3, 11, 13, 22, 26
Inter-organizational learning: 4, 15, 19, 21, 24, 29
Exploitative learning: 6, 8, 9, 16
Explorative learning: 17, 20, 27, 28

References

Akgun, A. E., Lynn, G. S., & Byrne, J. C. (2003). Organizational learning: Socio-cognitive framework. *Human Relations*, 56(7), 839–868.

Amabile, T. M., Conti, R., Coon, H., Lazenby, J., & Heron, M. (1996). Assessing the work environment for creativity. *Academy of Management Review*, 39, 1154–1184.

Amitay, M., Popper, M., & Lipshitz, R. (2005). Leadership styles and organizational learning in community clinics. *The Learning Organization*, 12(1), 57–70.

Argote, L., & Epple, D. (1990). Learning curves in manufacturing. *Science*, 247, 920–924.

Argote, L., & Miron-Spektor, E. (2011). Organizational learning: From experience to knowledge. *Organization Science*, 22(5), 1123–1137.

Argote, L., & Ophir, R. (2002). Intraorganizational learning. In Baum, J. A. C. (Ed.), *The Blackwell Companion to Organizations*. Oxford: Blackwell Business, 181–207.

Argyris, C., & Schön, D. A. (1978). *Organizational Learning: A Theory of Action Perspective*. Reading, MA: Addison-Wesley.

Avolio, B. J., Bass, B. M., & Jung, D. I. (1999). Re-examining the components of transformational and transactional leadership using the multifactor leadership questionnaire. *Journal of Occupational and Organizational Psychology*, 72, 441–462.

Baron, R. M., & Kenny, D. A. (1986). The moderator-mediator variable distinction in social psychological research: Conceptual, strategic, and statistical considerations. *Journal of Personality and Social Psychology*, 51, 1173–1182.

Bartko, J. J. (1976). On various intraclass correlation reliability coefficients. *Psychological Bulletin*, 83(5), 762–765.

Bass, B. M. (1985). *Leadership and Performance beyond Expectation*. New York: Free Press.

Bass, B. M. (1990). *From transactional to transformational leadership: Learning to share the vision. Organizational Dynamics*, (Winter), 19–31.

Bass, B. M. (1997). Does the transactional–transformational leadership paradigm transcend organizational and national boundaries? *American Psychologist*, 2(2), 130–139.

Bass, B. M. (1998). *Transformational Leadership: Industry, Military, and Educational Impact*. Mahwah, NJ: Lawrence Erlbaum Associates.

Bass, B. M., & Avolio, B. J. (Eds.). (1993). *Improving Organizational Effectiveness through Transformational Leadership*. Thousand Oaks, CA: Sage Publications Inc.

Bass, B. M., & Avolio, B. J. (1997). *Full Range of Leadership Development: Manual for the Multifactor Leadership Questionnaire*. Palo Alto, CA: Mind Garden.

Berends, H., Boersma, K., & Weggeman, M. (2002). The structuration of organizational leaning. *Human Relations*, 56(9), 1035–1056.

Berson, Y., Nemanich, L. A., Waldman, D. A., Galvin, B. M., & Keller, R. T. (2006). Leadership and organizational learning: A multiple levels perspective. *The Leadership Quarterly*, 17, 577–594.

Bhatnagar, J., & Sharma, A. (2005). The Indian perspective of strategic HR roles and organizational learning capability. *International Journal of Human Resource Management*, 16(9), 1711–1739.

Bogenrieder, I. (2002). Social architecture as prerequisite for organizational learning. *Management Learning*, 33(2), 197–212.

Bogenrieder, I., & Nooteboom, B. (2004). Learning groups: What types are there? A theoretical analysis and an empirical study in a consultancy firm. *Organization Studies*, 25(2), 287–313.

Bollen, K. A. (1989). *Structural Equations with Latent Variables*. New York: Wiley.

Bontis, N., Crossan, M., & Hulland, J. (2002). Managing an organizational learning system by aligning stocks and flows. *Journal of Management Studies*, 39(4), 435–469.

Brown, J., & Duguid, P. (1991). Organizational learning and communities of practice. *Organization Science*, 2(1), 40–57.

Bryk, A., & Raudenbush, S. W. (1992). *Hierarchical Linear Models for Social and Behavioral Research: Applications and Data Analysis Methods*. Newbury Park, CA: SAGE.

Bunderson, J. S. (2003). Management team learning orientation and business unit performance. *Journal of Applied Psychology*, 88(3), 552–560.

Calantone, R. J., Cavusgil, S. T., & Yushan, Z. (2002). Learning orientation, firm innovation capability, and firm performance in Chinese. *Industrial Marketing Management*, 31, 515–524.

Cameron, K. S., & Quinn, R. E. (1999). *Diagnosing and Changing Organizational Culture: Based on the Competing Values Framework*. Reading, MA: Addison-Wesley.

Campion, M. A., Medsker, G. J., & Higgs, A. C. (1993). Relations between group characteristics and effectiveness: Implications for designing effective work groups. *Personnel Psychology*, 46, 823–850.

Carlsson, B. (1995). R&D organizations as learning systems. In Kolb, D. (Eds.), et al., *The Organizational Behavior Reader* (6 th ed.). Englewood Cliffs, NJ: Prentice Hall.

Cavaleri, S., & Fearon, D. (1996). *Managing in Organizations That Learn*. Cambridge, MA: Blackwell.

Chadwick, I. C., & Raver, J. L. (2015). Motivating organizations to learn: Goal orientation and its influence on organizational learning. *Journal of Management*, 41(3), 957–986.

Chan, D. (1998). Functional relations among constructs in the same content domain at different levels of analysis: A typology of compositional models. *Journal of Applied Psychology*, 83, 234–236.

Chandler, D., & Hwang, H. (2015). Learning from learning theory: A model of organizational adoption strategies at the microfoundations of institutional theory. *Journal of Management*, 41(5), 1446–1476.

Chen, G. (2007). Study on learning ability system, learning-oriented human resource management system of learning organization and their relationship. *Chinese Journal of Management Science*, (11), 719–747.

Chen, G. (2016). Time space theory of organizational learning. *Technology Economics*, (8), 15–23.

Chen, G., & Bliese, P. D. (2002). The role of different levels of leadership in predicting self- and collective efficacy: Evidence for discontinuity. *Journal of Applied Psychology*, 87(3), 549–556.

Chen, G., & Ma, M. (2000). Research on organizational learning process model. *Journal of Management Sciences in China*, (3), 15–23.

Chen, G., & Zhao, C. (2010). An empirical study on the two-dimensional multilevel model of leadership influencing team members' learning ability. *Journal of Industrial Engineering and Engineering Management*, (4), 1–13.

Chen, G., & Zheng, H. (2005). An empirical study on the influence factors of organizational learning, learning ability and performance. *Journal of Management Sciences in China*, (1), 48–61.

Child, J. (2001). Learning through strategic alliances. In Dierkes, M., Antal, A. B., Child, J., & Nonaka, I. (Eds.), *Handbook of Organizational Learning and Knowledge*. Oxford: Oxford University Press, 657–680.

China Entrepreneur Survey System. (2006). Enterprise learning: Current problems and its impact on innovation and competitive advantage. *Management World*, (6), 92–100.

Choe, J. M. (2004). The relationships among management accounting information, organizational learning and production performance. *Journal of Strategic Information Systems*, 13(1), 61–85.

Cook, S., & Yanow, D. (1993). Culture and organizational learning. *Journal of Management Inquiry*, 2(4), 373–390.

Crossan, M., & Berdrow, I. (2003). Organizational learning and strategic renewal. *Strategic Management Journal*, 24, 1087–1105.

Crossan, M., Lane, H., & White, R. (1999). An organizational learning framework: From intuition to institution. *Academy of Management Review*, 24(3), 522–537.

Crossan, M., Lane, H., White, R., & Djurfeldt, L. (1995). Organizational learning dimensions for a theory. *International Journal of Organizational Analysis*, (3), 337–360.

Crossan, M., Maurer, C., & White, R. (2011). Reflections on the 2009 AMR decade award: Do we have a theory of organizational learning? *Academy of Management Review*, 36(3), 446–460.

Daft, R. L., & Weick, K. E. (1984). Toward a model of organizations as interpretation systems. *Academy of Management Review*, 9, 284–295.

Dai, W., Zhao, S., & Jiang, J. (2006). Research on dynamic model of complex system, knowledge management and organizational learning process. *China Soft Science*, (6), 120–128.

Day, G. S. (1994). Continuous learning about markets. *California Management Review*, 2, 9–31.

De Geus, A. P. (1988). Planning as learning. *Harvard Business Review*, March–April, 70–74.

DiBella, A., & Nevis, E. (1998). *How Organizations Learn*. San Francisco, CA: Jossey-Bass.

Dixon, N. (1999). *The Organizational Learning Cycle: How We Can Learn Collectively*. Gower: Gower Publishing Ltd.

Duncan, R., & Weiss, A. (1979). Organizational learning: Implications for organizational design. *Research in Organizational Behavior*, 1, 75–123.

Easterby-Smith, M., Crossan, M., & Nicolini, D. (2000). Organizational learning: Debates past, present and future. *Journal of Management Studies*, 783–796.

Edmondson, A. (1999). Psychological safety and learning behavior in work teams. *Administrative Science Quarterly*, 44, 350–383.

Ellinger, A. D., Ellinger, A. E., Yang, B. Y., & Howton, S. W. (2002). The relationship between the learning organization concept and firm's financial performance: An empirical assessment. *Human Resource Development Quarterly*, 13(1), 5–21.

Ellis, S., & Shpielberg, N. (2003). Organizational leaning mechanisms and managers' perceived uncertainty. *Human Relations*, 5(10), 1233–1254.

Fiol, C. M., & Lyles, M. A. (1985). Organizational learning. *Academy of Management Review*, 10(4), 803–813.

Fisher, S. R., & White, M. A. (2000). Downsizing in a learning organization: Are there hidden costs? *Academy of Management Review*, 25(1), 244–251.

Ford, C. M. (1996). A theory of individual creative action in multiple social domains. *Academy of Management Review*, 21, 1112–1142.

Fox, S. (2000). Communities of practice, Foucault and actor-network theory. *Journal of Management Studies*, 37(6), 853–867.

Garvin, D. A. (1993). Building a learning organization. *Harvard Business Review*, 71(4), 78–91.

Gherardi, S., Nicolini, D., & Odella, F. (1998). Toward a social understanding of how people learn in organizations. *Management Learning*, 29(3), 272–297.

Gnyawali, D. R., & Stewart, A. C. (2003). A contingency perspective on organizational learning: Integrating environmental context, organizational learning processes, and types of learning. *Management Learning*, 34(1), 63–89.

Goh, S. C. (1998). Toward a learning organization: The strategic building blocks. *SAM Advance Management Journal*, 63(2), 15–20.

Goh, S. C., & Rhan, P. J. (2002). *Learning capability, organizational factors and firm performance. Third European Conference on Organizational Knowledge, Learning and Capabilities*, Athens, Greece, April 5–6.

Goh, S. C., & Richards, G. (1997). Benchmarking the learning capabilities of organizations. *European Management Journal*, 15(5), 575–583.

Gómez, P. J., Lorente, J. J. C., & Cabrera, R. V. (2004). Training practices and organizational learning capability: Relationship and implications. *Journal of European Industrial Training*, 28(2–3), 234–256.

Greenleaf, R. K. (1977). *Servant Leadership*. Mahwah, NJ: Paulist Press.

Gupta, A. K., Smith, K. G., & Shalley, C. E. (2006). The inter-play between exploration and exploitation. *Academy of Management Review*, 49(4), 693–706.

He, H., & Peng, J. (2008). Working mechanism of human resource management practice on innovation performance: An integrated framework based on knowledge management and organizational learning. *Foreign Economies and Management*, (8), 53–59.

He, Y., & Tian, Z. (2008). The relationship between organizational learning and enterprise performance: An empirical study based on the perspective of adaptability. *R&D Management*, (1), 91–96.

He, Z.-L., & Wong, P. K. (2004). Exploration vs. exploitation: An empirical test of the ambidexterity hypothesis. *Organization Science*, 15, 481–494.

Hedberg, R. (1981). How organizations learn and unlearn. In Nystrom, P. C., & Starbuck, W. H. (Eds.), *Handbook of Organizational Design*. Oxford: Oxford University Press.

Hofmann, D. A. (2002). Issues in multilevel research: Theory development, measurement, and analysis. In Rogelberg, S. G. (Ed.), *Handbook of Research Methods in Industrial and Organizational Psychology*. Malden, MA: Blackwell Publishers, 247–274.

Hofmann, D. A., Griffin, M. A., & Gavin, M. B. (2000). The application of hierarchical linear modeling to organizational research. In Klein, K. J., & Kozlowski, W. J. (Eds.), *Multilevel Theory, Research, and Methods in Organizations: Foundations, Extensions, and New Directions*. San Francisco, CA: Jossey-Bass, 467–511.

Hofmann, D. A., Morgeson, F. P., & Gerras, S. J. (2000). Climate as a moderator of the relationship between leader-member exchange and content specific citizenship: Safety climate as an exemplar. *Journal of Applied Psychology*, 88(1), 170–178.

Hofmann, D. A., & Stetzer, A. (1996). A cross level investigation of factors influencing unsafe behavior and accidents. *Personnel Psychology*, 49, 307–339.

Holmqvist, M. (2003). A dynamic model of intra- and interorganizational leaning. *Organization Studies*, 24(1), 95–123.

House, R. J., & Aditya, R. N. (1997). The social scientific study of leadership: Quovadis? *Journal of Management*, 23, 409–473.

Howard, B. D. (2003). Organizational learning capacity in the context of the symlog most effective value profile. *Dissertation Abstracts-International*, 64(3-B), 1533.

Huber, G. P. (1991). Organizational learning: The contributing processes and the literatures. *Organization Science*, 2, 88–115.

Hult, G. T. M., & David, J. (Eds.). (2003). Organizational learning as a strategic resource in supply management. *Journal of Operations Management*, 21, 541–556.

Hult, G. T. M., & Ferrell, O. C. (1997). A global learning organizational structure and market information processing. *Journal of Business Research*, 40, 155–166.

Hult, G. T. M., Ferrell, O. C., & Hurley, R. F. (2002). Global organizational learning effects on cycle time performance. *Journal of Business Research*, 55, 377–387.

Hurley, R. F., & Hult, G. T. M. (1998). Innovation, market orientation, and organizational learning: An integration and empirical examination. *Journal of Marketing*, 62(7), 42–54.

Ingram, P. (2002). Interorganizational learning. In Baum, J. A. (Ed.), *Blackwell Companion to Organization*. Malden, MA: Wiley-Blackwell, 642–663.

Inkpen, A. C. (2000). Learning through joint ventures: A framework of knowledge acquisition. *Journal of Management Studies*, 37(7), 1019–1043.

Inkpen, A. C., & Crossan, M. (1995). Believing is seeing: Joint ventures and organization learning. *Journal of Management Studies*, 32, 595–618.

James, L. R. (1982). Aggregation bias in estimates of perceptual agreement. *Journal of Applied Psychology*, 67, 219–229.

James, L. R., Demaree, R. G., & Wolf, G. (1984). Estimating within-group interrater reliability with and without response bias. *Journal of Applied Psychology*, 69, 85–98.

James, L. R., Demaree, R. G., & Wolf, G. (1993). Estimating within-group interrater Rwg: An assessment of within group interrater agreement. *Journal of Applied Psychology*, 78, 306–309.

Jansen, J., Vera, D., & Crossan, M. (2007). *Strategic leadership for exploratory and exploitative innovation. 2007 Technology Transfer Society Conference*, UC Riverside Palm Desert Graduate Center, October 24–26.

Jerez-Gómez, P., Céspedes-Lorente, J., & Valle-Cabrera, R. (2005a). Organizational learning capability: A proposal of measurement. *Journal of Business Research*, 58(6), 715–725.

Jerez-Gómez, P., Céspedes-Lorente, J., & Valle-Cabrera, R. (2005b). Organizational learning and compensation strategies: Evidence from the Spanish chemical industry. *Human Resource Management*, 44(3), 279–299.

Jiang, C., & Zhao, S. (2006). The relationship between social capital and corporate entrepreneurship and performance: The mediating role of organizational learning. *Management World*, (10), 90–99.

Jiao, H., Wei, J., & Cui, Y. (2008). Path analysis of the construction of enterprise dynamic capabilities: From the perspective of entrepreneurial orientation and organizational learning. *Management World*, (4), 91–105.

Jung, D. I., Chow, C., & Wu, A. (2003). The role of transformational leadership in enhancing organizational innovation: Hypotheses and some preliminary findings. *The Leadership Quarterly*, 14, 525–544.

Katilac, R., & Ahujac, G. (2002). Something old, something new: A longitudinal study of search behavior and new product introduction. *Academy of Management Journal*, 45, 1183–1194.

Keller, R. T. (2006). Transformational leadership, initiating structure, and substitutes for leadership: A longitudinal study of R&D project team performance. *Journal of Applied Psychology*, 91, 202–210.

Kim, D. H. (1993). The link between individual and organizational learning. *Sloan Management Review*, Fall, 37–50.

Klein, K. J., Bliese, P. D., & Kozlowski, W. J., et al. (2000). Multilevel analytical techniques. In Klein, K. J., & Kozlowski, W. J. (Eds.), *Multilevel Theory, Research, and Methods in Organizations: Foundations, Extensions, and New Directions*. San Francisco, CA: Jossey-Bass, 512–553.

Knight, L. (2002). Network learning: Exploring learning by interorganizational networks. *Human Relations*, 55(4), 427–454.

Konovsky, M. A., & Cropanzano, R. (1991). Perceived fairness of employee drug testing as a predictor of employee attitudes and job performance. *Journal of Applied Psychology*, 76, 698–707.

Kozlowski, W. J., & Klein, K. J. (2000). A multilevel approach to theory and research in organizations: Contextual, temporal, and emergent processes. In Klein, K. J., & Kozlowski, W. J. (Eds.), *Multilevel Theory, Research, and Methods in Organizations: Foundations, Extensions, and New Directions*. San Francisco, CA: Jossey-Bass, 3–90.

Lahteenmarki, S., Toivonen, J., & Mattila, M. (2001). Critical aspects of organizational learning research and proposal for its measurement. *British Journal of Management*, 12, 113–129.

Lam, Y. L. (2002). Defining the effects of transformational leadership on organizational learning: A cross-cultural comparison. *School Leadership & Management*, 22(4), 439–452.

Lane, P. J., & Lubatkin, M. (1998). Relative absorptive capacity and interorganizational learning. *Strategic Management Journal*, 19, 461–477.

Lane, C. (2001). Organizational learning in supplier networks. In Dierkes, M., Antal, A. B., Child, J., & Nonaka, I (Eds.), *Handbook of Organizational Learning and Knowledge*, Oxford: Oxford University Press, 699–715.

Lee, S., Courtney, J., & O'Keefe, R. (1992). A system of organizational learning using cognitive maps. *International Journal of Management Science*, 20(1), 23–36.

Lee, S., Rittiner, F., & Szulanski, G. (2016). The past, present and future of organizational leaning research: A conversation with Professor Linda Argote. *Journal of Management Inquiry*, 25(1), 85–92.

Levinthal, D. A., & March, J. G. (1993). The myopia of learning. *Strategic Management Journal*, 14, 95–112.

Levitt, B., & March, J. G. (1988). Organizational learning. *Annual Review of Sociology*, 14, 319–338.

Li, C., & Shi, K. (2003). Research on the relationship between transformational leadership and leadership effectiveness. *Psychological Science*, (1), 115–117.

Li, C., & Shi, K. (2005). The structure and measurement of transformational leadership. *Acta Psychologica Sinica*, (6), 803–811.

Li, Y. (2003). Manifestations and types of organizational errors: Nuclear power and civil aviation. *Doctoral Dissertation of Institute of Psychology, Chinese Academy of Sciences*.

Li, Y. (2004). The study of organizational learning in the management innovation. *PhD Thesis of Fudan University of China*.

Lian, Y. (2002). Structure and performance of learning organization: A case study of a technology company in Taiwan. *Journal of Business and Management Technology*, (4), 337–358.

Liden, R. C., Wayne, S. J., Zhao, H., & Henderson, D. (2008). Servant leadership: Development of a multidimensional measure and multi-level assessment. *The Leadership Quarterly*, 19(3), 161–177.

Lindholm, N. (1997). Learning processes in international joint ventures in China. *Advances in Chinese Industrial Studies*, 5, 139–154.

Ling, W. Q., Chen, L., & Wang, D. (1987). Structure of CPM leadership behavior questionnaire. *Acta Psychologica Sinica*, 19(2), 199–207.

López, S. P., Peon, J. M. M., & Ordas, C. J. V. (2005). Human resource management practices, organizational learning and business performance. *Human Resource Development International*, 8(2), 147–164.

López, S. P., Peon, J. M. M., & Ordas, C. J. V. (2006). Human resource management as a determining factor in organizational learning. *Management Learning*, 37, 215–223.

Lowe, K. B., Kroeck, K. G., & Sivasubramaniam, N. (1996). Effectiveness correlates of transformational and transactional leadership: A meta-analytic review. *The Leadership Quarterly*, 7, 385–425.

March, J., & Olsen, J. (1975). Organizational learning under ambiguity. *European Journal of Policy Review*, 3(2), 147–171.

March, J. G. (1991). Exploration and exploitation in organizational learning. *Organizational Science*, 2(1), 71–87.

Marquardt, M. J. (1996). *Building the Learning Organization: A System Approach to Quantum Improvement and Global Success*. London: McGraw-Hill.

Marsick, V. J., & Watkins, K. E. (1999). *Facilitating Learning Organizations: Making Learning Count*. Aldershot: Gower.

Meyer, J. P., Allen, N. J., & Smith, C. A. (1993). Commitment to organizations and occupations: Extension and test of a three-component conceptualization. *Journal of Applied Psychology*, 78(4), 538–551.

Miller, D. (1996). A preliminary typology of organizational learning: Synthesizing the literature. *Journal of Management*, 22(3), 485–505.

Mills, D. O., & Friesen, B. (1992). The learning organization. *European Management Journal*, 10(2), 146–156.

Moilanen, R. (2001). Diagnostic tools for learning organizations. *The Learning Organization*, 8(1), 6–20.

Motowidlo, D. J., & Scotter, J. R. V. (1994). Evidence that task performance should be distinguished from contextual performance. *Journal of Applied Psychology*, 79(4), 475–480.

Mumford, M. D. (2000). Managing creative people: Strategies and tactics for innovation. *Human Resource Management Review*, 10, 313–351.

Nemanich, L., & Vera, D. (2007). *Transformational leadership and ambidexterity in the context of an acquisition, 2007 Technology Transfer Society Conference*, UC Riverside Palm Desert Graduate Center, October 24–26.

Nemanich, L., Vera, D., & Crossan, M. (2009). Transformaional leadership and ambidexterity in the context of an acquisition. *The Leadership Quarterly*, 20, 19–33.

Nevis, E., DiBella, A., & Gould, J. (1995). Understanding organizations as learning systems. *Sloan Management Review*, 36, 73–85.

Nonaka, I., & Takeuchi, H. (1995). *The Knowledge Creating Company*. London: Oxford University Press.

O'Reilly, C. A. (1990). Organizational behavior: Where we've been, where we're going. *Annual Review of Psychology*, 42, 427–458.

Örtenblad, A. (2002). A typology of the idea of learning organization. *Management Learning*, 33(2), 213–230.

Pawlowsky, P. (2001). The treatment of organizational learning in management science. In Dierkes, M., Antal, A. B., Child, J., & Nonaka, I. (Eds.), *Handbook of Organizational Learning and Knowledge*. Oxford: Oxford University Press, 61–81.

Pedler, M., Burgoyne, J., & Boydell, T. (1991). *The Learning Company: A Strategy for Sustainable Development*. London: McGraw-Hill.

Peng, X. M., Wu, X. B., & Wu, D. (2011). The evolution of enterprise networks based on the dynamic process of the second innovation and the evolution of the balance model of the organizational learning. *Management World*, (4), 138–166.

Rafferty, A. E., & Griffin, M. A. (2004). Dimensions of trans-formational leadership: Conceptual and empirical extensions. *The Leadership Quarterly*, 15, 329–354.

Redmond, M. R., Mumford, M. D., & Teach, R. (1993). Putting creativity to work: Effects of leader behavior on subordinate creativity. *Organizational Behavior and Human Decision Processes*, 55, 120–151.

Richter, I. (1998). Individual and organizational learning at the executive level: Towards a research agenda. *Management Learning*, 29(3), 299–316.

Ron, N., Lipshitz, R., & Popper, M. (2006). How organizations learn: Post-flight reviews in an F-16 fighter squadron. *Organization Studies*, 27, 1069–1089.

Rosengarten, P. G. (1999). The characteristics, outcomes and sources of the learning organization: The case of car component suppliers in Britain. *MPhil Thesis of London School of Economics and Political Science*. http://ourworld.compuserve.com/homepages/PRosengarten/LO.htm.

Rui, M., & Lv, Y. (2005). An empirical study on the influence of leadership behavior, organizational learning, innovation and performance. *Shanghai Management Science*, (2), 32–37.

Salk, J. E., & Simonin, B. L. (2003). Beyond alliances: Towards a meta-theory of collaborative learning. In Easterby-Smith, M., & Lyles, M. (Ed.), *The Blackwell Handbook of Organizational Leaning and Knowledge Management*. Oxford: Oxford University Press, 253–277.

Schein, E. (1992). *Organizational Culture and Leadership*. San Francisco, CA: Jossey-Bass.

Schwandt, D., & Maruardt, M. (2000). *Organizational Learning: From World-Class Theories to Global Best Practices*. Boca Raton, FL: ST Lucie.

Senge, P. (1990). *The Fifth Discipline: The Art and Practice of the Learning Organization*. New York: Doubleday Currency.

Shalley, C., & Gilson, L. L. (2004). What leaders need to know: A review of social and contextual factors that can foster or hinder creativity. *The Leadership Quarterly*, 15, 33–53.

Shrivastava, P. (1983). A typology of organizational learning systems. *Journal of Management Studies*, 20(1), 7–28.

Shu, C., Yi, F., & Jiang, X. (2015). Dual learning, knowledge acquisition and innovation performance in strategic alliances. *R&D Management*, (6), 97–106.

Silin, R. H. (1976). *Leadership and Value: The Organization of Large-Scale Taiwan Enterprises*. Cambridge, MA: Harvard University Press, 66–128.

Simon, H. A. (1991). Bounded rationality and organizational leaning. *Organization Science*, 2, 125–133.

Slater, S. F., & Narver, J. C. (1995). Market orientation and the learning organization. *Journal of Marketing*, 59(3), 63–74.

Stata, R. (1989). Organizational learning – The key to management innovation. *Sloan Management Review*, 1, 63–74.

Sun, R., & Zhao, C. (2017). Organizational emotional ability, organizational learning and innovation performance of high-tech enterprises. *Science Research Management*, (2), 93–100.

Sun, W., Liu, L., & Sun, M. (2005). An analysis of the influencing factors of organizational learning and knowledge sharing. *Science of Science and Management S&T*, (7), 135–138.

Sun, Y. F., Li, Y., & Liao, X. (2007). A study of corporate innovation and internal controls under heterogeneous strategic orientations. *Journal of Industrial Engineering Engineering Management*, 4, 24–30.

Tannenbaum, S. (1997). Enhancing continuous learning: Diagnostic findings from multiple companies. *Human Resource Management*, 36(4), 437–452.

Templeton, G. F., Lewis, B. R., & Snyder, C. A. (2002). Development of a measure for the organizational learning construct. *Journal of Management Information Systems*, 19(2), 175–218.

Tippins, M. J., & Sohi, R. S. (2003). IT competency and firm performance: Is organizational learning a missing link? *Strategic Management Journal*, 24, 745–761.

Tsui, A. S., Egan, T. D., & O'Reilly, C. A. (1992). Being different: Relational demography and organizational attachment. *Administrative Science Quarterly*, 37, 547–579.

Ulrich, D., & Brockbank, W. (2005). *HR Value Proposition*. Boston: Harvard Business School Press.

Ulrich, D., & Todd, J. (1993). High-impact learning: Building and diffusing learning capability. *Organizational Dynamics*, 3, 52–66.

Vera, D., & Manor, B. (2004). Strategic leadership and organizational learning. *Academy of Management Review*, 29(2), 222–240.

Waldman, D. A., Bass, B. M., & Einstein, W. O. (1987). Leadership and outcomes of performance appraisal process. *Journal of Occupational Psychology*, 60, 177–186.

Wang, R. (2002). System model and structure design of learning organization. *Doctoral Dissertations of Beijing University of Aeronautics and Astronautics*.

Watkins, K. E., & Marsick, V. J. (1993). *Sculpting the Learning Organization: Lessons in the Art and Science of Systemic*. San Francisco, CA: Jossey-Bass.

Wei, J., Ying, Y., & Liu, Y. (2014). A case study on the decentralization of R&D network, organizational learning order and innovation performance. *Management World*, (2), 137–151, 186.

Weick, K. E. (1991). The nontraditional quality of organizational learning. *Organizational Science*, (2), 116–124.

Westwood, R. (1997). Harmony and patriarchy: The cultural basis for paternalistic headship among the overseas Chinese. *Organization Studies*, 18(3), 445–480.

Wright, P. M., Gardner, T. M., Moynihan, L. M., & Allen, M. R. (2005). The relationship between HR and practices and firm performance: Examining causal order. *Personnel Psychology*, 58, 409–446.

Wu, C., Cao, A. F., & Zhou, C. H. (2009). The evolution of leadership styles in the process of corporate development: Case studies. *Management World*, (2), 123–137.

Wu, X. (1995). Cycle of secondary innovation and organizational learning model of enterprises. *Management World*, (3), 168–172.

Wu, Z. M., & Wu, X. (2006). The relationships between transformation leadership, organizational citizenship behavior. *Journal of Management Sciences in China*, (5), 40–47.

Xie, H., Wu, L., Wang, C., & Ge, Z. (2006). Antecedents and consequences of organizational learning: A new theoretical framework. *Science of Science and Management S&T*, (8), 158–168.

Xie, H. M., Luo, H. L., & Wang, C. (2007). Learning, innovation and core competence: Mechanism and path. *Journal of Economy Research*, (2), 59–70.

Yan, H. F., & Guan, T. (2006). The study of internationalization behaviors based on organizational learning. *Foreign Economies and Management*, (10), 34–42.

Yang, B. Y., Watkins, K. E., & Marsick, V. J. (2004). The construct of the learning organization: Dimensions, measurement, and validation. *Human Resource Development Quarterly*, 5(1), 31–55.

Yang, J., Wang, C., & Li, J. (2010). Research on the influence mechanism of organizational learning on organizational performance. *Science of Science and Management S&T*, (7), 158–162.

Yeung, A., Ulrich, D., Nason, S., & Glinow, M. (1999). *Organizational Learning Capability*. New York: Oxford University Press.

Yu, H., Fang, L., & Ling, W. (2004). Integrated theoretical model of organizational learning. *Advances in Psychological Science*, (2), 246–255.

Yu, H., Fang, L., & Ling, W. (2006). Learning structure of enterprise organization. *Acta Psychologica Sinica*, (4), 590–597.

Yu, H., Fang, L., & Ling, W. (2007). Empirical study on organizational learning and its effectiveness. *Journal of Management Sciences in China*, (5), 48–61.

Yu, H., Zheng, X., & Liu, C. (2008a). How to lead organizational learning: The relationship between transformational leadership and organizational learning. *Science of Science and Management S&T*, (3), 183–188.

Yu, H., Zheng, X., Fang, L., & Ling, W. (2008b). An empirical study on the balance between explorative learning and exploitative learning in Chinese enterprises. *Science Research Management*, (6), 137–144.

Yu, H., Zheng, X., Fang, L., & Ling, W. (2008c). How to lead organizational learning: The relationship between paternalistic leadership and organizational learning. *Science Research Management*, (5), 180–186.

Yu, W., Lv, X., & Wang, Y. (2002). Research on the organizational culture of continuous learning. *Psychological Science*, (2), 134–135 (151).

Yuan, X., Tan, Z., & Yi, J. (2006). Study on the interaction mechanism of learning and performance in organization. *Science Research Management*, (6), 136–143.

Yukl, G. (1999). An evaluation essay on current conceptions of effective leadership. *European Journal of Work and Organizational Psychology*, 8(1), 33–48.

Zhang, D., Zhang, Z., & Yang, B. Y. (2004). Learning organization in mainland China: Empirical research on its application to Chinese state-owned enterprises. *International Journal of Training and Development*, 8(4), 258–273.

Zhang, J., Liu, Y., & Lin, B. (2015). Theoretical review and future research prospects of organizational duality. *Economic Management*, (8), 181–188.

Zhang, L., Lei, L., & Guo, B. (2003). *Application of Multilayer Linear Model*. Beijing: Educational Science Publishing House.

Zhang, Z., & Yu, C. (2015). Research on the influence of utilizing and exploring learning on management innovation. *Journal of Management*, (2), 252–258.

Zhao, W. (2002). Factors promoting organizational learning. *Master's Thesis of Renmin University of China*.

Zheng, B. (2004). Chinese culture and organizational leadership: From phenomenon description to theoretical verification. *Indigenous Psychology Research*, (22), 195–251.

Zheng, B., Zhou, L., & Fan, J. (2000). Paternalistic leadership: The construction and measurement of ternary model. *Indigenous Psychology Research*, (14), 3–64.

Zheng, B., Zhou, L., & Huang, M. (2003). Three element mode of paternalistic leadership: Evidence from Chinese mainland enterprise organization. *Indigenous Psychology Research*, (20), 209–252.

Zheng, J., & Zhou, Y. (2001). Research on the evaluation questionnaire of learning organization. *Master's Thesis of Human Resources Research Institute of Taiwan Central University*.

Zhou, H., & Long, L. (2007). The relationship between paternalistic leadership and organizational justice. *Acta Psychologica Sinica*, (5), 909–917.

Zohar, D. (2000). A group-level model of safety climate: Testing the effect of group climate on micro accidents in manufacturing jobs. *Journal of Applied Psychology*, 85, 587–596.

Index

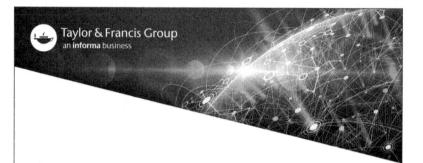

Printed in the United States
by Baker & Taylor Publisher Services